Prescription for a Successful Economy

OTHER TITLES BY LUTHER TWEETEN

The World Food Economy. Malden, Massachusetts: Blackwell, 2007.

Terrorism, Radicalism, and Populism in Agriculture. Ames: Iowa State Press, 2003.

Agricultural Policy for the 21st Century. Ames: Iowa State Press, 2002. (Editor; author of three chapters)

Promoting Third-World Agricultural Development and Food Security. Westport, Connecticut: Praeger, 1997. (Editor; author of two chapters)

Changing Trade Environment After GATT: A Case Study of Taiwan. Taiwan: Council of Agriculture, Executive Yuan, 1994. (Editor; author of two chapters)

Research Methods and Communication in the Social Sciences. Westport, Connecticut: Praeger, 1994.

Japanese and American Agriculture: Tradition and Progress in Conflict. Boulder, Colorado: Westview Press, 1993. (Editor; author of two chapters)

Agricultural Trade: Principles and Policies. Boulder, Colorado: Westview Press, 1992.

Agricultural Policy Analysis Tools for Economic Development. Boulder, Colorado: Westview Press, 1989. (Editor; author of five chapters)

Farm Policy Analysis. Boulder, Colorado: Westview Press, 1989.

Micropolitan Development: Theory and Practice of Greater-Rural Economic Development. Ames: Iowa State University Press, 1976.

Foundations of Farm Policy. Lincoln: University of Nebraska Press, 1970 and 2nd ed. 1979.

Roots of the Farm Problem. Ames: Iowa State University Press, 1965.

Resource Demand and Structure of the Agricultural Industry. Ames: Iowa State University Press, 1963.

Prescription for a Successful Economy

The Standard Economic Model

Luther Tweeten

iUniverse, Inc.
New York Lincoln Shanghai

Prescription for a Successful Economy
The Standard Economic Model

iUniverse books may be ordered through booksellers or by contacting:

iUniverse
2021 Pine Lake Road, Suite 100
Lincoln, NE 68512
www.iuniverse.com
1-800-Authors (1-800-288-4677)

ISBN-13: 978-0-595-39967-3 (pbk)
ISBN-13: 978-0-595-84355-8 (ebk)
ISBN-10: 0-595-39967-3 (pbk)
ISBN-10: 0-595-84355-7 (ebk)

Printed in the United States of America

PREFACE

Major preventable afflictions of the planet—abject poverty, hunger, and treatable disease—have festered too long. It is not that nothing can be done. Dozens of nations and billions of people have been freed from these afflictions. The maladies have causes and cures. Diagnoses and cures do not come from economics alone. This volume draws widely from sociology, anthropology, and other disciplines as well as economics and much experience to set forth the ingredients for socioeconomic success of any country. Of course any country can reject the proven prescription, but at vast cost in human suffering.

I learned a few things from four decades of experience with observing and fostering socioeconomic development. One is that countries with sound policies and institutions overcome problems of abject poverty, hunger, and treatable diseases without relying on charity from other countries. I also learned that countries rejecting sound policies and institutions do not overcome their afflictions even with charity from other countries. Roads, sanitary water supplies, or irrigation facilities provided by donors are unsustainable in a toxic economic environment.

The *Standard Economic Model* had a long gestation period. I had the good fortune of working with the venerable Professor Bruce Johnston when I was a visiting professor at Stanford University. We spent a few weeks together in Ghana in 1967 working on an economic development project in agriculture. My interest in economic development intensified when I became heavily involved in the USAID-sponsored Agricultural Policy Analysis Project for about a decade beginning in 1981. Research, lectures, consulting, and managing workshops in approximately 50 countries over my career taught me much about what makes an economy fail or succeed.

I was struck by how heavily the economic success of individuals and firms depended on national economic policies, institutions, and culture. I observed that household and community projects such as safe water and health clinics were successfully initiated, financed, and sustained with little or no outside help if the national policies and institutions were supportive of economic development. I also observed what I call the macroeconomic degradation process. That process began with a nation trying to live beyond its means, spending more than it earned, borrowing more than it lent, and importing more than it exported. After borrowing to the extent possible in domestic and international financial markets, nations turned to creating money which in turn generated inflation. With the home currency often tied to the dollar or other hard currency, the result of domestic inflation was overvalued local currency. With imports cheap and plentiful and exports overpriced and difficult to sell, the result was depletion of foreign exchange reserves. This caused severe, painful belt tightening at best and collapse of the economy at worst as imported fuels and spare parts became unavailable.

I concluded that these and the many other economic difficulties encountered by countries mostly traced to unintended or willful neglect of a relatively few rules of sound economic policy (and institutions). I have summarized these rules in the *standard economic model* laid out in this volume. The rules, though few, and the environment needed to implement them are not necessarily easy to follow. But this volume is dedicated to the proposition that knowledge of the model and the immense cost of ignoring the model will motivate change.

I have watched the economies of India, Vietnam, Estonia, and Chile come to life after economic reforms. I have been in Mexico and South American countries where rigorously trained economists replaced socialist and populist economists as advisors to government. Poor and nonpoor people alike made great progress as economic reforms emerged out of sound economic advice. This volume attempts to continue that tradition of informing public policy. This volume identifies why China and South Korea, for example, which not long ago lay in economic ruin, now prosper while sub-Saharan Africa continues to be mired in abject poverty, disease, economic stagnation, and hunger.

Prescription for a Successful Economy: The Standard Economic Model is intended for all students of public policy where "student" is broadly defined to include laypersons, academics, practitioners, and decision makers concerned with economic and social development. Development literature has suffered from fragmentation: economists emphasize income growth, the World Bank and International Monetary Fund focus on finance, sociologists trumpet equity, nongovernment organizations promote community improvement, anthropologists obsess with preserving culture, and environmentalists peddle doomsday. This volume attempts the formidable but essential process of integrating these various streams of knowledge to provide a paradigm that successfully addresses poverty, hunger, disease, and the environment.

The book is aimed especially at poor countries, but applies also to rich countries. For example, the macroeconomic degradation process is apparent in the United States and not just in poor countries in recent decades. As a huge, wealthy economy, the U.S. can be abused longer and deeper than weak economies. The lessons of the *standard model* apply nonetheless.

I am grateful to my colleagues for their inputs. Emeritus Professors Douglas Graham and Norman Rask, illustrious colleagues in the Department of Agricultural, Environmental, and Development Economics at Ohio State University, read draft chapters and shared insights from their long careers in international finance and development. My cherished wife Eloyce has been a patient and strong supporter of my efforts; for this I am very thankful. My son Lon designed the book cover—I owe him one. I, of course, am solely accountable for shortcomings of this volume.

Luther Tweeten

CONTENTS

1

Introduction

The standard economic model (or simply "standard model" or "SM") is a set of best practices for economic development. SM is a proven framework for socio-economic development and emerges from decades of empirical evidence of what works. The model is market-oriented, while recognizing the crucial role of institutions and culture in development. The model arguably is the most important development in economics in decades.

No one should accept that bold statement on faith. This volume establishes the conceptual and empirical case for the model. Many elements of SM are not new—some trace at least to Adam Smith. What is new is the coming together of the various pieces of the development puzzle in a workable framework for providing equitable and efficient economic progress.

Almost everyone rejoices over prospects to end scourges such as smallpox and polio. With leadership from the World Health Organization, vaccines have been made available to all at an affordable price. The felicitous result is that smallpox has been eliminated and polio nearly eradicated. Millions of lives have been spared. Polio has not been eliminated, because unscrupulous people have convinced some persons in northern Nigeria and a few other places that polio vaccination is harmful. A consequence is that travelers from the few remaining pockets of polio carry the disease around the world, rendering eradication impossible.

The standard model is the economic equivalent of a cure for polio and smallpox. Empirical evidence attests that following the standard model's economic policies and institutional requirements can assure any country of economic progress. SM policies do not necessarily make a country rich, but they do provide sufficient economic progress for a country to afford alleviating poverty and the accompanying problems of hunger, ill health, and environmental degradation.

With few exceptions, economists are inept moralizers. About as close as they get to moralizing is to contend that devoting resources to investments with benefit-cost ratios greater than 1.0 is "good" and devoting resources to investments with benefit-cost ratios of less than 1.0 is "bad." Because markets strive to devote resources to investments where benefits exceed costs, it follows that the market-oriented standard model (with appropriate adjustments for the marginal utility of income to serve equity and for externalities to align social with private incentives) outlined in this volume serves morality.

The morality of the standard model can be expressed in less academic terms. Adolph Hitler, Mao Zedong, and Joseph Stalin occupy the top positions in the pantheon of human villainy. They respectively accounted for fifty million, seventy million, and thirty million deaths during three decades of the twentieth century. (See chapter 3 for some alternative estimates.) That appalling death toll averaging 5 million per year is only half the more than 10 million children, the vast majority in poor countries, under five years of age who now die each year from treatable diseases ("In Brief," p. 2). Because of tragic economic policies, neither parents nor other potential sources of help in the country can afford to provide necessary health care.

Or consider the numbers of children and adults who die well before their time for lack of resources to acquire medication for just three treatable diseases: tuberculosis, malaria, and AIDS. Together, these illnesses take six million lives each year (Farmer, p. 22). Thus 150 million lives will be sacrificed, largely in poor countries, in just twenty-five years in the twenty-first century, to these three treatable diseases because individuals and countries lack the buying power to obtain effective treatment. The needless deaths continue.

Thus opinion makers and decision makers in poor countries who reject standard-model policies and institutions overshadow the depredations of the "big three" villains as measured by annual deaths alone. Such failure might have been dismissed in the past as excusable ignorance of medicine and economics. With the standard model and more effective medical treatments, that excuse falls flat. Excusable ignorance turns into willful ignorance, a far more serious offense. Opinion makers and decision makers in poor countries are now culpable for treatable disease, chronic hunger, and abject poverty.

Some will say that the standard model is unnecessary—caring, rich individuals and nations will provide for the sick and hungry in poor countries. I am a strong supporter of private and public charity, and I personally support an AIDS orphan project in Africa. I am also a realist. Private and public charity from local or foreign sources has never adequately addressed—and will never adequately address—hunger and disease in poor countries. To properly and fully address these scourges, poor countries must reform their policies and institutions.

Mere numbers cannot express the pain and suffering caused by needless morbidity and mortality resulting because food and proven methods of health care are unaffordable. But numbers from the IMF ("Checking up on Health," pp. 8, 9) provide further clues. Life expectancy in poor countries averages about sixty years compared to eighty years in rich countries; thus, on average, twenty years of life are lost. An estimated forty-five million people lived with HIV/ AIDS in 2003, most of them in sub-Saharan Africa, where an estimated 2.4 million people died of the disease and its complications in that year. Tuberculosis killed 1.7 million people in 2000, two-thirds of them in low-income countries. Malaria killed 1.1 million people in 2000, some ninety percent of them in Africa. Some five million children are included in the eight million people estimated to die from hunger-related causes each year (see Falcon and Naylor, p. 1114). Many people die each year in poor countries from measles, whooping cough, diarrhea, malaria, tuberculosis, and other diseases that need not be fatal, but find opportunistic victims in families and countries that cannot afford adequate diets and health care.

The standard model is more important for the world's welfare than is any disease cure. The reason is that research and application of numerous disease cures await resources that will be made available only through economic development. No country has too few natural resources, too fecund people, or too ignorant and ungifted a population to be forever condemned to the economic doldrums (Box 1).

Box 1. My wife taught music in public schools. Each student aspiring to be in the school chorus had to submit to a tryout. The young boy sitting beside her on the piano bench was a monotone who sang only one note as my wife played up the music scale. Finally, the tryout boy sighed in frustration and concluded, "Teacher, I don't think I can go any higher!" Many poor countries are like that about development, aspiring to economic progress but getting nowhere. While frustrated, unlike "Johnny One-Note," they are not congenitally condemned to underperformance. Appropriate policies can move any poor country up the economic scale. Although they may blame multinational corporations, affluent nations, an international economic system rigged against them, and a host of other outside factors for lack of economic progress, the enemy in fact is within—their own attitudes, institutions, and misguided policies.

Some contend that standard-model policies are not necessary to alleviate problems of poverty and of hunger and disease that attend poverty. The longevity of residents of socialist Cuba and Kerala, India, is cited as evidence that socialism works. The attention of these very poor countries to health and education is commendable, and many other developing countries could learn from their experience. But neither man nor woman lives by health care alone. People seek a higher standard of living, freedom, and democracy. People have fled Cuba in droves. Kerala is economically stagnant. Its economic base to maintain social services depends on remittances from 3.5 million of its citizens working abroad, especially in oil-rich countries of the Middle East.

A country does not have to be rich for its people to live long; Portugal is an example. However, no country, including Portugal, has been able to attain even a minimally adequate standard of living and freedom without harnessing the wealth-generating power of markets.

Economic progress attainable by any poor country following the standard model eventually will allow aid from other countries to be phased out. Once-destitute countries will be able to afford their own poverty, health, education, and food programs. On the other hand, countries rejecting the standard model can expect to persistently depend on donors for such programs, a precarious existence indeed, given the vagaries of international politics and donor fatigue. Economic success does not come overnight if a country embraces the standard model, but economic development will forever elude poor countries rejecting the model.

This conclusion is not a mandate to end foreign aid. Here it is important to make a distinction between two types of assistance: *humanitarian aid* to treat acute problems of health and nutrition and *developmental aid* to promote economic progress so that countries can become self-reliant over time in addressing their own needs. For humanitarian reasons, rich countries cannot ignore hunger and disease in a poor country, even if the country's problems and policies are of its own leaders' making. Humanitarian food and medical aid saves lives. Humanitarian aid can ease the transition to sound economic policies. Following policy and institutional reform, development can be speeded by donors' provision of public goods such as agricultural research, infrastructure, and education. Giving only humanitarian assistance but withholding economic development assistance until economic reform may appear heartless, but it makes sense to provide assistance where it is used well, rather than where it is wasted. Economic development aid to countries following bad policies delays needed policy reform; meanwhile, aid pays off handsomely in a poor country that adopts and maintains standard-model policies.

Seeking Economic Equity and Efficiency

The standard model is for rich and poor countries. Not even the wealthiest countries have enough resources to meet all the health, retirement, safety, educational, and environmental wants of its residents. Needs are especially acute in poor countries, however, and SM prescriptions are particularly germane to them. Rich countries (unless they struck oil) have followed enough SM policies to be successful. Poor countries have not been following SM policies for long, or they wouldn't be poor. Such countries desperately need additional income to address poverty and other problems.

Standard-model policies are often criticized when an indebted poor country living beyond its means is required by the International Monetary Fund (IMF) or another lender to make cost-cutting reforms to restore fiscal order. So-called "structural adjustment" programs of the IMF can do more than they traditionally have to cushion the impact of national austerity measures on the poor. But this volume calls for countries to follow sound economic policies so they will not face financial crises, structural adjustment measures, and the need for debt forgiveness.

The standard model mostly is about how to raise real national income, and not about how that economic "pie" should be divided. Economics doesn't have a rigorous framework for specifying what the income distribution ought to be, although considerable progress has been made on that issue in recent years. Much is said in this volume about policies that at once promote equity *and* efficiency. Conventional wisdom to the contrary, growing empirical evidence indicates that national economic growth does not necessarily cause income to become more unequally distributed—as measured by the proportion of income going to the richest or poorest segments of the population (Gini coefficient). However, much scope remains to make economic policy more pro-poor.

This volume addresses several troubling puzzles. If a proven economic prescription is available to provide any country with sufficient income to end abject poverty and hunger, why do so many countries reject that prescription? What is an appropriate role for rich countries and multilateral agencies to play in promoting economic development in general and the standard model in particular? Before addressing such puzzles, however, I lay out the standard model in chapter 2. Of particular interest is the role of the public and private sectors in that model. Chapter 3 provides compelling empirical evidence that the standard model works to bring development. Chapter 4 outlines the conceptual framework explaining why following standard-model policies saves lives and improves the well-being of people. Chapters 5 and 6 lay out innovative SM policies to provide economic equity and public goods.

Standard-model policies are on the ascendancy in much of the world, with especially telling benefits in countries such as China and India that together account for two-fifths of the world's inhabitants. While the economic vital signs of much of the world are turning up, they are turning down in sub-Saharan Africa. Chapter 7 addresses the problems of Africa. Opening trade and investment channels offers so much promise for poor countries that chapter 8 is devoted to the topic.

The consequences of adoption of the standard model are, for the most part, predictable and salutary. Some consequences are unintended. A falling world population would have huge consequences. Chapter 9 is devoted to that issue. Finally, chapter 10 provides the summary and conclusions.

The general public, by and large, knows little of the standard model, though it is straightforward and simple enough that its principal components can be listed on the back of an envelope. This volume attempts to remove ignorance as an excuse for egregious, unnecessary global mortality and morbidity arising from failure to follow standard model policies. It is a challenge indeed to convince countries of the benefits of sound economic policies and of rejecting appealing, simple, but wrong populist and counterculture proposals for economic success.

The old saying that "If dreams were horses, beggars could ride" could be reworded to state, "If lofty goals were bread, the poor could be fed." The right to food has been widely asserted at least since the adoption of the Universal Declaration of Human Rights in 1948. The 1974 World Food Conference proclaimed that "every man, woman, and child has the inalienable right to be free from hunger and malnutrition in order to develop their physical and mental faculties." This was to have been achieved "within a decade." At the World Food Summit of 1996, leaders from over 185 countries pledged by the year 2015 to halve the number of the world's hungry people from the 800-million-person benchmark in 1990. "Millennium Development Goals" (MGDs) were established by the 191 member states of the United Nations meeting in New York City in September 2000, and were reaffirmed at the United Nation's World Food Summit by over 180 countries in 2002. The eight MGDs pledged, from a base of 1990, by year 2015 to:

1. Reduce extreme poverty (people living on less than $1 per day) and hunger by half.
2. Achieve universal primary education, ensuring that all children are able to complete primary education.

3. Eliminate gender disparity in primary and secondary schooling, and in general to promote gender equality and empower women.
4. Reduce the mortality rate of children under five by two-thirds.
5. Improve maternal health; reduce the maternal mortality rate by three-fourths.
6. Combat diseases, halting and beginning to reverse HIV/AIDS and other diseases.
7. Ensure environmental sustainability. Cut in half the proportion of people without sustainable access to safe drinking water and sanitation.
8. Develop a global partnership for development. Reform aid and trade, with special treatment for poor countries.

With a decade remaining to reach MGD targets, the United Nations Development Program's *Human Development Report* 2005 (UNDP, p. 17) summarized progress to date thus:

If current trends continue, the MGDs will be missed by a wide margin. Instead of seizing the moment, the world's governments are stumbling towards a heavily sign-posted and easily avoidable human development failure—a failure of profound implications not just for the world's poor but for world peace, prosperity, and security.

The target for reducing child mortality will be missed. An estimated additional 4.4 million children will die in 2015 if the 2005 trajectory is continued versus meeting the MDG target (UNDP, p. 18). Some 380 million more people will live in abject poverty in developing countries in 2015 if current trends continue versus achieving the MDG target.

Real income per capita mostly trends upwards worldwide and shows modest increases since 2000, even in sub-Saharan Africa, where it has been falling for decades. However, the Human Development Index compiled by the UNDP to include the income, education, and health aspects of well-being fell in twelve countries with 240 million people in sub-Saharan Africa between 1990 and 2003 (UNDP, p. 21). The former Soviet Union accounted for the other six countries where the Human Development Index fell between 1990 and 2003.

Given the urgency of dealing with poverty and hunger to improve the well-being of people in developing countries, it is good to review progress by world region over time. Only developing countries, which account for the poorest three-fourths of the world's more than six billion people, are considered in table 1.1. Data in the table are for undernutrition, defined as persons whose average calorie intake falls below the minimum required to maintain metabolism and perform light activity.

Table 1.1 Undernutrition in Developing Countries

Region	1969–71	1979–81	1990–92	1995–97	2000–02
	Million Persons				
	(Percent of region total)				
Latin America and Carib.	53 (19)	48 (14)	59 (13)	55 (11)	53 (10)
South Asia	238 (33)	303 (34)	291 (26)	287 (23)	301 (22)
East and Southeast Asia	475 (41)	378 (27)	277 (16)	221 (12)	217 (11)
Near East and North Africa	48 (27)	27 (12)	25 (8)	35 (10)	39 (10)
Sub-Saharan Africa	103 (38)	148 (41)	170 (36)	197 (36)	203 (33)
Total developing countries	917 (35)	904 (28)	824 (20)	797 (18)	815 (17)

Source: FAO, 1996; 2004

East Asia and Southeast Asia alone accounted for over half of undernourished persons in poor countries in 1969–71. Mainly because of falling numbers of undernourished persons in China, by 1990–92 South Asia (mostly the Indian subcontinent) had overtaken East Asia and Southeast Asia as the region with the greatest number of undernourished persons. Very soon, sub-Saharan Africa will have greater numbers of undernourished persons than South Asia. Portents for Africa are not favorable, also based on the incidence of malnutrition as measured by the proportion of persons in each region who are undernourished. While the incidence of malnutrition fell sharply for most regions between 1969–71 and 2000–02, it fell very little in sub-Saharan Africa. The growing number of undernourished persons since 1995–97 is of serious concern, because it reverses decades of progress. The situation needs to be monitored as future nutrition data become available.

Poverty and undernutrition are closely related, as is apparent from the data in tables 1.1 and 1.2. Most of the some 800 million undernourished people are also numbered among the 1.1 billion very poor people living on less than one dollar per day. Some differences in year and among countries selected for inclusion in regions preclude precise comparisons, but it is notable that the largely comparable East Asia and Southeast Asia region (table 1.1) and the East Asia and Pacific region (table 1.2) had respectively the highest incidence of undernutrition and of abject poverty in early years. (Data are not shown, but the incidence of poverty was high in East Asia in 1970.) In recent years, the sub-Saharan region has had by far the highest incidence of undernutrition and poverty. The Latin America and the Caribbean region and the Middle East and North Africa region had relatively low levels of abject poverty and undernutrition. With the exception of sub-Saharan Africa, the incidence of poverty fell dramatically since 1981 in all regions and for poor countries as a group. As in the case of undernourishment, global numbers in poverty would not have dropped without the success of China; however, the percent of persons in abject poverty would have fallen from twenty-eight percent to twenty-four percent in 2001, even excluding China. We observe in chapter 3 that the success of nations in raising income and in addressing poverty and undernutrition is closely related to how closely they have followed the standard model.

Conclusions

The number of persons who rarely get enough to eat has remained stuck at approximately 800 million in recent decades. Excluding China, the numbers of hungry people have grown. The MGDs are worthy goals by well-intentioned people, but they never had a chance to be realized. Unrealistic goals arise from unrealistic notions of what is required to achieve success. Inordinate emphasis was placed on what developed countries must do, and too little emphasis was placed on the vital ingredient for success—the policies (and institutions) of poor countries themselves!

Table 1.2. Number of Persons and Percentage of Region in Abject Poverty (less than $1 per day) by Region for Selected Years

Region	1981	1990	1993	1996	1999	2001
		Million persons (Percent of region total)				
Latin America and Carib.		48				50
	(9.7)	(11.3)	(11.3)	(10.7)	(10.5)	(9.5)
South Asia		466				431
	(51.5)	(41.3)	(40.1)	(36.6)	(32.2)	(31.3)
East Asia and Pacific		470				271
	(57.7)	(29.6)	(24.9)	(16.6)	(15.7)	(14.9)
Middle East and North Africa		5				7
	(5.1)	(2.3)	(1.6)	(2.0)	(2.6)	(2.4)
Sub-Saharan Africa		241				313
	(41.6)	(44.6)	(44.1)	(45.6)	(45.7)	(46.4)
Total		1,237				1,089
		(28.3)				(21.1)

Source: World Bank, 2004, p. 46; 2005a, p. 21; 2005b.

Unreachable goals inspire despair and cynicism, not commitment. To succeed in addressing hunger, disease, and poverty, poor countries will need to buy into substantive elements of the standard model. This volume lays out what works to achieve development goals. The requirements are daunting and long-term. Critics will find fault and look for shortcuts. There are none—history is littered with the carcasses of failed alternatives.[1] If the numbers of people in

---

1   The annual global shortfall of income below the abject poverty threshold of one dollar per day could be closed with cash outlays to the poor of $124 billion, or about 0.6 percent of rich-country GDP. This compares with a UN target of 0.7 percent and the actual average of 0.2 percent of GDP provided by donors to economic assistance of various types. A cash payment is not administratively feasible. Even if it were, it would

chronic hunger and poverty are to fall, the way people think and act will need to change. That is what this volume is about.

References

"Checking up on Health." *Finance and Development.* Washington DC: International Monetary Fund, March 2004.

Falcon, Walter and Rosamond Naylor. "Rethinking Food Security for the Twenty-First Century." *American Journal of Agricultural Economics* 87: 1113–27, December 2005.

FAO. *The State of Food Insecurity in the World 2004.* Rome: Food and Agriculture Organization of the United Nations, 2004.

FAO. *Data of Food and Agriculture 1996.* Rome: Food and Agriculture Organization of the United Nations, 1996.

Farmer, Paul. *Pathologies of Power.* Los Angeles: University of California Press, 2005.

"In Brief: Aid must be Better Targeted." *Finance and Development.* International Monetary Fund, June 2006.

UNDP. *The State of Human Development 2005.* New York: United Nations Development Program, 2005.

World Bank. *Global Economic Prospects 2004 (and 2005).* Washington DC: World Bank, 2004, 2005a.

World Bank. *World Development Indicators.* Washington DC: World Bank, 2005b.

---

only temporarily end *income* poverty. It might detract from ending structural general poverty, which depends on accumulation of human and other forms of capital, including one's attitudes, as explained in chapter 4.

2

Defining the Standard Model

The standard model, a proven prescription for economic development, has a neoclassical, market-oriented lineage but is not chosen for its ideology. It is chosen because it works. The model relies on the market through the price system in a supportive institutional environment to make most of the millions of decisions required daily in an economy regarding what, when, where, and how to produce. Many countries have eliminated abject poverty (income less than one dollar per person per day), but none has done so without harnessing the efficiency of markets.

Without an economic pie, issues of how to divide the pie equitably are moot. Economies such as the former Soviet Union, Cuba, and North Korea that have relied on bureaucrats in government to make such decisions have failed spectacularly. For economic efficiency—getting the most real output out of limited resources—no substitute has been found for the market price system. Today, almost no one doubts that markets are essential for economic success. At issue is how large a role markets versus other means should play in allocating resources and outputs.

Critics have savaged markets, sometimes with reason. They note that the market is impersonal. A well-functioning market unceremoniously culls unprofitable, redundant, and poorly performing workers and firms without regard to race, creed, or status in society. Famed economist Joseph Schumpeter labeled this phenomenon "creative destruction." A well-functioning market does not ask whether participants have political connections when making decisions. Instead, it allocates resources to the highest and best use; *i.e.,* uses providing the highest monetary return but presumably also contributing most to the well-being of people.

To be sure, governments often intervene to unduly protect a politically influential corporation or family, but that is a fault of government as much as (or more than) of markets. Government-directed economies offer far more scope for political favoritism than do market-driven economies. Organized labor can thwart markets, as in the case of General Motors, forcing the company to continue paying workers who have been laid off because of falling demand for cars. Workers' success in thwarting change is temporary—when the company goes bankrupt, thousands of workers are left with neither jobs nor company retirement and health-care benefits. (Problems of economic equity and of economic versus social well-being will be addressed in a subsequent chapter; here the focus is mostly on economic efficiency.)

The market also is faulted because it does not force people to make choices recommended by an elite composed of "experts" or persons in authority. The flip side of that criticism is that markets allow people (voting with buying power) rather than elites the freedom to choose how best to allocate resources and income. Well-functioning markets constitute what economists call a positive-sum game; that is, market participants benefit because exchange does not take place unless both buyer and seller perceive gains from the transaction. This volume proposes several remedies for situations where power is concentrated to favor one over another party in market transactions.

Given that salubrious case for private markets, it may come as a surprise that most of this chapter's description of the standard model will center on the role of the public sector. The reason is that markets work on "automatic pilot," and little need be said of them if the public sector provides a supportive institutional environment. Getting that institutional environment right is far more important than getting prices right, because prices will be right if the institutional environment is right. The issue of what activities are best left to the public sector and what to the market is critical to any successful economy and hence to the standard model. That important issue requires dealing with some abstractions and therefore is relegated to an annex to this chapter, but it is recommended reading for all students of public policy.

Regarding poor countries, the standard model calls for a lean public sector doing a few things well. The principal roles of the public sector are to provide so-called public goods (and services) and to provide a safety net for those who have too few personal, family, or charitable sources to provide necessities for living. The height of the public safety net is a social, moral, and political decision as well as an economic decision. The economics discipline has been much more rigorous in specifying what policies are appropriate to raise national income (efficiency) than how that income should be distributed (equity). The proper size of the safety net is not specified here, except to state that a high safety net is likely to sacrifice national income. One way to minimize such onerous tradeoffs is with public policies that simultaneously promote economic progress *and* a more nearly even distribution of income. Human resource investments, such as in basic health care and universal education through at least elementary school, are especially effective in promoting such broad-based, pro-poor development.

The following sections of this chapter list antecedents of the standard model, priorities for development, and the role of foreign assistance. But first, the standard model is defined under six components: governance, macroeconomic policy, foreign trade, infrastructure, services, and environment.

Standard Model Components

This section defines the standard model, especially the role of government, based on the public requirements for economic progress outlined in the annex. Subsequent chapters will elaborate on several of the components.

1. Governance:
- Security, stability, order. The rule of law and order is the single most important policy and institutional element for the economic progress of any country. Government needs to strive for an environment where business plans (contracts) can be made and carried through. Contracts must be enforceable. Firms must be confident that violence will not interfere with normal, legal economic transactions. Adherence to the rule of law in no way implies a police state, violation of individual rights, or oppression in any form. A proper rule by law requires an independent judicial system to hear grievances, interpret laws, and administer justice.
- Honesty and competence in public administration. Corruption in government undermines economic progress (Sachs, 1997). Corruption, like sin, cannot be eliminated but can be minimized by measures such as civil-service examinations, merit hiring and promotion, public administration training, competitive pay scales, transparency in public records, a free press, protections against administrative employee discharge for political reasons, and enforcement of laws against bribes and kickbacks.
- Property rights. To encourage investment and improvements in property, investors must be able to "reap what is sown." Property rights allow property to be used as collateral for loans. A favorable investment climate avoids capital flight and attracts foreign direct investment.
- Competition. Competition along with property rights promotes productivity, obtaining the most output from always limited resources. Governments need to avoid giving protection to firms exercising monopoly power. In the case of natural monopolies (only one firm can operate at low cost per unit of output), regulation or cooperatives are sometimes helpful; but open trade to countervail the economic power

of domestic firms is often the most effective option. Parastatals (state-owned enterprises) need to be avoided where possible.

2. Macroeconomic policies:[2]

- Fiscal responsibility. Countries need to avoid deficits in their government operating account. A deficit is justified in the capital account only for investments with the strong chance of a return that will at least pay the principal and interest. Governments may attempt to follow a desirable countercyclical stabilization policy, running a budget deficit in the depressed phase and a surplus in the boom phase of the business cycle; however, few poor countries have the will or means to follow such a Keynesian policy. Because political leaders never seem to believe their country has reached full employment, countercyclical policy intentions tend to morph into a ruinous policy of perpetual deficit spending.

- Monetary restraint. A useful rule of thumb is to increase money supply at the real GDP growth rate, with appropriate adjustments for foreign exchange and direct investment. A central bank "at arm's length" from political pressure adjusts the money supply, interest rates, and reserve requirements with the objective of price stability. An annual inflation rate of up to three percent can be tolerated and even helpful by creating real wage and price flexibility. Sticky (inflexible downward) wages can be adjusted downward in real terms as the nominal wage/price is held steady while inflation changes buying power.

- Appropriate taxation. An onerous challenge for any developing country is to collect taxes to pay for even minimal public services. Successful governments tax "bads" (consumption, tobacco, alcohol, toxic emissions), not "goods" (investment, exports). They charge user fees to cover costs for electricity, irrigation water, and the like provided by the public sector. Sales tax, value-added tax, and property tax distort the economy less than taxes on corporate profits and exports. Taxing at

---

2   Failure to pursue sound macroeconomic policy energizes the *macroeconomic degradation process* (Tweeten, 1989). The process sequence usually is as follows: (1) Government attempts to live beyond its means, as apparent in domestic government budget and foreign trade deficits. (2) The government borrows to the limit, perhaps first domestically and then internationally. Debt service becomes high relative to export earnings. (3) To meet payrolls and debt obligations, in desperation, the government "prints" money. The result is inflation. (4) With exchange rates in the developing country pegged to one or more hard currencies, inflation causes an overvalued exchange rate. (5) Foreign exchange is depleted as the overvalued currency discourages exports and encourages imports. (6) Shortages of fuel, spare parts, and other critical imports emerge, creating a national crisis in the worst-case scenario.

a flat rate allows taxes to be taken out at the source rather than from individual recipients of income, simplifying procedures and minimizing tax avoidance. Exempting food or providing a lump-sum payment to low-income families and individuals can minimize the regressiveness of flat-rate taxation. Taxing services and housing as well as goods broadens the tax base and helps to keep overall marginal tax rates commendably low. Taxing gifts (including inheritance) progressively and using the proceeds to educate poor people can promote a more even distribution of income without materially distorting market signals.

3. Utilizing foreign markets. Chief elements of a liberal trade policy include:

- Properly valued foreign exchange. The preferred alternative is flexible exchange rates set by supply and demand for currency in international markets. For poor countries with undeveloped banking systems, high inflation, and unstable currency values set in markets, a useful alternative is an occasional market float along with interim period fixed exchange rates adjusted periodically (e.g., monthly with high inflation) for inflation rates at home relative to those of trading partners.

- Open economy to investment. Foreign direct (private) investment (FDI) dwarfs official (public) development assistance (ODA). FDI brings capital, management, technology, and access to foreign markets. It can quickly transform an economy for the better, as illustrated by China. On the other hand, shorter-term financial capital can be flighty, moving out as quickly as (or more quickly than) it came in. The result of that capital outflow can energize financial crises, as in East Asia and Southeast Asia in 1997. Thus, developing countries may wish to discourage speculative financial capital flows while encouraging equity capital inflow.

- Free trade. Uniform, if any, taxes on imports. Countries are tempted to tax imports to promote infant industries. Unfortunately, taxes on imports become taxes on exports when exports are produced using imported inputs. If imports are to be taxed at all, duties are best kept low and uniform. Taxes on exports are especially undesirable because they tax domestic industries—exporters cannot pass the higher taxes to buyers in highly price-responsive foreign markets.

4. Infrastructure investments. Examples are:

- All-weather roads for food security and commercial activity consistent with comparative advantage.

- Bridges, seaports, airports, electricity, and the like. Numerous infrastructure investments show high social rates of return on investment, but each project is unique (Tweeten and McClelland, chapter 4). Hence, these and other infrastructure, such as dams and irrigation facilities, need to pass the benefit-cost test.

5. Public services.

- Agricultural research offers unusually high returns on investment, but Africa spends less than 0.5 percent of agricultural GDP on agricultural research. Raising public and private spending to one percent of agricultural GDP could pay high dividends, because agriculture frequently accounts for sixty to eighty percent of the labor force and forty to sixty percent of GDP in developing countries.

- Human-resource investments are essential for broad-based development for all regions and for women and men, including minorities. Because rates of return on elementary-schooling investment are especially high, universal elementary schooling is a priority for food security and development. Sanitation for economic development and food security requires attention to water and waste. Parasites and bacteria interfere with digestion of food and sap vitality.

- Health clinics staffed by volunteers and paraprofessionals can provide low-cost services such as immunization, vitamin supplements, oral rehydration, family planning, HIV/AIDS prevention, pre-and post-natal health care, and bed nets to protect against malaria-carrying mosquitoes.

6. Environment. For development to be sustainable, attention must be given to the environment. This is especially urgent where poverty attends high population growth and density. Agriculture can benefit from integrated crop management (forage and tree legumes for nitrogen, alley cropping, etc.), conservation tillage (no-till, ridge till, mulch till), integrated pest management (an economic threshold of pest infestation required before intervention, biological pest controls, pest-resistant crops and livestock, "best management practices"), integrated crop-livestock systems including forage legumes, and integrated forest management (plantation forests, ecotourism, firewood, etc.).

The foregoing six components constituting the standard model are for the most part pro-poor. The education and health provisions serve both equity and efficiency. Property rights and the rule of law benefit the poor as well as the rich. The poor are especially disadvantaged by anarchy, because they lack access to lawyers and government officials. The poor in developing countries benefit from export expansion made possible by free trade, because the countries specialize in exporting labor-intensive products employing lower-skilled workers.

The poor are most disadvantaged by a highly regulated economy stifled by pay-offs to corrupt officials for licenses and permits to conduct business.

Thus, the standard model makes possible a two-front attack on poverty. One front is direct addition to income. China's successful attack on poverty came not from income transfers but from additional earnings that attended economic development. Without any significant new redistribution policies or foreign aid, but by adopting elements of the standard model, China by 2005 already had met the UN's Millennium Development Goal of reducing abject poverty to half the 1990 level. In contrast, sub-Saharan Africa, where poverty is high and adherence to the standard model is low, had made little progress in reducing poverty by 2005.

The second front of the two-front attack of the standard model on poverty is to provide the income essential to fund a food and income safety net. The public safety net is for those unable to depend on themselves, the market, family, or other private sources. Landless peasants, smallholders, and the urban poor are especially vulnerable to economic setbacks. Women and children are more vulnerable than men. The form of safety net depends on the stage of development and the administrative capabilities of a country. A very poor country may afford only charitable contributions provided and administered by families, churches, and other charitable organizations. Targeted humanitarian assistance options include medications and food for education (*e.g.,* school lunches) or for work. Foreign donors are an important source of food and medicine. As nations grow in wealth and administrative capabilities, the safety net can come in forms such as food stamps, whereby a poor household pays a proportion of its income to a public agency in return for food stamps sufficient to purchase an adequate diet. Similar income-conditioned programs can provide low-income persons with medical care and housing.

Some forms of safety net can seriously impede economic progress. Germany and France, for example, provide generous unemployment allowances that diminish incentives for the jobless to return to work. The countries also require firms to provide large severance packages and other benefits to laid-off workers. A consequence is high unemployment rates, because firms that find it costly to release workers don't hire workers.

Governments seek safety nets that transfer income to the poor with minimal cost in lost national income. Some affluent nations find wage or earnings supplements attractive to target low-income persons by generating jobs for disadvantaged workers. Chapter 5 depicts in more detail various forms of safety nets targeted to the needs of rich and poor countries.

The height and breadth of the safety net is a political decision and is not dictated by the standard model. A high safety net, as characterized by the term "welfare state," often means slow economic growth due to lack of incentives, flexibility, and "creative economic destruction" pruning economic deadwood. The safety net of necessity must begin low, but it is expected to expand as development progresses. Table 2.1 suggests limits to the size of the safety net as measured by the proportion of a nation's gross domestic product (GDP) in the public sector. In 1990, ten industrial countries listed in table 2.1 devoted over half their GDP to the public sector. Nine of those ten countries reduced the public-sector share by 2006. The one exception is France, which increased its public-sector share from 50.7 percent in 1990 to 53.9 percent in 2006. Judging by its double-digit unemployment and slow economic growth in recent years, France appears to have exceeded the optimal level of government in its economy, as measured by regulations and government GDP. The country seems destined for economic reforms restoring business and employment incentives consistent with the standard model.

Table 2.1. Government Outlays as Percent of Gross Domestic Product, OEDC Countries

Country	1990	2006	Country	1990	2006
Australia	36.2	35.4	Luxembourg	43.2	45.6
Austria	51.6	48.2	Netherlands	54.8	47.8
Belgium	53.4	49.1	New Zealand	53.3	39.1
Canada	48.8	38.9	Norway	54.0	45.3
Czech Republic	n/a	45.2	Poland	n/a	45.1
Denmark	57.0	54.1	Portugal	42.1	47.3
Finland	48.7	50.4	Slovak Republic	n/a	38.1
France	50.7	53.9	Spain	43.4	40.1
Germany	44.5	46.1	Sweden	63.5	56.7
Greece	50.2	48.1	Switzerland	30.0	35.2
Hungary	n/a	50.0	United Kingdom	42.2	45.2
Iceland	42.4	43.6	United States	37.0	35.7
Ireland	43.2	34.3	Euro area	48.7	47.7
Italy	54.4	48.7			
Japan	31.7	37.5	Total OECD	40.3	40.4
Korea	19.5	28.3			

Source: OEDC, 2005

Antecedents of the Standard Model

The standard model has antecedents in the Washington Consensus, a term coined by John Williamson in 1990 to describe the set of policies endorsed by the U.S. Treasury, the Federal Reserve Board, the International Monetary Fund, and the World Bank (all located in Washington DC) to address the financial crisis gripping several countries in Latin America in the 1980s. The ten elements of the Washington Consensus were:

1. Fiscal discipline
2. Redirection of public expenditures toward high-return, pro-egalitarian investments in human resources and infrastructure
3. Tax reform to lower rates and broadening the base
4. Interest-rate liberalization
5. A competitive exchange rate
6. Trade liberalization
7. Foreign direct investment liberalization
8. Privatization
9. Deregulation
10. Secure property rights

It is obvious that the Washington Consensus, sometimes referred to as neo-liberalism, contains much wisdom for today's world, although it was intended only for a single region, Latin America, experiencing a macroeconomic financial crisis in the 1980s.

The Washington Consensus had flaws. The Post-Washington Consensus of the late 1990s attempted to correct some of the flaws by incorporating institutions, finance, and good governance. The augmented Washington Consensus called for better corporate governance, flexible labor markets, World Trade Organization agreements, and for financial codes and standards. Williamson himself noted in 1999 that the policy prescription would generalize better if the term "interest-rate liberalization" were replaced by "financial liberalization," but with the elaboration that the financial system needs some public regulation and disclosure to protect depositors and investors. Furthermore, he recognized that "flighty" short-term and intermediate-term financial capital might need some regulation to avoid capital flight, which raised havoc with several East Asian and Southeast Asian economies in the financial crisis of 1997. Chile, for example, has successfully employed policies to minimize instability from capital flight. Credit for consumers and businesses does not have externalities that make it a public good to be provided by government, but it requires government oversight regarding disclosure and fiduciary responsibility.

The Washington Consensus was viciously attacked. Critics said it promoted a race to the environmental bottom as competition forced nations to cut costs by ignoring the environment. Critics faulted the Consensus for diminishing the capacity of nations to tax and pay for public services. Critics labeled it ideological, moralistic market-fundamentalism and said it failed requirements for sustainable development, democracy, and competition policy. The unkindest cut of all was a charge that the Consensus policies were pro-rich and anti-poor.

These criticisms do not stand scrutiny. The Washington Consensus was never intended to be comprehensive. It said next to nothing about the environment, agriculture, competition, and democracy, because it was mostly about fiscal, monetary, and trade policy. It was intended to address acute financial problems of nations rather than broader issues of economic development. Like the standard model, the Consensus was designed to express what works, and not an ideology. The standard model builds on the Washington Consensus to provide a more comprehensive blueprint for economic development, but any general policy formulation must be tailored to specific circumstances.

Was the Washington Consensus pro-rich and anti-poor? Some background regarding Latin America in the 1980s is helpful in understanding the origins of the Washington Consensus. Multinational banks in the West were seeking outlets for deposits they had amassed from petrodollar-flush oil producers, mostly in the Middle East. To curry favor with constituents, populist governments in Latin America eagerly borrowed money that was spent to promote consumption rather than high-payoff investments. The attempt to live beyond their means energized the macroeconomic degradation process (defined in footnote 2) in Latin America. Financially overextended countries eventually had no alternative but to cut consumption. Without the assistance of the IMF, even more of the burden of adjusting to financial realities would have fallen on the poor. The governments of the bankrupt countries, rather than the International Monetary Fund and other multinational banks, decided the incidence of inevitable sacrifice. The time to avoid a hangover is "the night before." So too, sound economic policies must be adopted before financial crisis to avoid subsequent sacrifice, burdening the poor and others.

Rodrik (p. 2) comments on the current status of the Washington Consensus: "While the lessons drawn by proponents and critics differ, it is fair to say that nobody really believes in the Washington Consensus anymore. The question is not whether the Washington Consensus is dead or alive; it is what will replace it."

The logic and empirical data presented in subsequent chapters of this book indicates that the standard model has no peers, hence appropriately replaces the Washington Consensus as a template for economic progress.

Rodrik proposes his own framework for economic growth that unintentionally reveals shortcomings of omitting the standard model. His growth strategy (p. 17) has three components: (1) a *diagnostic analysis* to identify the most significant constraints on economic growth, (2) a "creative and imaginative" *policy design* to target the identified growth restraints, and (3) the means to *institutionalize* the processes of (1) and (2). Diagnosis and remediation are useful indeed, but Rodrik omits an essential component: a framework of what constitutes a successful economy and a checklist of what to look for when the economy fails to perform. The shortcoming can be illustrated by the challenge of fixing a car whose engine will not run. A clueless mechanic who checks the tires, paint, and bumpers to fix a stalled engine will soon be unemployed. In contrast, a mechanic who knows that an empty gasoline tank is often the cause of engine failure will have more success with "policy design." Furthermore, if the gas tank is empty because of too many miles between service stations and mechanics, someone might "institutionalize" the solution by asking motorists to carry extra gas or by seeing that more service stations are built. Rodrik's growth strategy is helpful, but it complements rather than replaces the standard model or other development framework.

At about the same time the Washington Consensus was taking shape, the United States Agency for International Development (USAID) asked me to chair a task force examining operational changes needed in the agency after the U.S. Congress requested that the agency change its mission from promoting economic development to promoting food security in poor countries. The task force saw no substantive distinction between policies for economic development and food security. An exception is that the latter called for greater attention to broad-based development, including a food safety net (Tweeten *et al.,* 1992). The task force's final report contained many elements of the standard model. It was comprehensive enough to emphasize the rule of law, including the importance of property rights. Hernando de Soto has often articulated that the poor, because they lack access to law enforcers, attorneys, and legislators, are the most disadvantaged in a society lacking property rights. Standard-model policies also are important in protecting wildlife and biodiversity. Open-access property is overexploited in the "tragedy of the commons" as people grab resources such as plants, animals, and minerals "before the hoarders get them." Controlling common property access to preserve the environment requires standard-model policies to pay the bill for competent administration and law enforcement.

Prioritizing Standard-Model Components

All elements of the standard model cannot be pursued simultaneously. Setting priorities is a daunting task for any government. Needed reforms are unique to each country. No country can afford to skimp on the technical and analytical capabilities required to determine where public resources best can be devoted for economic success in the short and long run. Constraints standing in the way of an economy achieving goals set for it (hopefully by representative governments) need to be identified and diminished, if not removed.

Economists like to set investment priorities on the basis of benefits relative to costs or, equivalently, the rate of return on investment. The market performs that prioritization in the private sector. The task of prioritizing is more elusive in the public sector, because many public services, policies, infrastructure elements, and natural resources lack reliable prices. The implementation of best policies inevitably will be somewhat thwarted by self-serving political interests, but without a vision of the possible, there is little hope of success. Countries experiencing general poverty and chronic food insecurity are not following the standard model, hence the highest payoff in those countries is from policy and institutional reform. Careful studies for developing countries often find high rates of social returns for public investments in agricultural technology (adaptation and diffusion), elementary schooling, and some forms of infrastructure (Tweeten and McClelland).

The difficulty of choosing among investment alternatives is illustrated by the development economist Jeffrey Sachs' priorities for development for a poor village in Kenya. As explained in more detail in chapter 7, his (Sachs, pp. 234–36) economic prescription to alleviate poverty in a village of five thousand residents in Sauri, Kenya is to spend seventy dollars per person in the village on fertilizers and improved fallow for farmland, a clinic staffed by a doctor and nurse dispensing antiviral drugs and malaria control, a village truck for running errands, modern cooking fuel for schools, a few cell phones for communication, a grain storage facility, electricity for the school and clinic, water wells and storage for the community, a station to charge batteries used to power light bulbs provided to residents, and finally various outlays to improve community management and services.

Sachs' proposal has flaws. The community and donor administrative capacity is inadequate to direct funding to the activities he favors. Considerable funds probably would go to corrupt officials and administrators. Sachs' (p. 236) program for Kenya would require $1.5 billion of donor support, or fifteen times the current support of $100 million. Donors will be able to provide that level of support for only a few fortunate communities. A serious shortcoming is that the proposal does not address the institutional and cultural environment keeping Kenya from building capital and income to address its own problems of hunger, disease, and poverty. As explained in chapter 7, sub-Saharan Africa needs improved agricultural technology development and diffusion to raise productivity and conserve soil. It needs investments in infrastructure, such as farm-to-market roads and irrigation systems. It needs more training for teachers, to improve education; for civil servants, to reduce corruption; and for decision makers, to improve governance through sound economic policies. Sachs' community improvements will not be sustained and roads will fall into disrepair if Kenya and other countries in Africa continue to neglect economics.[3]

A sustainable alternative much less costly to Kenya and international donors is for Kenya to adopt standard-model policies and institutions to raise income, which in turn could finance worthy projects such as those identified by Sachs. Based on the equations predicting income in chapter 3, improving Kenya's policies and institutions from the current level to the modest levels of Botswana or Estonia could raise Kenya's income by multiples of the seventy dollars per capita that Sachs considers necessary for Sauri.

The Role of Foreign Economic Assistance

The critical importance of economic policy implies that economic development assistance is successful only if recipients recognize their problems and "take ownership" of needed reforms. That ownership is apparent when poor countries demonstrate a commitment to reform *before* significant aid begins. (An exception is warranted for humanitarian food and medical assistance.)

Foreign assistance is especially critical in early stages, when the economic base of a developing country is too low to provide even minimal development tools, such as improved agricultural technology. Development assistance can be

3   I have noted recurring instances in Africa of donors, after observing the decrepit state of agricultural research in a country, agreeing to fund the building of research facilities and training of scientific personnel for say five to ten years, after which the recipient country is to continue funding and control. Often, however, the research effort collapses as donor support ends.

decisive for countries to break the poverty trap of too little income to support infrastructure, technology, and education necessary to raise income. Developed countries have commendably shared technical and scientific knowledge with poor countries and will continue to do so, but a more important and difficult contribution of rich countries to developing countries is open global markets.

Because agriculture typically accounts for three-fourths of employment and a significant share of GDP in poor countries, the long road to economic development must begin with agriculture. However, many poor countries, especially in Africa, will not be able to prosper on agriculture alone. They will need to shift to manufacturing products for export after improvements in agriculture first provide the economic base to improve human capital essential for competing in non-farm industries and attracting foreign direct investment. The long progression will be from farming to light, labor-intensive, low-wage manufacturing, to capital-intensive industry, and finally to higher-paying service industries.

Food security ranks high in Abraham Maslow's or anyone else's hierarchy of needs. It is well to consider how foreign assistance needs change as food security needs change over time. In the short run, with given food supplies, the challenge is plentiful international buffer stocks, relocation of supplies, and open trade and aid to match food availability with individual food needs. In the intermediate run, the challenge is economic growth featuring greater productivity to raise food production and consumer buying power. In the long run, the challenge is for the demographic transition to run its course to zero population growth (ZPG), as portrayed in chapter 9. Family planning alone will not suffice; higher incomes are necessary to provide environmental protection, schooling, urbanization, gender equity, health care for child survival, social security, and other contributors to lower birth rates and ZPG in developing countries.4

Developed countries are mostly near or even below total fertility rates needed for ZPG. The *food security dilemma* is how to raise incomes of the masses in developing countries of sub-Saharan Africa, South Asia, and elsewhere to levels bringing ZPG without jeopardizing the global environment and natural resource stocks over time. Measures such as petroleum or carbon taxes to cut or slow greenhouse gas formation in the United States and other countries not

---

4   Studies (Westoff, pp. 74–80) show that desired total fertility rates, though less than actual total fertility rates, are still well above ZPG total fertility rates of about 2.1 child per woman in most developing countries, but especially in sub-Saharan Africa. Hence, family planning enabling parents to have their desired number of children will not alone bring ZPG.

charging the full social cost of energy use can make tradeoffs less globally disruptive for developing countries.

Concluding Comments

How does the standard model differ from previous prescriptions to foster economic progress? One major difference is that the standard model treats institutions and culture and not just public policy as instrumental variables in the effort to promote economic progress and alleviate poverty, hunger, and disease. The standard model acknowledges the importance of getting agriculture moving to jump-start growth in poor countries with most of their population in agriculture. The standard model recognizes that it is inappropriate to promote just agriculture or just industry to create jobs—all sectors work synergistically to promote economic progress.

The standard model recognizes what might be called the *turnpike theory*; *i.e.*, the quickest and easiest route to success in addressing poverty is not to rely solely on the direct "two-lane" road of direct subsidies to poor people. Rather, the preferred route is the "superhighway" of building human and other assets of people, so they can permanently work themselves out of poverty (see footnote 1 in chapter 1), even if getting to that superhighway means traveling some difficult back roads. The standard model places the principal burden of development on poor countries themselves, although rich countries can be important catalysts. The standard model recognizes that sustainable progress at the individual, firm, and community level depends on supportive institutions and policies at the national and international level. In short, the standard model stresses that successful development is integrated and holistic.

The standard model is useful in identifying what governments need not do; for example, provision of credit and farm-commodity price supports. Such programs, on which governments lavish hundreds of billions of dollars each year, are neither public goods nor equitable. On average, the benefits of such subsidized programs go to persons with above-average income and wealth.

Helping poor countries meet immediate short-run critical needs for food and health care is essential. Even more important in the intermediate to long run is helping poor countries to recognize the seminal importance of standard-model policies and institutions for addressing underdevelopment and poverty. Countries following standard-model policies will grow out of the need to rely on foreign donors and nongovernment organizations to treat hunger, disease, and environmental problems. It is sad commentary that some nongovernment organizations and humanitarians fight the standard model because the prospect of being out of their job is unsettling.

The next chapter makes a case that the standard model outlined in this chapter is a proven tool of economic progress. Nonetheless, adoption by countries of the standard model is a choice, not a mandate. The model must be tailored to the circumstances of each country. SM, like the Linux operating system, is open-source. If science and experience can convincingly show better guidelines for development, the model needs to be modified.

Following standard-model policies is not easy for a nation, partly because political power is likely to be in the hands of those who gain from current policies, however damaging those policies may be. Subsequent chapters will introduce the notion that policy and institutional change may need to be attended in some instances by cultural change.

Decision makers considering whether to embrace standard-model policies (and institutions) must balance the cost of imposing standard-model policies against the egregious cost of continuing current policies with the attendant hunger, disease, war, and early death that attends poverty and slow economic growth. The costs of poverty are not borne only by residents of poor countries. War, disease, and hunger in poor countries spill over boundaries to affect the lives of people everywhere.

References

de Soto, Hernando. *The Mystery of Capitalism: Why Capitalism Triumphs in the West and Fails Everywhere Else*. New York: Basic Books, 2000.

Maslow, A. H. "A Theory of Human Motivation." *Psychological Review* 50: 370–96, 1943.

Persaud, Suresh and Luther Tweeten. "Impact of Agribusiness Market Power on Farmers." Chapter 7 in L. Tweeten and S. Thompson, eds., *Agricultural Policy for the 21st Century*. Ames: Iowa State Press, 2002.

OECD. Paris: Organization for Economic Cooperation and Development. http://www.oecd.org/dataoecd/5/51/2483816.xls, 2005.

Rodrik, Dani. "Goodbye Washington Consensus, Hello Washington Confusion." (Paper prepared for the *Journal of Economic Literature*.) Cambridge, Mass.: Harvard University, January 2006.

Sachs, Jeffrey. "The Limits of Convergence." *The Economist*. July 14–20, 1997, pp. 19–22.

Sachs, Jeffrey. *The End of Poverty*. New York: Penguin Press, 2005.

Tanzi, V., and L. Schuknecht. *The Growth of Government and the Reform of the State in Industrial Countries*. IMF Working Paper. Washington DC: International Monetary Fund, December 1995.

Tweeten, Luther. "The Economic Degradation Process." *American Journal of Agricultural Economics*. 71: 1102–1111, December 1989.

Tweeten, Luther. *Terrorism, Radicalism, and Populism in Agriculture*. Ames: Iowa State Press, 2003.

Tweeten, Luther, John Mellor, Schlomo Reutlinger, and James Pines. *Food Security Discussion Paper*. Prepared for U.S. Agency for International Development. Arlington, Virginia: AID Development Information Services Clearinghouse, May 1992.

Tweeten, Luther and Donald G. McClelland, eds. *Promoting Third World Development and Food Security*. Westport, Conn.: Praeger, 1997.

Westoff, Charles. "Reproductive Preferences and Future Fertility in Developing Countries." Chapter 4 in Wolfgang Lutz, ed., *The Future Population of the World*. Luxembourg, Austria: International Institute for Applied Systems Analysis, 1996.

Williamson, John. "What Washington Means by Policy Reform." In John Williamson, ed., *Latin American Adjustment: How Much Has Happened*. Washington DC: Institute for International Economics, 1990.

Williamson, John. "Implications of the East Asian Crisis for Debt Management." In A. Vasudevan, ed., *External Debt Management: Issues, Lessons, and Preventive Measures*. Mumbai: Reserve Bank of India, 1999.

Chapter 2 Annex: Market versus Public Goods

A central issue in the standard model is what goods (and services) should be provided by the public sector and what should be provided by the private sector to improve the well-being of people. The former are called *public goods* and the latter are called *market goods*. Careful use of property rights, regulations, and incentives often can convert public goods into private goods allocated efficiently by markets. All this will be explained with (hopefully) some clarity in chapters 4 and 6. Because of its extreme importance in establishing the division of public-sector versus private-sector activity in the standard model, the distinction between public and private goods and services is addressed in the following paragraphs.

It makes sense to produce and consume another unit of a good if the benefit to society of that incremental unit exceeds the cost to society. Cost is the value of inputs used to produce the good or, equivalently, the value of other goods foregone by producing and consuming the good in question. As will be shown in chapter 4, a private market responding to price incentives will do a pretty good job of that if private costs (benefits) to individuals and firms do not differ from costs (benefits) to society. For example, a large livestock farm may have low private costs of production only because it passes the cost of odor, flies, and polluted water to neighbors. These latter, uncompensated costs, called negative *externalities* by economists, added to the private cost borne by the producing firm, constitute the total or social cost. Because in this example the private cost is below the social cost, it follows that a firm producing in a competitive market at the output where private incremental cost equals the demand price will produce too much.

The first law of welfare economics is that *goods characterized by externalities are candidates for government intervention with taxes, subsidies, or other measures, so that private firms or public agencies operate at the output where incremental social cost is equal to incremental social benefit.* The second, often overlooked law of welfare economics to raise the well-being of people is the caveat that *government intervention in private markets is justified only if the cost of government intervention (e.g.,* in mismanagement and corruption) *is less than the cost to society of allowing the externality to continue.*

Market goods are rival, exclusionary, and transparent; public goods lack one or more of these attributes. The term "rival" means that consumption by one consumer means less of a good is available for other consumers. The term "exclusionary" means that consumers can be excluded from consuming a good if they do not pay for it. The term "transparent" means that the properties of goods must be knowable by market participants. If a good such as a bridge is non-rival, so that consumption by one does not reduce consumption of the good by another, then the good needs to be provided free to maximize benefits to society. A private firm that charges each car to cross that bridge will unduly restrict the benefits to society.[5] Where a good is not transparent, so that consumers do not know what they are buying, markets are subject to failure, in part because of unscrupulous demagogues who peddle "snake oil" (see Tweeten, 2003, p. 71). Patients' difficulty in judging the quality of medical care is one reason why the allocation of medical resources is not left solely to markets. Before getting too carried away by the transparency issue, it is well to point out that markets will supply information regarding goods and services if it pays to do so. In fact, markets flood consumers with "information" in the form of advertising that the public sector often finds misleading.

The major impediment to the market is not the rival and transparency requirements, but rather is the exclusionary problem. That problem precludes firms from supplying goods, because they cannot obtain enough market receipts to cover their costs of operation—even though the social benefits exceed the social costs. An example of a non-exclusionary public good is basic research to develop a new technology, such as a soybean variety or disease cure, whose development costs cannot be recovered in the market. Farmers who plant a new soybean variety, for example, may sell their production to neighbors for seeding while the seed firm that developed the technology goes broke. The private, uncorrected market produces too little of the good, because not enough of the perhaps considerable social benefits of production can be captured as monetary gain by the firm to cover its development cost.[6] Governments bestow intellectual property rights such as patents, copyrights, and trademarks to give market power to firms so they can raise prices to cover costs.

---

5   The obvious question is "Who will pay for the bridge?" The answer is the public sector, using tax revenues. A problem is that many governments are too riddled with lethargy, special interests, ignorance, and penury to supply needed public goods.

6   The government may directly provide public goods such as public administration, grades, standards, antitrust enforcement, national defense, and the like. Or the government may hire private firms or bestow property rights to private firms to perform needed functions. It can be shown that the three public goods properties listed in the text resolve to externalities causing social costs (benefits) to deviate from private costs (benefits).

The ideal is to have many firms in an industry, so that no one can influence the competitive market price, which will be equal to the incremental cost of production. Such competitive industries are rare today. Some markets are characterized as "natural monopolies," where only one firm can operate and achieve economies of size minimizing production costs. To provide an alternative to monopoly pricing by a private firm in such situations, farmers often have formed cooperatives to gin cotton or mill and store grain.

In today's high-tech, high-information economies, huge development or overhead (fixed) costs characterize many industries, and incremental variable costs often fall as output expands. Firms in such industries are characterized by economies of size. Firms cannot recoup their overhead cost and survive in such circumstances with competitive pricing; *i.e.,* with the price for output only covering the incremental variable cost. The few firms able to survive in an industry characterized by economies of size may control enough of the market to exercise market power. Encouraging innovation by letting firms use market power to price above incremental cost and thereby cover fixed cost is common and ordinarily provides greater economic efficiency than relying on state-owned and-operated businesses. In U.S. agribusiness industries, the cost savings seem to predominate over the exercise of market power, so that consumers have fared well, despite increasing concentration in industry (Persaud and Tweeten). Market studies indicate that it does not take very many firms in an industry to foster competition, particularly if markets are open to competition from abroad.

Two additional "laws" of welfare economics are instructive to policymakers. One is that *it is appropriate for externality originators to pay costs of correcting for negative externalities and for externality recipients to pay the costs of correcting for positive externalities.* In the case of a negative supply externality, for example, the farmer ordinarily should not be paid to stop doing "bad things," such as allowing soil erosion to deposit sediment and harmful chemicals in an urban reservoir being used for drinking water. That negative supply externality could be corrected by requiring conservation tillage of the farmer, or, perhaps better yet, by a "cap and trade" pollution control system outlined in chapter 6. In the case of a positive demand externality, such as a scenic farm view prized much more by urban dwellers than by the farm operator, it is appropriate for city dwellers to raise taxes to pay the farmer for preserving and enhancing that view.

The fourth law of welfare economics is that *benefits of public programs tend to go disproportionately to the wealthiest within the group eligible for benefits.* Most government transfers do not go to the poor. Those with more income also tend to have the talents, political influence, and drive to aggressively procure cash transfers or other benefits. The lesson of that fourth law is that public programs to improve welfare must be carefully crafted and administered to avoid leakage and instead to target subsidies to those who most need help.

Table 2.1 suggests that there is no single optimal size for the public sector. However, Tanzi and Schuknecht (1995) concluded that economies with the lowest rise in public spending from 1960 to the 1990s were more efficient and innovative and had more rapid employment and patent registration growth. Some countries have prospered with less than ten percent of their economies in the public sector by minimizing military spending and privatizing social security and health care. On the other hand, some Western European "welfare state" market economies have prospered, with approximately half of their economy in the private sector, by taxing consumption and minimizing incremental direct taxes on private savings, investment, and firm profits (table 2.1). Thus there is no single optimal size for the public sector, but a large public sector itself may need embedded market-price incentives to encourage efficiency.

3

Empirical Evidence for the Standard Model

The case for the standard model rests on whether it in fact serves societal objectives such as economic efficiency, equity, freedom, and security. This chapter presents empirical evidence for and against the model. Chapter 4 will lay out the conceptual framework, establishing reasons to expect success from the standard model.

We have observed that countries such as the former Soviet Union, North Korea, and Cuba deviating sharply from the standard model have failed by almost every standard, while the Asian tigers, Chile, Ireland, and Estonia, following SM policies, have fared well. Such anecdotal evidence for the standard model is telling, but rigorous analytical studies make the case even more compelling (Agarwala; Bale and Lutz; Gwartney *et al.*; Holmes and Kirkpatrick; Zhao *et al.*). Many of these studies quantify how market distortions reduce national income.

More definitive judgments are possible from recent, more comprehensive studies of standard-model policies and institutions. In an extensive survey of literature, Niclas Berggren (2003) provides an especially compelling case that standard-model policies generate economic growth. Berggren reviewed the results from a large number of empirical studies expressing economic growth as a function of the Economic Freedom Index (EFI) or its components. The single EFI variable, a proxy for standard-model policies, aggregates thirty-seven component variables into five groups: (1) size of government as measured by expenditures, taxes, and state enterprises; (2) legal structure and security of property rights; (3) access to sound money; (4) freedom to exchange currency with foreigners; and (5) regulation of credit, labor, and business.[7] Typical reforms consistent with the standard model outlined in chapter 2 include privatizing state-owned enterprises, deregulating commerce, reducing government spending, balancing government budgets, removing internal and foreign trade barriers, devaluing currency (or allowing markets to value currency) in foreign exchange, reducing corruption in government, and creating an independent

---

7   For a listing of component variables, see Roll (pp. 60–62).

central bank whose role is to stabilize the general price level. The thirty-seven components of FYI reflect most such policies.

The Economic Freedom Index is misnamed. It measures standard-model policies more than economic freedom. In fact, the name reveals a fortuitous confluence: standard-model policies presumed to be consistent with economic progress are consistent with another prized attribute—the freedom of firms and individuals to make production and consumption decisions.

In studies reviewed by Berggren, annual data were employed for five-year intervals from 1975 to 2000 for 123 countries in 1995 and 2000, but fewer countries in earlier years, relating the EFI to economic performance. The some twenty-five empirical studies reviewed by Berggren found that standard-model policies, as represented by the EFI or its components, were consistently linked statistically to economic progress, with the exception of size of government. The latter seemed to be nonlinearly linked to growth: governments must be large enough to provide a supportive institutional framework for markets to work, but a very large government is dead weight holding back the economy. Standard-model policies were consequential indeed for economic growth: the quintile of countries with the lowest standard model (EFI) scores experienced, on average, a 0.86 percent annual decline in national income per capita from 1990 to 2000, whereas the quintile of countries with the highest standard-model scores experienced a 2.56 percent annual increase in national income per capita in the same decade. No clear-cut relationship was found in the many studies cited by Berggren between EFI and the proportion of income going to poor people. However, standard-model policies were positively correlated with political freedom.

EFI and analytical studies using the index are imperfect. Empirical studies may be faulted for omitting or failing to control for variables such as natural resource endowments and culture that cause economic progress to differ among countries adopting the standard model. Still, analysts regressing per capita income on disaggregated variables (beyond just those in EFI) find the variables included in EFI to be especially significant. For example, an extensive statistical analysis of up to eighty-six countries over various periods from 1965 to 1995 by Barro (chapter 9) found that economic growth was positively and significantly increased by "the rule of law" and by international openness and negatively influenced by high inflation and government consumption. Each of these variables is accounted for in EFI. By disaggregating components of EFI, Roll (chapter 3) accounted for just over eighty percent of the variation in per capita income among up to 157 countries from 1995 to 1999. The strongest variables "explaining" per capita income positively were property rights and negatively were informal markets. The latter variable probably was a proxy for the negative impact of excessive taxes and regulations driving businesses underground.

EFI is used extensively in the following analysis. It is convenient and contains variables that are not only very important for the economy, but also ones that a country can control.

Recent Data Linking the Economic Freedom Index to Economic Progress

Table 3.1 shows for each country with an EFI below 7.0 (out of a possible range of 0, the worst, to 10, the best) its 2003 income level (GDP per capita in 1995 U.S. dollars, corrected for purchasing-power parity) and also real growth rate over the 1994–2003 decade. For comparison purposes, similar income series are shown in table 3.2 for countries with EFIs of 7.0 or more. Striking differences appear in both income level and growth rate among countries ranked by EFI.

Table 3.1. Real Gross Domestic Product (GDP) per Capita Level in 2003 and Growth Rate over 1994–2003 Decade for Seventy-six Countries with an Economic Freedom Index (EFI) below 7.0

Country	2002 EFI	2003 GDP/ cap in 1995 U.S. PPP $	Annual % GDP incr.,1994–2003	Country	2002 EFI	2003 GDP/ cap in 1995 U.S. PPP $	Annual % GDP incr.,1994–2003
Congo, Dem. R.	4.4	586	-4.18	Croatia	5.9	9,687	4.79
Central Afr. Rep.	4.5	943	-0.84	Haiti	6.0	1,422	-1.20
Algeria	4.6	5,433	1.89	Iran	6.0	6,214	2.54
Venezuela	4.6	4,269	-2.64	Sri Lanka	6.0	3,284	2.61
Guinea-Bissau	4.8	592	-3.31	Bulgaria	6.0	6,789	1.98
Burundi	4.9	545	-2.54	Fiji	6.0	4,798	0.81
Congo, Rep. of	4.9	824	0.99	Brazil	6.2	6,755	0.84
Russia	5.0	7,997	2.65	Egypt	6.2	3,435	2.34

Togo	5.1	1,328	-0.25	Paraguay	6.2	4,108	-0.90
Gabon	5.1	5,335	-0.35	Slovenia	6.2	16,784	3.64
Sierra Leone	5.2	483	-3.67	Tanzania	6.3	531	1.68
Rwanda	5.3	1,103	4.98	Tunisia	6.3	6,160	2.77
Ukraine	5.3	4,759	0.75	India	6.3	2,530	3.79
Niger	5.3	719	-0.11	Ghana	6.3	1,943	2.06
Colombia	5.3	5,899	0.24	Nicaragua	6.4	2,194	-0.69
Chad	5.4	1,049	2.91	Poland	6.4	10,108	4.42
Syria	5.4	3109	0.90	Guyana	6.4	3,647	1.06
Romania	5.4	6,280	1.89	Namibia	6.4	5,544	0.52
Benin	5.4	978	2.23	Guatemala	6.4	3,584	0.75
Madagascar	5.5	703	-0.84	Kenya	6.4	900	-0.82
Turkey	5.5	5,869	1.79	Honduras	6.4	2,312	-0.05
Malawi	5.5	538	1.79	Malaysia	6.5	8,432	2.45
Mali	5.6	864	3.45	Mexico	6.5	7,945	0.76
Cameroon	5.6	1,799	1.62	Bolivia	6.5	2,215	0.76
Ecuador	5.6	3,203	0.38	Zambia	6.6	768	0.26
Barbados	5.6	13,665	1.52	Uganda	6.6	1,279	3.52
Pap. New Guinea	5.6	2,179	-1.40	Slovak Rep.	6.6	11,713	3.55
Nepal	5.6	1,233	1.25	Dominican Rep.	6.6	5,829	3.37
Albania	5.7	3,975	5.38	Philippines	6.6	3,758	1.10
Pakistan	5.7	1,714	0.60	Thailand	6.7	6,592	1.92
China	5.7	4,344	6.75	South Africa	6.8	9,124	0.76
Nigeria	5.7	891	1.05	Lithuania	6.8	9,784	5.33
Senegal	5.8	1,463	2.02	Peru	6.8	4,580	1.40
Indonesia	5.8	2,926	1.24	France	6.8	23,765	1.40
Cote d'Ivoire	5.8	1,277	-0.86	Uruguay	6.8	7,201	-0.74
Argentina	5.8	10,075	-0.63	Greece	6.9	17,370	3.29
Bangladesh	5.9	1,553	2.81	Czech Rep.	6.9	14,304	2.62
Morocco	5.9	3,489	0.81	Jamaica	6.9	3,639	0.41
Average	5.4	3,000	0.80		6.4	6,343	1.71

Source: World Bank (2005); Gwartney and Lawson

The seventy-six low-EFI countries in table 3.1 and the thirty-four high-EFI countries in table 3.2 were each divided into the best half and worst half by EFI score in their group. Average income level and growth rate consistently increased as EFI improved across the four resulting categories. The low-half EFI countries in table 3.1 scored on average 5.4 in EFI, $3,000 in per capita income, and 0.80 percent annual income growth. This contrasts with the top half of "poor" performers shown in table 3.1, which scored on average 6.4 on EFI, $6,343 on income, and 1.71 percent on annual income growth.

Turning to countries with EFIs of 7.0 and higher in table 3.2, the lower half averaged an EFI of 7.2, average income of $15,189, and annual income growth of 2.17 percent. The top half of high-EFI countries averaged an EFI score of 7.9, average income of $25,485, and an income growth rate of 2.55 percent.

Table 3.2. Real Gross Domestic Product (GDP) per Capita Level in 2003 and Growth Rate over 1994–2003 Decade for Thirty-four Countries with an Economic Freedom Index (EFI) of 7.0 and above

Country	2002 EFI	2003 GDP/ cap in 1995 U.S. PPP $	Annual % GDP incr.,1994– 2003	Country	2002 EFI	2003 GDP/ cap in 1995 U.S. PPP $	Annual % GDP incr.,1994– 2003
Japan	7.0	24,491	0.96	Botswana	7.4	7,269	2.72
Italy	7.0	23,524	1.33	Austria	7.5	26,065	1.66
Jordan	7.0	3,756	0.24	Denmark	7.6	27,507	1.95
Norway	7.0	32,232	1.78	Iceland	7.6	26,662	2.00
Latvia	7.0	8,680	5.51	Estonia	7.7	11,605	6.02
Trinidad & Tob.	7.1	8,675	3.03	Netherlands	7.7	25,578	2.04
Spain	7.1	19,362	2.35	Finland	7.7	23,700	2.55
Costa Rica	7.1	8,252	2.36	Luxembourg	7.8	54,652	4.82
Panama	7.2	5,631	1.48	Ireland	7.8	31,981	7.32
Portugal	7.2	16,039	2.37	Canada	7.9	26,492	1.93
Mauritius	7.2	9,790	3.41	Australia	7.9	25,344	2.04
El Salvador	7.2	4,343	1.16	Switzerland	8.2	26,251	0.26
Hungary	7.3	12,673	3.54	United States	8.2	32,483	1.65
Chile	7.3	8,875	2.68	United Kingdom	8.2	23,573	1.95
Sweden	7.3	23,181	2.01	New Zealand	8.2	18,416	1.02
Germany	7.3	24,010	1.03	Singapore	8.6	21,289	2.20
Belgium	7.4	24,694	1.67	Hong Kong	8.7	24,373	1.26
Average	7.2	15,189	2.17		7.9	25,485	2.55

Source: World Bank (2005); Gwartney and Lawson

Statistical analysis confirmed the strong positive relationship visible between EFI and income level and growth in the tables. EFI alone explained fifty-five percent of the variation (the adjusted $R^{2)}$) in per capita income among the countries in tables 3.1 and 3.2. The statistically very significant coefficient of EFI in a simple regression of EFI on per capita income indicated that an increase of EFI by just one unit increased per capita income by $7,077. Of course, predictions of income from that coefficient are inexact for any one country and are especially hazardous outside the EFI's data range of 4.8 to 8.7.

A look at figure 3.1 indicates that income per capita increases at an increasing rate with higher values of EFI. A regression of per capita income on the linear and squared values of EFI gave highly significant coefficients on the EFI variables and an adjusted R^2 of 0.62.[8] Of note is the different response to an increase in EFI in poor versus in rich countries. The simple linear equation predicts that each unit increment in EFI raises per capita income by $7,077 in any country. In contrast, the nonlinear equation in footnote 8 predicts that a unit increase in EFI from the respective group mean adds only $2,698 to income of the lower half of poor countries (table 3.1), $6,812 to the upper half of poor countries (table 3.1), $10,103 to the lower half of rich countries (table 3.2), and $11,337 to the upper half of rich countries (table 3.2). One explanation for the rising response is that unfavorable economic policies and institutions characteristic of poor countries carry momentum not easily or quickly overcome following reform.

The highly significant coefficient on EFI regressed on income growth rate in 109 countries indicated that a unit rise in EFI was associated with a 0.75 percentage point increase in annual income growth rate.[9] A unit increase in EFI is well within the reach of any poor country. Increasing EFI by one unit for the lowest-scoring half of poor countries in table 3.1 would reduce the time to double income from nine years to 4.7 years.

Although a given improvement in policies may impact rich countries most strongly (as indicated by the equation in footnote 8), for several reasons the annual percentage growth rate tends to slow as countries get richer. One reason is that a rich country operating at the frontiers of technology finds it challenging and expensive to develop productive new technology. It is easier to follow a prepared path than to break trail. A poor country can utilize technology developed by rich countries.

---

8   The equation is per capita predicted income $Y = 47,956 - 19,518 EFI + 2,057 EFI^2$. The standard error of the EFI coefficient is 6,486 and of the EFI^2 coefficient is 500.

9   Luxembourg was dropped from the data set because it is very small, had unique characteristics, and was a clear outlier.

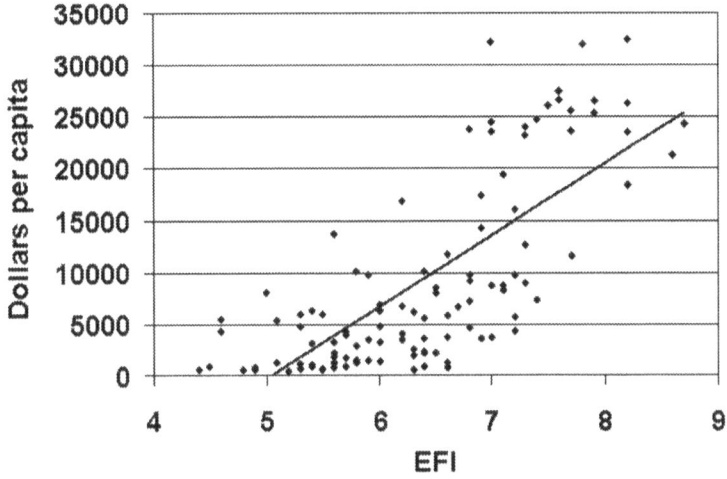

Figure 3.1. Predicted (line) and Actual (dots) Real Gross Domestic Product per Capita in 2003 by Country as a Function of the Economic Freedom Index (EFI) in 2002

Source: Basic data from World Bank (2005); Gwartney and Lawson

Other factors also retard growth in rich countries. One of the signal advantages of high income is the creation of options to use wealth. The income growth rate can slow over time as a rich country opts to sacrifice economic growth in order to raise the health and income safety net. Many people and countries use their affluence to purchase security, benevolence, environmental amenities, leisure, and the like, which are not apparent in the growth rate of income. Countries do not all choose the same economic growth versus socio-environmental tradeoffs, hence it is no surprise that the adjusted R^2 of EFI "explaining" income level is 0.55 to 0.62 but explaining income growth rate is only 0.12.

Variables other than EFI are available to measure the influence of public policy on economic development. One such variable is the economic incentive regime variable (EIR) compiled by the World Bank (2006). EIR measures barriers to trade, the regulatory climate, and rule of law—the latter based on the crime rate, quality of the judiciary, and the enforcement of contracts. EIR is highly correlated with EFI (r=0.75) and gross domestic product per capita (r=0.84), but has the same low correlation (r=0.34) as EFI with the annual rate of increase in GDP per capita.

The foregoing data indicate that poor countries willing to follow standard-model policies can generate the means to attack hunger, poverty, and disease. The equation in footnote 8 predicts that moving countries from an EFI mean of 5.4 for the low-scoring half of countries in table 3.1 to the mean of the upper half of low-scoring countries in the same table (EFI 6.4) adds an estimated $4,755 to per capita income. The cross-sectional data used to estimate equations expressing income as a function of EFI probably reflect long-term rather than short-term impacts. Even if ten years are required to obtain the benefits predicted from a higher EFI, the gains are impressive.

It may be argued that regression results do not apply to Africa, because EFI omits the region's immutable disadvantages of culture, location, disease, and natural resource endowments slowing economic progress. To test that proposition, a discrete variable (with sub-Saharan African countries assigned 1.0 and all other countries 0.0) along with the single-variable EFI were regressed on the level of income, using data for countries (except Luxembourg) from tables 3.1 and 3.2. The coefficient for African countries, minus $2,950, was statistically significant at the six percent probability level. The adjusted R^2 was raised by only one unit, from 0.55 to 0.56, by including the variable for sub-Saharan Africa. The very highly significant coefficient of EFI, $6,449, indicates that just 0.5 units of EFI can offset the unique disadvantages of sub-Saharan Africa. The implication is that Africa is not uniquely poor, but is poor because it does not attend to the institutional and policy variables in EFI.

Of course, culture and other difficult-to-change elements underlie some components of EFI. Plenty of policy variable components of EFI can be changed, however, reinforcing the thesis of this volume that every country, given some time to change, has the capacity to deal effectively with hunger, poverty, and treatable disease.

Sound methodology calls for examining whether data can reject the hypothesis of this chapter. Can we select data from individual countries in tables 3.1 and 3.2 to refute the hypothesis that higher income and growth are associated with adherence to standard-model policies as represented by EFI?[10] We must scrutinize economically underperforming countries with high EFI scores and economically overperforming countries with low EFI scores. El Salvador and

---

10 Critics often list Argentina as Exhibit A of the failure of the standard model. The country embarked on free-market reforms in the 1990s, mostly consistent with the standard model. A fatal deviation from the model was adopting a fixed exchange rate while pursuing an expansionary fiscal policy. Rising domestic wages and prices cut exports and increased imports, energizing the macroeconomic degradation process and culminating in default on international debt in December 2001. The standard model calls for monetary, fiscal, and exchange-rate policy to work in harmony.

Jordan have poor economic performance, given their relatively high EFI scores. El Salvador's economy continues to be hobbled by the devastation remaining from civil war in the 1970s and 1980s. Jordan's economy has struggled to absorb massive numbers of destitute refugees from the Israeli-Palestinian conflict. Jordan's water resources for irrigation, essential to food and fiber production in that arid land, are severely limited by the outcome of armed conflict that gave Israel control of water from the Jordan River.

Even with a relatively well-managed economy, as evident from an EFI of 7.4 in 2002, Botswana managed an income of only $7,269 in 2003. Easterly (p. 26) comments that "Botswana registered 6 percent per capita growth over the [1960–present] period, a historically unprecedented number for so long a period." The country embraced democracy and was favored by diamond mines. On the other hand, economic success in recent years has been slowed by the debilitating influence of the highest HIV/AIDS rate in the world, nearly two out of five adults.

The economies of other sub-Saharan African countries fared much worse. One reason is that sub-Saharan countries have rejected the standard model—nineteen of the thirty-five lowest-EFI countries were in sub-Saharan Africa in 2002. Only Botswana among sub-Saharan African countries has an EFI above 6.8.

Another type of error in predicting income from EFI occurs for high-income countries with low EFIs. France and Greece have higher incomes than their EFIs would seem to support, as noted in table 3.1. The economic performance of the two countries has faltered since 2002. Growth might be slower in the two countries without their membership in the European Union and sharing the culture and institutions of Europe (not registered in EFI). Numerous European countries have benefited from standard-model policies, as noted by their strong representation among countries with high EFIs and incomes in table 3.2.

Critics charge that the Washington Consensus has failed in the region it targeted—Latin America. The critics are at least half wrong. Some countries indeed heeded advice and made progress towards balancing government budgets, slowing inflation, devaluing currency, and reducing foreign debt and trade deficits. These policy reforms are consistent with the Washington Consensus but Latin American reforms stopped well short of fulfilling the standard-model prescription. As noted in tables 3.1 and 3.2, Latin American countries with few exceptions such as Chile are low in the Economic Freedom Index, ranking above only the African countries. They have incomes to match. Today, rigid labor laws discourage companies from hiring workers. The International Finance Corporation of the World Bank notes that it costs more to start a business in Latin America than in any other region except Africa and the Middle

East. Government rules, regulations, and arbitrary enforcement of laws inhibit entrepreneurs. Poverty and economic inequality, perennial curses of Latin America, endure. Inequality is perpetuated as tax dollars are lost through energy subsidies or consumed as generous pay and pensions to civil employees and tertiary education for the rich rather than invested in infrastructure and in common schooling for the poor. Populist governments arising out of frustration with the status quo only exacerbate economic problems as governments live beyond their means, consume rather than invest, harass private enterprise, and nationalize multinational firms.

Case Studies

Some recent examples of the success of standard-model policies come from the ten countries, most of them in Eastern Europe, joining the European Union (EU) in 2004. Membership in the EU is contingent on institutional reform. The European Commission, the administrative arm of the European Union, provides a reform blueprint containing several elements of SM. That blueprint establishes the framework for monetary, fiscal, and trade policy. The required rule of law, secure individual and property rights, business codes, judicial protections, and competition policy rule out the "power capitalism" of industry under a small number of oligarchs characterizing the Russian economy. Following the EU blueprint brought economic success worth more to new members than EU subsidies—judging by the impressive economic progress made by the ten new members. Data are not available for all countries, but as an example, the three Baltic countries (Estonia, Latvia, and Lithuania) grew on average by 5.33 to 6.03 percent annually in the decade prior to membership in the EU (see tables 3.1 and 3.2). It is no coincidence that among Eastern European countries, Estonia has the highest economic growth rate and also most closely follows standard-model policies.

This example provides some valuable lessons. The "carrot" of reward for institutional reform can work; reform need not be forced. By requiring reform before the reward (EU membership) is bestowed, countries must demonstrate unequivocal commitment to change. (Too often, under the tutelage of the International Monetary Fund and the World Bank, countries have reneged on promised reforms once rewards were given.) Reform requirements for EU membership must not be too onerous, or there would not be such a clamor by numerous additional countries for membership. Perhaps country leaders use EU membership as a cover for making overdue reforms hitherto deemed impossible because of the power of domestic special interests. One can argue that institutional reform provides its own reward, but that begs the question of why so many poor countries reject the standard model. This issue is addressed elsewhere in this volume.

Three additional examples, Australia, China, and India, are discussed briefly below to illustrate how standard-model reforms can transform for the better the economy of a rich or poor nation. Numerous other examples such as Ireland, New Zealand, and Vietnam could be discussed but are omitted to save space.

It took Britain, "breaking trail" beginning about the year 1750 with the industrial revolution, sixty years to double its income. Following a well-marked trail in recent decades, China and India took only eight and twelve years respectively to double real income, because the world's capital and technology were available to them. China and India also illustrate tradeoffs in the standard model—their industrious, thrifty, and enterprising people offset the drag of weak institutions barely up to the task of fostering development.

Australia offers a recent example of the success of even partial adoption of standard-model policies. Australia had such abundant natural wealth at the time it became an independent federation in 1901 that it could afford to neglect standard-model policies (Lockwood, pp. 3–4). Misguided policies stifled progress over time, however, and Australia fell from being the highest per capita nation on the planet in 1901 to the eighteenth by 1990. Reforms in the 1980s and thereafter to reinvigorate the economy include fiscal restraint—moving from budget deficits to budget surpluses that nearly eliminated the nation's debt. Notable achievement included the introduction of a value-added tax—a tax prized for its efficiency in raising funds with minimal reduction in national income—and giving independence in inflation control to Australia's central bank in 1996. International trade barriers were reduced. A notable achievement was a bilateral free-trade agreement with the United States.

China is today the world's most dynamic economy. In 1978, China introduced the household responsibility system, allowing farmers to profit by privately marketing some of their output. Chinese farmers had not been soporific long enough under communism to lose their considerable work and enterprise ethics. Chinese rulers, notably Deng Xiaoping, surmised that what worked for the farming economy just might be good for industries throughout the nation. Markets spread. China's GDP, which had increased only 4.0 percent annually on average in the 1970s, accelerated to an annual increase of 8.3 percent in the 1980s. China made another true leap forward when it joined the World Trade Organization in December 2001, thereby opening its doors to international commerce. Annual national income increased on average by 8.6 percent from 1990 to 2003. From a dismally low income of $717 (constant U.S. $2000) in 1979, per capita income increased to $4,726 in 2003. In 1979, per capita income in China was similar to that in many countries in sub-Saharan Africa. China's income increased sevenfold without aid donations from rich countries; meanwhile, income per capita stagnated in Africa, despite billions of dollars of official development assistance. Chen and Ravallion (p. 15) observed that "There were 400 million fewer people living on under $1 per day in China in 2001 than 20 years earlier," and "China's incidence of poverty was roughly twice that for the rest of the developing world [in 1981]; by the mid-1990s, [it] had fallen well below average."

China's welcoming of foreign private investment contributed massively to the country's economic growth. Foreign, mostly private, direct investment in China alone of $50–70 billion per year equaled the whole of annual official, mostly government, development assistance to *all* of the world's poor countries in recent years. Investment poured in especially from overseas Chinese in Taiwan, Hong Kong, and Singapore. China itself (like India and Brazil, but unlike most other developing countries) invested heavily in agricultural science and technology. Agricultural technology, including cutting-edge transgenic crop varieties, made huge strides. China is credited with developing and in 1990 commercially growing the world's first transgenic crop, tobacco engineered to resist a plant virus. Some of China's technical universities, like some in India, are becoming world-class institutions. China is building infrastructure, including roads and ports, at a furious pace.

China's reforms are far from complete by standard-model criteria. Since 1978, when almost its entire industry was state-owned, China has released some twenty to thirty million workers from state-owned enterprises (SOEs). Most of those workers found far more productive employment in the private sector (Miles, p. 12). Some 140,000 SOEs remained in 2006, however, one-third of them making no return on investment. Millions of the remaining forty million workers employed in SOEs could be released for more productive employment elsewhere. In China today, financial and material infrastructure remains inadequate. The rule of law barely suffices. Intellectual property rights are regularly violated. Democracy remains a distant dream, but the rapidly expanding middle class will push for it.

Economic reform came more recently in India. In 1991, the country nearly ran out of foreign exchange to purchase imports. Avoiding a humanitarian catastrophe required immediate major reforms. The country began to dismantle the "license raj" system of suffocating regulations and red tape that had tethered the economy to mediocrity since independence. Central planning was de-emphasized, industrial licensing was liberalized, capital markets were opened, the rupee was devalued, and import duties and import controls were diminished. The Indian economy responded magnificently. Xenophobia, perhaps a holdover from colonial domination before independence in 1947, along with nationalism and populism, had long been used to justify protectionism. In January 1995, however, India joined the World Trade Organization. The resulting opening of markets to international trade, though incomplete, was another boost to the economy. Even in the face of a population growing 1.66 percent annually to 1.1 billion people in 2003, real gross domestic product growth increased 5.9 percent annually from 1992 to 2002.

The impact of standard-model reforms is apparent from the success of India and China in reducing food insecurity. India has made less progress although, unlike China, it is a democracy. Between 1990–92 and 2000–02 the proportion of people who were undernourished fell from sixteen to eleven percent in China and from twenty-five to twenty-one percent in India. During that period, the number of undernourished people in India *increased* from 215.8 million to 221.1 million. The number of persons in poverty (living on less than one dollar per day in purchasing power parity) in the last two decades of the twentieth century fell by about four hundred million in China and by seventy million in India.

What accounts for the greater success of China in reducing poverty and hunger? Indian reforms began later and remain more incomplete than China's. India especially needs fuller implementation of standard-model policies to maintain growth momentum. Government regulations on Indian industry have kept manufacturers from hiring millions of impoverished but able workers from the massive farming sector. China did not make that major regulatory mistake.

Both countries were once brutally poor and suffered recurring famine, which took millions of lives. India has not experienced famine since it became a democracy, however; whereas China under Mao Zedong suffered the most severe man-made famine in history in the "Great Leap Forward" of 1958–61. China attempted to modernize quickly by "appropriate" small-scale industrialization of rural areas. Small-scale steel furnaces and other industrial technologies were highly inefficient, and agriculture was neglected. The result was the loss of some thirty-eight million lives to famine in 1959–61 (see Chang and Halliday; Clark).

Many Chinese also lost their dignity and lives during the Cultural Revolution of 1966–76, which attempted to return the country to its supposed proletarian roots. Chang and Halliday estimate that the communist dictatorship of Chairman Mao Zedong cost seventy million lives in so-called peacetime purges, the Cultural Revolution, and the "Great Leap Forward." Neither Joseph Stalin nor Adolph Hitler can match that villainy.

Dictatorships more than democracies can lurch rapidly among policies. EFI scores of 5.7 for China and 6.3 for India in 2002 leave much scope for improvement in both countries (see table 3.1). China has enough rule of law to attract massive foreign direct investment, but the country's one-child policy will create high dependency rates and labor bottlenecks in the future, severely constraining economic potential.

Meanwhile, the "license raj" continues to stifle commerce in India. Democracy dominated by special interests has been used to distort the market economy to benefit a privileged few, at a loss to society as a whole. Agriculture provides ready examples. In the breadbasket of India, Punjab, the government supports the price of rice (a heavy irrigation water user) well above market levels. Such prices generate surpluses, which are too often left to rot or be eaten by weevils. In addition to price supports for rice and wheat, Punjabi farmers receive free electricity from the government to run irrigation pumps. Excessive pumping has dropped the underground water table to alarmingly low levels. As the water table drops, the cost of pumping rises. With time, water for irrigation could become prohibitively expensive. Thus Punjab agriculture, as currently practiced, is unsustainable.

As a successful world-class competitor in the outsourcing of services, India is well known for the superior skills of the workers in its information technology industry. This achievement masks the reality of a nation with high illiteracy rates. Females especially lack access to schooling. In the future, India will be severely constrained by its lingering caste system and underinvestment in elementary education and infrastructure.

These realities demonstrate that India has far to go to implement standard-model policies that could end poverty, hunger, and illiteracy in the country that soon will surpass China as the world's most populous nation. The major impetus for further economic reform in India is likely to come from competition with a dynamic China.

Continuing application of standard-model policies in India and China will result in these two countries dominating global manufacturing in the twenty-first century. Should the rest of the world welcome or fear such industrial behemoths? The following considerations indicate that there is more to welcome than to fear.

In a provocative book published in 1995, Lester Brown raised the specter that China would starve the world by crowding out other buyers to corner available world food exports. Such concerns were dismissed by most agricultural experts as unduly alarmist and did not materialize. But in the early 2000s, China drove up world petroleum and other mineral prices by importing to supply its burgeoning industry. In a world of more open markets, India and China, as low-cost producers of manufactured goods, will at least initially retard industrialization and job creation in Africa, which has followed too few standard-model policies to be competitive. It may be argued that this is a problem that Africans rather than the Chinese, Indians, or anyone else must solve. In the longer run, rising living standards and wages in successful developing countries will drive their labor-intensive industries to countries such as Africa offering cheaper labor. Firms in newly developed nations will become better markets and also bring to poorer countries desperately needed technology, capital, management, and access to world markets.

Interactions between China and the United States illustrate conundrums in dealing with a growing Chinese economy. In theory, it is possible that the rising global costs of petroleum and basic metals, caused by the rise of the large Chinese economy, raise basic commodity prices in the United States and elsewhere enough to offset the usual gains from trade. On the other hand, China has made positive contributions to the U.S. economy that probably offset any negative influences. A purportedly undervalued Chinese currency has caused a huge trade surplus with the United States, especially in labor-intensive manufacturing goods. The United States has lost manufacturing jobs, but consumers have enjoyed low prices on the many goods they purchase labeled "Made in China."

America's growing, full-employment economy, characterized by a five-percent unemployment rate, is evidence that new and often better jobs are replacing manufacturing jobs lost to competition from low-cost imports from China and other developing countries. Nonetheless, the United States could do a better job of providing trade adjustment assistance in the form of job training and mobility assistance to displaced workers, so that even fewer workers are made worse off by trade.

The Chinese-American commercial interaction based on an undervalued Chinese currency and huge U.S. budget deficits is not sustainable. The undervalued Chinese currency implies that Chinese leaders would rather see their workers employed than see consumers live well. Millions of Chinese workers, plants, and equipment that could be producing for the domestic market instead are producing exports to accumulate dollars. The continuing accumulation of dollars by China is not possible, though. At some point, China's authorities will realize that it is better for consumers to live well (by spending for imports) than for the country to continue its mercantile policy of accumulating "funny money."

At some point, panic over devaluation of the dollar could cause a frenzied global selling of dollars. With China holding approximately $800 billion of dollar reserves in 2006 and U.S. currency overvalued twenty to forty percent, China could quickly experience a wealth loss of $200 billion with currency realignment. An international financial crisis would cost the United States thousands of jobs and buying power, as interest rates would rise (to attract dollars from abroad to finance America's debt) and the economy would slide into recession. Housing values and banks could collapse as mortgage holders find their interest payments unmanageable. The prices of imports would increase, creating inflationary pressures. Financial troubles of large economies are contagious, and an international financial crisis could emerge. That doomsday scenario may seem overdrawn, because China and the United States alike have a stake in avoiding such "mutually assured destruction." The surest way to avoid a crisis is to avoid massive financial imbalances that provide the tinder for global economic conflagration.

It is important to recognize that some aspects of dollar accumulation have served the world well. For example, trade has served East Asians, who have a high propensity to save and work, and it has served Americans, who have a high propensity to consume. Chinese households save one-fourth of their income, while American households save almost none, on average. The billions of dollars accumulated in China by households and businesses have been invested in American financial securities, thereby financing budget deficits and allowing the United States to live beyond its means. Low-priced imports from China have allowed the American Federal Reserve Bank to maintain a loose, growth-stimulating, low-interest monetary policy without at the same time causing inflation.

The American economy has been a world economic engine for growth, providing markets for East Asia when domestic markets failed. Outsourcing of computer software and information technology jobs serves American firms, who find American workers unprepared with mathematical and scientific expertise for such jobs, while giving China and especially India the opportunity to profit from skills in this field. On the other hand, a sizable portion of the massive and continuing American current trade and services account deficit arises because of large U.S. federal budget deficits. The meager saving of U.S. households, joined by corporate saving in the form of retained earnings, fall far short of being able to finance the huge annual investment required for a growing and prosperous America; hence the federal deficit can only be financed with billions of dollars from abroad. Those "savings" by foreigners come from their trade surpluses with the United States, made possible by an overvalued dollar. Egregious imbalances cannot go on, however, not just because foreigners will tire of accumulating dollars, but also because eventually the entire American GDP would go for interest payments on debt, much of it owed to foreigners.

Advances in communication and transportation technologies have indeed made the world a more competitive place. Nations heeding standard-model policies, exploiting comparative advantage, will prosper as never before in such a world. Nations, even rich ones, that become complacent and fail to develop human and other resources will fall behind. The economic success of countries such as India and China will spill over their borders as wages rise and markets mature at home. As nations progress economically, they are able to contribute world-class science and technology, as evidenced by India in information technology, China in genetic engineering, and South Korea in cloning[11]. The world will no longer need to depend on a few Western countries for scientific "miracles." These formerly poor nations will share technology with the rest of the world. Their firms will look for new places to produce and sell.

If Africa and other lagging regions follow standard-model policies, they will be recipients of technology, capital, and access to markets afforded by new developed countries such as China and India. Economic growth will cause wages to rise in once-poor countries, so that rich countries will no longer be able to complain that they cannot compete with cheap labor in poor countries. Africa someday will be far enough along in this development process to be able to financially support and conduct basic research and be a source of scientific breakthroughs to improve the health and welfare of people everywhere. That is the way development proceeds if the policies outlined in chapter 2 are followed.

Flaws in the Standard Model

The standard model is a framework for an economy to be successful, but it needs to be tailored to unique local and national settings. Sachs (p. 81) is critical of what he calls the "structural adjustment era," ushered in by the likes of Prime Minister Margaret Thatcher of the United Kingdom, whom many economists regard as the savior of the British economy from the depredations of Fabian socialism. Fabian socialism, featuring central planning and "benign" state ownership of the means of production, was taught in British universities after World War II. This was precisely when many students from Africa were being educated in Britain and when African colonies were gaining independence. Not surprisingly, African students returning from British universi-

11 Fraudulent research by South Korea's cloning scientist Hwang Wu Suk and uncovered in 2005 should not be interpreted as representative of the country's capabilities. The country has world-class cloning and stem-cell research scientists and infrastructure.

ties became leaders and economic advisors in their newly independent home countries. Also not surprisingly, the new countries adopted the very policies that brought the British economy to its knees. A consequence is that African countries got poorer rather than richer with independence.

The IMF, the World Bank, and aid-donor governments called for reforms, originating what Sachs (p. 81) describes as the structural adjustment era:

> The rich countries told the poor countries: 'Poverty is your own fault. Be like us (or what we imagine ourselves to be—free market oriented, entrepreneurial, fiscally responsible) and you, too, can enjoy the riches of private-sector led economic development.' The IMF-World Bank programs of the structural adjustment era were designed to address the four maladies assumed to underlie all economic ills: poor governance, excessive government intervention in the markets, excessive government spending, and too much state ownership. Belt tightening, privatization, liberalization, and good governance became the order of the day.

Nongovernment organizations (NGOs) also have widely criticized the International Monetary Fund and the World Bank for structural adjustment policies that called for devaluation of currency, cutting government spending, and tightening money supply when countries had bankrupted themselves by living beyond their means. The antiglobalization movement has assembled tens of thousands of demonstrators, some of them violent, at meetings of the IMF, World Bank, and World Trade Organization to protest structural adjustment policies, foreign trade, multinational corporations, export cropping, and the presumed nefarious international financial establishment (see Tweeten, chapter 3).[12] Sachs (p. 355) applauds the antiglobalization movement: "The antiglobalization movement has made its mark, and in my view, mostly for the good (except for the moments of violence that fringe elements of the movement incite)." In seeming contradiction to this statement, he (p. 355) volunteers that "Globalization, more than anything else, has reduced the numbers of extreme poor in India by 200 million and in China by 300 million since 1990."

---

12 NGOs are commendably engaged in charitable activities such as providing sanitary water and distributing the food provided by the World Food Organization, the United States, and the European Union to poor people. A cynical view is that NGOs oppose standard-model policies because it will put them out of a job, as well-run economies earn sufficient income to provide their own food and water, right down to the village level. A more realistic view is that economics is not the strong suit of the fine people in NGOs.

Paul Stiles makes the case that markets generate wealth that in turn is insep-arable from the immiserating rat race, urban sprawl, gas-guzzling cars, pol-lution, endless commuting, social isolation, single working mothers, obesity, and (yes) terrorism. In the same year, economist Benjamin Friedman made the contrary case that increases in income (not just high income) enhance well-being by promoting a more open, tolerant, generous, democratic, and just soci-ety. Chapter 6 of this volume provides empirical evidence that income growth above some income threshold is good for the environment.

The debate over the merits of economic growth will continue in perpetuity, but most observers conclude that economic development improves well-being in poor countries. Arguments are more about whether growth is edifying for rich countries. One answer is that growth creates options. A household in a rich country has numerous options to sacrifice income to take a less stressful job, lobby for environmental protection, drive a fuel-efficient car, eat less, live in a smaller house, and skip visits to the doctor. The issue is choice, and people almost everywhere prefer more to less choice and more to less income. Even for those who do not prefer more, the standard model and the improved produc-tivity attending it allow people to use *fewer resources* to attain their preferred level of income. Finally, the "gate test" of people voting with their feet is telling. In the absence of border controls, tens of millions of people would migrate from poor countries to rich countries.

The above criticisms of economic progress itself and how the standard model contributes to growth are mostly unjustified. The explanations for economic development contained in this volume do not include but could include dis-ease, geography, and climate variables, as called for by Sachs. Natural resources are not a reliable predictor of economic progress, however. And disease and parasites are as much an effect as a cause of poverty. Much of the debt provided to poor countries by public and quasi-public lenders should never have been provided and will never be repaid; hence it is being written off. Private-sector loans and public grants make more sense for the future. Structural adjustment programs will remain a fact of life.

The United Nations calls for rich developed countries to give 0.7 percent of their GDP to poor countries. Achieving that target would raise world official development assistance (ODA) from $53 billion or 0.2 percent of GDP in 2002 to $175 billion per year, and U.S. aid would increase from $15 billion or 0.14 percent of GDP in 2004 to $75 billion per year. To reap the funding from the United Nations and from the Millennium Challenge Account offered by the United States, recipient countries would have to demonstrate, through concrete action, their commitment to good governance and efficient administration of funds and programs. This requirement is also consistent with the directions called for by the Meltzer Commission, this volume, and past structural adjustment. Nonetheless, one can question whether the provision will be enforced.

At issue is whether it should be enforced. It is unfortunate that critics of structural adjustment have not separated the issue of need for policy reform from the issue of undue burden on the poor of such reform. The need for reform is self-evident. More can be done to cushion impacts on the very poor when nations inevitably must learn to live within their means.

Concluding Comments

Empirical evidence strongly supports the conclusion that any nation following standard-model policies (and institutions) can be an economic success. The nation may not become rich, but it can be wealthy enough to alleviate treatable disease, hunger, abject poverty, and environmental problems. Standard-model policies also contribute to freedom, democracy, stability, and peace. Equity is served by the model's call for broad-based development policies with access to health and education services for every race, gender, and region of each country.

Given that the Economic Freedom Index is a useful proxy for major components of the standard model, Berggren's statement after an extensive EFI literature review is a fitting conclusion to this chapter (p. 201):

> No results showing that economic freedom hampers growth or that it is associated with lower GDP per capita have been reported. To the contrary, the results in general show that an increase in economic freedom exerts a positive influence on the development of economic wealth.

Perhaps the direction of causality is reversed. Perhaps high and increasing levels of income and wealth cause standard-model policies. Employing Granger causality, Dawson (pp. 481–94) found that *increases* in EFI and economic growth seem to be jointly determined, whereas the absolute *level* of EFI seems to cause growth. Some components of EFI, such as use of markets and property rights, tend to cause growth, while other components are jointly determined by economic growth. Standard-model policies and socioeconomic variables reinforce one another as development proceeds at least to a point. That observation helps to explain why an increment in EFI has a greater impact in rich than in poor countries. A challenge is to jump start that synergism.

With the exception of some oil-rich countries, no country has become affluent without ranking quite high in standard-model attributes. Some countries, notably in Latin America, have experienced growth spurts by following popu-list policies of "eating their seed." Such exceptions prove the rule, because prof-ligate economies collapse and require austerity when finances are exhausted. It is important to emphasize that following the standard model is especially criti-cal to supply even the most basic necessities in countries with the least favor-able attitudes and natural resources.

This chapter placed considerable reliance on per capita income to measure welfare. Other measures also have merit, including the Human Development Index (HDI) assembled and published by the United Nations Development Program (UNDP). The index accounts for life expectancy, education, and income per person. Given the latter variable, the index obviously is closely related to income. Norway ranks at the top and Niger at the bottom of the HDI. Measures of poverty, HDI, and other variables supplement income in measur-ing welfare in this volume. All are highly correlated.

Leaders from all over the world gathered at the United Nations to review progress toward the Millennium Development Goals (see chapter 1) by 2015. It was evident by the 2005 assessment that the goals would not be met. Some countries such as Bangladesh, Brazil, and Indonesia showed promise of meet-ing the goals, in part because they ranked thirty-fourth or higher in EFI and had positive income growth in the 1994–2003 decade. As the richest nation in the world, the United States has especially been criticized for falling short of the UN target donation. The United States can do more. But it is also important to note that the Millennium Development targets were unattainable even if the U.S. contribution had been the UN's requested 0.7 percent of GDP annually. Foreign development assistance is wasted on countries that fail to address their problems of violence, corruption, mismanagement, and lack of commitment to economic progress.

Some might paraphrase Winston Churchill's famous quip by saying that the standard model is the worst form of policy, except for all the rest. Creative destruction is painful for the worker or firm being destroyed. Nonetheless, the alternatives to the standard model have not stood the test of implementation and time. Marxism, socialism, import substitution, central planning, industrial policy, and other significant departures from the standard model have been tried and have fallen short. Each of these requires an enlarged role of govern-ment that in turn depends heavily on "good" people making the right deci-sions to serve the public interest. Import substitution calls for public officials to carefully select and nurture industries that are able to become efficient and profitable. A political following forms to continue protection whether or not the "infant" industry grows into a world-class competitor. Industrial policy, whereby governments champion the growth of favored industries, suffers from similar pitfalls. Government chooses and nurtures—through low-interest financing and other subsidies—domestic industries to become globally competitive.[13] Governments need to do indicative planning and analysis, but central planning in its various guises has fallen into disfavor, because it has not worked as well as markets to guide the economy.

References

Agarwala, R. 1983. Price Distortions and Growth in Developing Countries. *Staff Working Paper* 575. Washington DC: World Bank.

Bale, M. D., and E. Lutz. "Price Distortions in Agriculture and Their Effects: An International Comparison." *American Journal of Agricultural Economics.* 63: 8–22, 1981.

Barro, Robert. "Economic Growth Across Countries." Chapter 9 in Marc Miles, ed., *The Road to Prosperity.* Washington DC: Heritage Books, 2004.

Berggren, Niclas. "The Benefits of Economic Freedom." *The Independent Review.* 8(2): 193–211, Fall 2003.

Brown, Lester. *Who Will Feed China? Wake-up Call for a Small Planet.* London: Earthscan Publications, 1995.

Chang, Jung and Jon Halliday. *Mao: The Unknown Story.* New York: Knopf, 2005.

Chen, S. and M. Ravallion. "How Have the World's Poorest Fared Since the Early 1980s?" Policy Research Working Paper No. 3341. Washington DC: World Bank, 2004.

Clark, Colin. "Economic Development in Communist China." *The Journal of Political Economy.* 84(2): 239–64, 1976.

13 South Korea's automobile industry is frequently cited as an exception. Governments following the "industrial policy" model sometimes end up with a winner. The many losers get less publicity. It is extremely difficult to end subsidies once started, as evidenced by farm commodity supports. My judgment is that if a poor country must favor an infant industry, an import duty of no more than ten percent may be tolerated and may be applied across the board.

Dawson, John. "Causality in the Freedom-Growth Relationship." *European Journal of Political Economy*. 19(3): 479–95, September 2003.

Easterly, William. *White Man's Burden: Why the West's Efforts to Aid the Rest Have Done So Much Ill and So Little Good*. New York: Penguin Press, 2006.

Friedman, Benjamin. *The Moral Consequences of Economic Growth*. New York: Knopf, 2005.

Gwartney, James, Robert Lawson, and Walter Block. *Economic Freedom of the World: 1975–1995*. Vancouver, Canada: Fraser Institute. London: Institute of Economic Affairs, 1996.

Gwartney, James and Robert Lawson. *Economic Freedom of the World: 2004 Annual Report*. Vancouver: The Fraser Institute. Data retrieved from www.freetheworld.com, 2004.

Holmes, Kim, and Melanie Kirkpatrick. "Freedom and Growth." *The Wall Street Journal*, December 16, 1996, p. A12.

Lockwood, Christopher. "A Survey of Australia." *The Economist*. May 7, 2005, pp. 3–16.

Miles, James. "A Survey of China." *The Economist*. March 25, 2006, pp. 2–16.

Roll, Richard. "Economic and Political Freedom: The Keys to Development." Chapter 3 in Marc Miles, ed., *The Road to Prosperity*. Washington DC: Heritage Books, 2004.

Sachs, Jeffrey. *The End of Poverty*. New York: Penguin Press, 2005.

Stiles, Paul. *Is the American Dream Killing You?* New York: HarperCollins, 2005.

Tweeten, Luther. *Terrorism, Radicalism, and Populism in Agriculture*. Ames: Iowa State Press, 2003.

UNDP. *The State of Human Development 2005*. New York: United Nations Development Program, 2005.

World Bank. *Economic Development Indicators*. *http://devdata.worldbank.org/ dataonline*. Washington DC, 2005.

World Bank. *Knowledge for Development*. http://info.worldbank.org/etools/kam/ kei_table.asp?tid=0&year=2002&sortby=EIR&sortorder=ASC. Washington DC, 2006.

Zhao, Fenkum, Fred Hitzhusen, and Wen Chern. "Impact and Implications of Price Policy and Land Degradation on Agricultural Growth in Developing Countries." *Agricultural Economics* 5: 311–24, 1991.

4

Does the Standard Model Work in Theory?

Epistemology requires two things for reliable knowledge: (1) a plausible conceptual framework establishing logical cause and effect among variables, and (2) empirical evidence that the postulated causal variables in fact predict effects within acceptable statistical limits of probability. The previous chapter made a compelling *empirical* case that markets offer unmatched economic efficiency essential for alleviating poverty, hunger, disease, and environmental degradation. No country has successfully addressed these problems without harnessing the wealth-generating capabilities of markets.

A well-worn joke is one economist saying to another, "It works in practice, but will it work in theory?" This chapter risks living the joke. Although scientific methodology usually begins with a conceptual framework followed by empirical verification or refutation of the hypotheses suggested by theory, chapters 3 and 4 reverse that order. The reversal is because some readers may wish to learn only that the standard model works; they would just as soon skip the theory; yet the conceptual framework is extremely important in explaining the conditions necessary for markets to serve the public interest (see also the annex to chapter 2). Subsequent chapters propose remedies for situations where laissez-faire markets fail. Some readers may wish to omit the abstractions of this chapter and move on to issues addressed in subsequent chapters.

Following the abject failure of nonmarket economies by the end of the twentieth century, almost no one now denies that the market must be the core of any successful economy.[14] Neither is there denial that the public sector must play a crucial role in any successful economy. The remaining, perennial issue is how big a role each sector should play. The annex to chapter 2 listed criteria for determining what is a public good (or service) best provided by government and what is a market good most efficiently provided by the private sector.

Another dichotomy, in addition to the public versus market good distinction, is economic equity versus efficiency. In keeping with the aphorism that

---

14 Even the counter-culture, postmodernist philosophers who have replaced Marxist philosophers as the gurus of today's radical left protesters pretty much accept markets, even as they reject globalization and corporatism (Tweeten 2003, Chapter 2).

"When your only tool is a hammer, every problem looks like a nail," economists devote most of their ink to efficiency, because their tools are best adapted to that issue. Other social scientists, perhaps following the aphorism that (like Charlie Brown) they are "best at things that are a matter of opinion," emphasize economic equity. They render to economic efficiency the obscurity that economists give to equity. Both dimensions of economics are important and treated in this volume. This chapter will emphasize efficiency; matters of justice in access to resources and wealth will be addressed in chapter 5.

The General Concept of Economic Development

Economic development is defined here as an increase in the well-being of people, preferably on a sustained basis over time. The raison d'être of this chapter is to show how markets and economic development in theory promote a better life for people. The conceptual process of development is described with the aid of figure 4.1, depicting the "rocket" that propels an economy. The goal is to place the payload or satellite—the well-being of people—in "orbit." The launching pad and rockets depicted in figure 4.1 are merely means toward that goal. The payload is the product, not just of the level and distribution of income, but also of freedom, justice, stability, and other components determining quality of life.

The launching pad for the development rocket has three main foundation stones. The first is natural resources, including air, soil, water, climate, minerals, and biodiversity. Such resources are regarded by many as the most important ingredients for economic development.[15] Natural resources are important indeed, and if used wisely and shared through open trade, they are sufficient globally to provide a good living for everyone for a very long time. Consequently, natural resources in any particular country are less important ingredients than institutions and attitudes for economic progress. Japan, Hong Kong, and Singapore demonstrate that high living standards and food security are attainable in a country short on domestic natural resources. Of course, these countries have geographic location advantages that may be regarded as natural resources. Location is important but is not decisive for economic success. The prairie provinces of Canada, the mountain and prairie states of the

15 The biosphere as an ecosystem provides raw materials such as petroleum and phosphate, but it also provides a "sink," absorbing effluents. Some (see Daly) contend that future living standards of people will be more constrained by lack of absorptive capacity of natural resources as a sink than by limits on the supply of fossil fuels and other stock resources.

United States, and much of Australia demonstrate that being landlocked and remote do not condemn a geographic area to poverty. The conclusion is that other basic ingredients are more important than natural resources as a launching pad for economic progress.

Inclusiveness would list raw labor as a resource in figure 4.1. It is omitted because raw labor adds very little to output. Economic development in figure 4.1 is about enlarging well-being and income per capita. Additional raw, unskilled labor adds more to the denominator, population, than it adds to the numerator, income; hence it detracts from economic development.[16] Income per capita rises only if expansion in raw labor and population are attended by an expansion in human and other forms of capital.

The second basic foundation stone for real economic progress is institutions such as government, markets, and laws (figure 4.1). Institutions constitute the organizations and rules of the game for allocating resources to meet the wants of people. Institutions such as universities are repositories of accumulated knowledge, and gene banks are repositories of biodiversity essential to agricultural science and technology. Institutional innovations, such as limited liability joint stock corporations, legally enforceable property rights, and investment banks, invigorate markets. In many ways, institutions are mediators between attitudes, the third ingredient of economic progress, and natural resources; however, over time, institutions such as government, judicial systems, and markets change culture.

I view policy as a form of institution, but some analysts make a distinction between policy and institutions. Pritchett (p. 21) observes the work of numerous analysts who seem to think "the primary determinant of a country's level of income is the quality of its institutions." Then he (p. 21) makes a distinction along with a dash of humor when he quotes an anonymous source with the statement "…policies are what can be purposively changed and institutions are what cannot." We defer to later in this chapter the issue of what foundation stones can be moved.

---

16 Consider a Cobb-Douglas production function

$$Q=aK^bL^c$$

where Q is output, K is human and material capital, L is raw labor, and a and b are elasticities of production. If labor is proportional to population, output per capita is

$$Q/L=aK^bL^{c-1}.$$

If b=0.6 and c=0.4, then a ten-percent increase in raw labor reduces output per capita by 10 (c-1) or 6 percent.

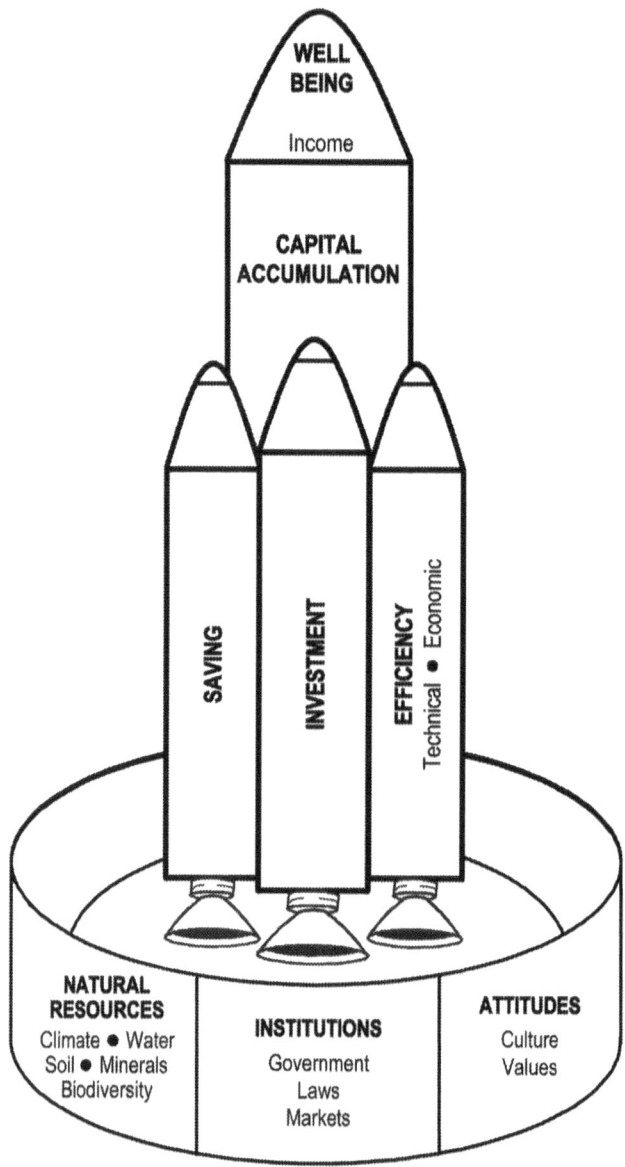

Figure 4.1. Elements of Economic Development

Attitudes, the third and most important basic ingredient of economic progress, constitute a range of attributes commonly called culture, goals, beliefs, and values of society. Attitudes conducive to economic progress and food security include morality *(e.g.,* not taking advantage of others, even if presented the opportunity), enterprise (entrepreneurship), industriousness (work ethic), thrift (deferred gratification), acquisitiveness (wealth seeking), intellectuality (desire for learning), and fraternity (sense of community). Most of these attributes are self-explanatory and need little elaboration. The Protestant ethic (Tawney; Weber) and Confucian ethic (Johnston) contain elements of morality, work ethic, and enterprise believed to be conducive to economic progress in northern Europe and East Asia, respectively.

Is there a national will for economic progress? Psychology professor David McClelland (1961) and his associates examined representative children's stories in various countries, looking in those stories for achievement images that might signal a collective drive for economic success. Achievement images could include satisfaction from the accumulation of wealth, triumph of the human spirit over impediments to economic success, and the thrill of succeeding in business after taking risks. If these images reflect a collective drive for success in the culture or impart a drive for success in the children, persisting until they became adults, countries with more achievement images would have higher economic growth rates. McClelland (p. 105) concluded thus:

A concern for achievement as expressed in imaginative literature—folk tales and stories for children—is associated in modern times with a more rapid rate of economic development. The generalization is confirmed not only for Western, free-enterprise democracies like England and the United States but also for communist countries like Russia, Bulgaria, and Hungry, or primitive tribes that are just beginning to make contact with modern technological society. It holds in the main whether a country is developed or underdeveloped, poor or rich, industrial or agricultural, free or totalitarian. In other words there is a strong suggestion here that men with high achievement motives will find a way to economic achievement given wide variations in opportunity and social structure. What people want, they somehow manage to get, in the main and on the average, though other factors can modify the speed with which they get it.

The results serve to direct our attention as social scientists away from the exclusive concern with the external events in history and toward the "internal" psychological concerns that in the long run determine what happens in history.

More recent evidence supports McClelland's conclusion that cultural attitudes conducive to development not only are important but also can be changed. Thomas Sowell (p. 345) credits much of Japan's economic success to "social and political attitudes that made economic development a priority bordering on an obsession." Government bureaucracies as well as businesses there were caught up in pursuing economic development. For bureaucracy in East Asian countries to be committed to development objectives is exceptional: the stereotypical bureaucrat in developing countries too often seeks personal security, wealth, and influence to the detriment of national economic progress.

I, like Sowell, have observed the widespread positive commitment to socioeconomic progress among the people of East Asia. Positive attitudes persist among citizens of formerly poor East Asian countries with an unfortunate legacy of cruelty inflicted by colonialism and war. This contrasts with the attitudes of victimhood pervading some perennially poor countries of Africa and Latin America. Self-pity is a toxic attitude for socioeconomic progress. Blaming one's current poverty on the West, multinational corporations, export cropping, or an international financial system cabal may be personally cathartic, but by diverting attention from the present need for domestic institutional and policy reform, self-pity robs a country of future socioeconomic progress.

Other attitudes have received increasing attention in recent decades. For example, intellectuality or scholarship (apparent in the commitment to education as a means to economic progress) has played no small part in the human resource development and economic success of Indians and East Asians in their home countries and elsewhere. If India and China continue to reform their long-stifling institutions and thereby unleash their suppressed spirit of learning and enterprise in an environment featuring standard-model economic policies, they will come to dominate the global economy.

"Sense of community" or fraternity is one of the more elusive and controversial attitudinal ingredients for growth. The attitude in a citizen implies solidarity with or tolerance for others in the community and nation. The attitude is revealed in mutual trust, collective identity, a shared future, and a willingness to work together and to sacrifice (*e.g.,* pay taxes) for community benefit. The importance of national community is apparent especially in the negative—lack of a sense of national community, evident in tribalism or sectarianism, has been the major cause of the civil violence underlying most famines since World War II.

Solidarity is easier to build at the local level than the national level. Much can be said for the principle of *subsidiarity,* which I define as government by the most local unit within which benefits and costs are internalized. People are more willing to bear tax burdens if they see the benefits. Thus, local government best administers local schools and roads, whereas national defense is the responsibility of central government.

Economists Paul Krugman and Jeffrey Sachs view as unhelpful the introduction of values as an element explaining or contributing to economic progress. Krugman (p. 29) summarized disapprovingly the *Washington Consensus* as "the belief that Victorian virtue in economic policy—free markets and sound money—is the key to economic development." Sachs (p. 317), a "clinical economist," to use his term, alleged, "The idea that whole societies are condemned to poverty because of their values has a long history, but one that is seldom useful." Fortunately, he disregarded that notion only two sentences later, recognizing the importance of cultural values such as the role of women in the labor market, household fertility choices, and school attendance of children. He (p. 317) went on to an even more important insight: "Values deemed to be inimical to economic development are rarely—if *ever*—unalterable features of the society." It follows that values are potential instrumental variables capable of being changed in pursuing socioeconomic progress.

Uganda provides an example of induced cultural change to foster social and economic progress. President Yoweri Museveni, noting the high and rising incidence of HIV/AIDS virus in the population, went village to village with a message against promiscuity and in favor of safe sex. Sexual behavior is cultural and not easily changed, but Museveni's message (with help from nongovernment organizations and the provision of condoms) influenced behavior. It is said to have reduced Uganda's incidence of HIV/AIDS from fifteen percent in the 1980s to five percent in 2005—quite a feat, even conceding that AIDS-related deaths inflated the appearance of success.

Fundamental ingredients for economic development have numerous trade-offs. Favorable attitudes or institutions can compensate for a lack of natural resources. For example, an abundance of natural resources in one country can offset a scarcity of resources in another country, if countries are open to trade; thus, a lack of agricultural resources in a country does not relegate it to poverty or hunger. Similarly, with open investment, a very low propensity to save in a country such as the United States can be offset by inflow of financial capital from other countries such as China and Japan with a high propensity to save. And enterprising people and a strong work ethic can offset inadequate institutions, as in China.

Attitudes that were highly functional in a traditional society can inhibit economic development toward an affluent society. Many poor countries have a culture of sharing within an extended family system. Any hungry family member is entitled to obtain food at no charge from any extended family member who has food. Such sharing is highly functional, averting starvation during famines.

The downside of continuing that tradition is that one's incentives to accumulate even modest wealth offered by today's technology and global commerce are compromised when the fruits of one's enterprise must be shared among extended family members. In Africa, I have observed well-educated, well-paid workers holding critical jobs relinquish their positions out of frustration over relatives and friends persistently at their doorsteps, demanding assistance.

It would be tempting but incorrect to conclude that market-oriented economic development would, unfortunately, erode a culture of sharing. Abigail Barr (pp. 24–7), studying social capital formation in Africa since 2000, concluded, "Where involvement in market exchange is rare, individuals are more selfish and less altruistic."

The African tribal tradition has been for the chief not only to hold a position of authority within the tribe, but also to visibly display the fortunes of the tribe. In both roles, the chief was given wide leeway to employ whatever methods he deemed appropriate to look good, so that the tribe looked good. This tradition contributed to tribal pride when almost everyone was poor, but in today's African nation-states, it contributes to corruption among leaders. Former president Mobutu Sese Seko of Zaire, when asked by a reporter to explain the alleged $5 billion he had pilfered from Zaire and deposited in Belgian and other European banks, replied, "How can I be accused of stealing from Zaire when I am Zaire?" The attitude that a leader is the servant rather than the master of people is too rare.

The role of culture in development has been a source of disagreement, not just among economists, but also between economists and other social scientists. I complained to a sociologist friend that the literature of his discipline offered little insight regarding means to change a culture from one stifling to one supportive of economic progress that is essential to alleviate hunger, disease, and poverty. His response was, "Sociologists don't change culture; they celebrate it." Upon reflection, he may have realized that his facile reply was disingenuous. Sociologists and anthropologists unabashedly and appropriately (in my value system) promote the virtues of gender and racial equality.

Kuran (p. 115) notes, "Multiculturalists generally maintain that globalization, by destroying local cultures, harms the affected communities, even humanity as a whole [see Box 4.1]. There is a need, they say, to resist the homogenizing influences of modern civilization by nurturing cultural differences." Preserving traditional culture in the face of globalization is difficult indeed. Modern media technology, such as radios and cassette players, is cheap and ubiquitous. Traditional cultures exposed to modern technology are eager to adopt modern medicine, machines, literacy, and other trappings of globalization and a better life. Even defenders of traditional culture would not deny locals education for literacy, antiretroviral drugs to treat HIV/AIDS, antibiotics to treat bacterial infections, and surgery to remove an infected appendix. These "essentials" must be paid for, and that requires a source of income. Earning that income is likely to require wage labor, the growing of cash crops, and dealing with merchants and employers from outside the community. Subsistence farming is not an option. Development cannot be separated from cultural change.

> **Box 4.1.** The readings and lectures in a university cultural anthropology course I sat in on in 2004 lamented the damage imposed on poor countries by international free trade, growing crops for export, multinational corporations, and multilateral institutions such as the World Bank, the International Monetary Fund, and the World Trade Organization. The instructor was genuinely distressed by the hunger and disease endemic to these poor countries. She was dedicated to a better life for traditional societies. But the lectures and assigned readings called for economic policies that if followed would condemn traditional cultures to a Hobbesian existence. The conflict between preserving traditional culture and alleviating hunger, poverty, illiteracy, and disease was palpable. The instructor either did not understand the tradeoff or would elect to preserve traditional culture at much cost in human misery.

The process of economic development itself changes culture. Beyond that, interventions in culture to promote development should not be undertaken lightly. Despite convincing evidence that a nationwide developmental zeitgeist promotes development in a poor country, promoting such a zeitgeist is a job for the poor country's citizens and leaders and not for outsider development zealots.

Promoting other types of cultural change to further development is less controversial (Box 4.2). Education to change culture is warranted if tribal animosities are causing genocide or if corruption in leaders is perennially condemning large segments of the population to poverty. Education to change values is appropriate if women are being mistreated by genital mutilation, forbidden to own property, or raped by older men attempting to end their HIV-positive status.

Box 4.2. The charity versus cultural change debate over Africa and other poor regions has its counterpart in the work of Christian missionaries. At issue is whether to save souls or bodies. No strategy is pure, but Roman Catholics lean toward providing education and health care to save bodies, while Protestant Evangelicals lean toward saving souls. Anthropologists and many political liberals condemn the latter activity as an unwarranted attempt to change culture. The issue is complex, as will become apparent below, and I find it difficult to take sides in the charity versus cultural change debate.

The case for material assistance is clear. The case for evangelism may be less obvious, so let me review. As noted, many problems of corruption and tribal animosities retarding economic development in Africa and other poor regions trace in no small part to the neglect of simple virtues. The bible teaches that everyone is created in God's own image and hence has personal worth and dignity. It teaches Christians to "love thy neighbor." The Ten Commandments contain strictures against killing, stealing, and false witness, and hence against violence and corruption. The virtue of enterprise is taught by the biblical parable of the servant who won praise for multiplying the talents placed in his hands. The book of Genesis teaches that we are stewards of God's creation, and hence of the environment. Protestant Evangelical church organization, for the most part, is democratic, and it rejects authority from the top down—the latter being a cultural trait that has ravished many a poor nation. Thus, the biblical message of honesty, openness, and tolerance, if taught fully, is constructive for cultural change and economic reform important to poor countries.

Economic progress is furthered by attitudes of (1) secular asceticism apparent in honesty, the work ethic, and deferred gratification; and (2) the risk-taking apparent in enterprise. These two dimensions often conflict. Christian teachings focus more on the former than the latter, but it is not difficult to find examples such as the early Congregational missionaries to Hawaii who "came to do good but ended up doing well." The Protestant ethic was a perhaps rare coming together of (1) and (2).

In conclusion, I see merit in the mission of Evangelicals emphasizing the Gospel that in the long run brings useful changes in culture, *and* in the mission of mainline Christians emphasizing the social gospel supplying immediate necessities for a better life among the disadvantaged.

Support from all three basic launch-pad components in figure 4.1 ensures economic development takeoffs. Economic development is largely a matter of accumulating capital per unit of raw labor ("booster rockets" in figure 4.1). Saving, investing, and in general devoting resources into high-payoff activities build capital. Saving is income not consumed. Nonetheless, if it is stashed in a mattress, it fails to accumulate capital or income. It must be invested to create capital. That investment will create no capital and generate no income unless it is used in positive-payoff activities. Investment in an unproductive asset is worthless, as many punters in the stock market have discovered.

Industrious people and businesses with a high propensity to save (defer consumption out of income) and to invest wisely in high-payoff public and private activities (efficiency) create capital that in turn generates a stream of income. That process began eons ago. Early man took some time away from gathering berries and hunting game to build capital in the form of snares, pots, knives, bows, and arrows. As a consequence of this accumulation of capital, the standard of living climbed.

Today, capital can take many forms, including material, technological, human, and social capital. Defining capital as durable inputs requiring scarce resources to accumulate and giving off services over several periods of time, we observe that some of the highest-payoff activities are investments in schooling (human capital) and technology. Based on data in table 4.1, it would be difficult to overestimate the importance of human capital to development. In the poorest regions of Africa and Asia in 1994, human resources comprised sixty percent of all assets, whereas "natural" capital, including agricultural land, comprised only ten to twenty percent (Dixon and Hamilton, p. 16). Of the $16 trillion in U.S. wealth in 1990, up to eighty-five percent was human capital and only four percent was farm real estate (Tweeten, 1997, chapter 9). The United States, early on, taxed an abundant resource, land, to build a scarce resource, human capital formed in local schools. In 1862, land grant colleges were established on the same principle, which gave the working class access to education that previously had been accessible only to the wealthy.

An extensive review of investments in developing countries found typical rates of return of near forty percent on elementary education, agricultural research, and some types of infrastructure, such as roads (Tweeten and McClelland). The rate of return can be defined as the highest rate of interest that can be paid on investment in a capital item and just break even on the investment. Typical private investments yield real returns of about eight percent, and many public investments yield negative returns. Hence, the ability to earn returns of forty percent or more makes a strong case for more investment in elementary schooling, roads, and agricultural research in poor countries.

Table 4.1. Wealth per Capita and Components, 1994

Region	Human capital	Produced capital	Agricultural land	Other natural	Total wealth	
	(Percent of total)				Percent	$/capita
North America	76.2	19.0	2.5	2.2	100.0	325,274
Australia, Japan, New Zealand	67.6	29.6	1.8	1.0	100.0	303,389
Western Europe	74.3	23.3	1.6	0.8	100.0	236,164
Middle East	38.2	18.7	4.7	38.4	100.0	146,243
South America	73.9	16.9	4.8	4.4	100.0	94,086
East Europe & Central Asia	48.8	35.6	7.8	7.8	100.0	62,500
North Africa	68.3	26.5	1.9	3.3	100.0	54,185
Central America	78.7	15.1	4.7	1.4	100.0	51,612
Caribbean	68.5	20.8	8.8	1.8	100.0	47,338
East Asia	76.4	15.7	6.2	1.7	100.0	46,076
Southern & East Africa	65.4	24.6	6.5	3.5	100.0	29,863
West Africa	60.0	18.6	16.0	5.3	100.0	22,036
South Asia	64.3	19.0	15.0	1.7	100.0	21,704

Source: Dixon and Hamilton, p. 16.

Saving, investing, and accumulating capital are not ends in themselves but are merely "booster rockets" in figure 4.1. The boosters contribute to acceleration of the main rocket, increased real income per capita. But income also is only a means, not an end, and it is valued because it adds to the well-being of people. As stated earlier, well-being derives from the distribution (equity) as well as from the level (a larger economic "pie") of income and wealth. Food security and health, for example, are best served when economic progress is broad-based, with human resource investments and opportunities open to the disadvantaged, minorities, women, and others. Opening access by women to education, property rights, inheritance, and occupations brings higher family income, improved nutrition and education of children, and reduced birth rates. Ultimately, economic development reduces birth rates more than death rates so that population falls—an issue to be explored in chapter 9.

Institutions and attitudes listed as part of the launching pad for economic progress in figure 4.1 are sometimes called, respectively, *institutional capital* and *social capital*. They are a form of capital if they need not be taken as "givens" but instead can be created by judicious investments in people. A sense of community is sometimes viewed as an immutable cultural legacy but alternatively can be social capital created by educating people to be tolerant. If a sense of community is social capital, it should be listed as a product of investment (a rocket engine in figure 4.1), rather than a foundation stone in the launching pad.

Finally, we come to the ultimate payload or satellite, the well-being of people, for the development rocket in figure 4.1. Economic development, defined as an increase in real income per capita (the core rocket), is the means to the ultimate end of improving the lives of people. That well-being depends on health, education, distribution of income, freedom, security, justice, and the like. Markets, some say, are about profit and not about what really counts: freedom, democracy, and justice. Some say that food should be for people and not for profit. How does the market-oriented standard model stack up in serving these sometimes intangible but important objectives of a successful society?

Data presented in chapter 3 and elsewhere in this volume leave no doubt that the standard model is consistent with freedom, security, and preservation of the environment. Although the Economic Freedom Index was designed to measure economic freedom rather than political freedom, the two freedoms are closely linked. It is no accident that no socialist economy has been a democracy. And China is showing that no successful market economy can remain socialistic.

Socialist economies of necessity are bureaucratic, command and control economies. Autocrats and bureaucrats running such countries must make a very large number of important decisions each day, many of which make many people worse off. Leaders of such an economy can ill afford the time or patience required for democratic consensus on each decision. The billions of decisions that markets make each day in a market economy frees time for politicians and bureaucrats to make a few decisions well. Thus it comes as no surprise that democracy is tenuous or nonexistent in countries ranking low in economic freedom in table 3.1. In contrast, political democracy predominates among countries ranking high in economic freedom in table 3.2.

Judging by East Asian countries with great economic progress but little democracy or personal freedom, the most basic ingredients for economic success are attitudes, markets, and the rule of law. Again judging by East Asian countries, the demand for personal freedom, justice, and democracy is positively correlated with income. As autocratic countries become more affluent, the growing middle class insists on the personal freedom, representation in government, and rules of political succession attainable only by embracing democracy. Perhaps someday China will demonstrate, as Taiwan already has, that freedoms associated with markets are contagious, bringing political democracy.

The world, according to Coyle, is experiencing what she calls a "new capitalism" that paradoxically promotes the very values its vociferous critics, the anti-globalists, champion. Coyle reasons that the new capitalism, with its greater openness to trade, investment, and cultural mixing, promotes not just higher living standards, but also justice, fairness, freedom, and a voice for those previously marginalized. The new, dynamic, information-age capitalism weakens opportunities for corporate hierarchies and governments to be overbearing and intrusive.

The case can be made that standard-model policies promote another vital dimension of well-being—peace. In 2003 alone, nineteen armed conflicts were underway in eighteen locations. The majority (seventeen) of these were civil (intrastate) wars, although little about them was civilized. The majority of the wars were in poor countries of Asia and Africa. Crude calculations by Collier and Hoeffler (p. 44) placed the average cost of a civil war at $54 billion per involved poor country and $64 billion if the cost to other countries is included. With an average of two new civil wars per year, the cost is $128 billion annually. Rich democracies do not have a record of civil war or waging war against each other. It follows that the standard model, which supports economic progress and democracy, serves the cause of world peace. Causality works both ways—the rule of law attending peace energizes standard-model policies.

Promoting Development through Supply and Demand

Markets operate through supply and demand to promote saving, investment, efficiency, capital accumulation, and income generation central to economic development, as depicted in figure 4.1. Inevitably, economics is about tradeoffs. Something must be sacrificed to get more of something else. For example, cutting greenhouse gas emissions to reduce global warming means sacrificing fossil fuel energy used to keep us warm in winter and cool in summer. Another tradeoff is between using less fossil fuels to reduce global warming versus more fossil fuels for supplying fertilizers and power to the food economy. Such tradeoffs work through supply and demand, setting prices and clearing markets.

Demand

Demand is defined as the schedule of quantities taken in the market at various prices for a good q (figure 4.2). Alternatively, demand may be viewed as the schedule of prices in the market associated with various quantities taken by consumers. The schedule applies to a specific unit of time *(UT)*, such as a week or a year.

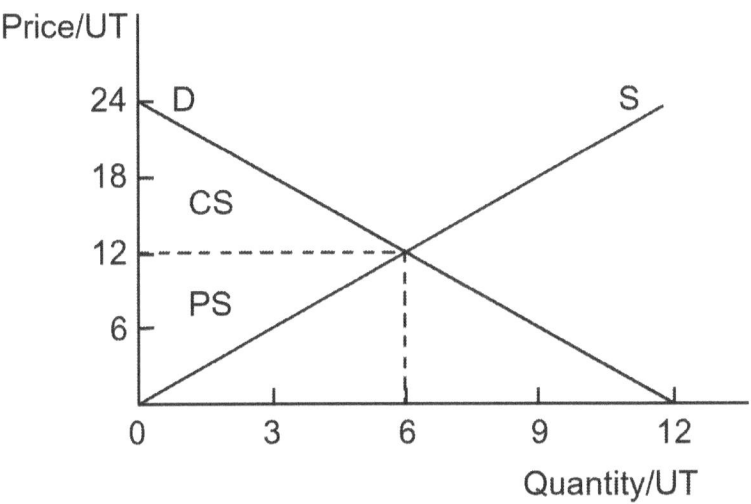

Figure 4.2. Demand *(D)* and Supply *(S)* per Unit of Time *(UT)* for quantity *q* and price of *q* in dollars

Demand curve D in figure 4.2 graphically displays a hypothetical demand schedule as follows:

Price	Quantity
0	12
4	10
8	8
12	6
16	4
20	2
24	0

Demand curves such as D generally slope downward to the right because of *diminishing marginal utility;* that is, consumers derive the most satisfaction from the first unit of *q* and derive successively less satisfaction from each additional unit consumed. Consequently, they are willing to pay the highest price for the first unit and successively lower prices for additional units of q. Thus, consumers are willing to pay twenty-two dollars for the first unit, twelve dollars for the sixth unit, and nothing for the twelfth unit of q in figure 4.2. (If we are examining markets for a country, these values of q may refer to billions of units.)

Changes in population, income, and tastes can shift the demand curve. Ernst Engel, a Prussian economist, in the nineteenth century noted from budget studies that as the income of consumers increases, the proportion of their income spent on food decreases. This relationship is called Engel's Law. The proportion of income spent on food falls, because people prefer to spend additional income on education, health care, recreation, and other goods and services. The falling proportion of income spent on food, coupled with rising labor productivity in agriculture under economic growth, causes agriculture to become a smaller part of the economy.

Supply

Supply is defined as the schedule of quantities of a good q that producers will deliver to the market at various prices of q (figure 4.2). If producers act rationally to increase their net income, they will supply another unit to the market if the price of the good covers the cost of producing another unit, called the *marginal cost* of production.

In figure 4.2, the supply schedule is depicted as the supply curve S per unit of time, as follows:

Price	Quantity
0	0
4	2
8	4
12	6
16	8
20	10
24	12

Producers are willing to supply one unit of q to the market at the price of two dollars. They require a much higher price to supply more—to supply the tenth unit they require a price of twenty.

The supply curve ordinarily slopes upward to the right, as in figure 4.2, because of *diminishing marginal returns*, sometimes called the *law of variable proportions*. That is, supplying the first ton of wheat from the field to the market may cost little, because it was raised on very fertile land; however, the marginal cost of production rises for additional output, because more fertilizer, irrigation water, and pesticides are required as inferior hectares are cropped. Stated in terms of the law of variable proportions, the incremental cost of producing another ton of wheat rises because more and more inputs must be applied on each additional hectare as cropping is extended to inferior land.

The supply curve shifts because of technology and weather. Weather is unpredictable and causes mostly random shifts in the supply curve. Technology, which raises output for a given amount of conventional production inputs at a given price, is largely the product of nonconventional inputs such as education, science, and human ingenuity. In American agriculture, farm production inputs such as labor, land, and on-farm capital increased very little in aggregate over the past century, while farm output quadrupled, mainly due to nonconventional inputs of education, infrastructure, and research. Improved capital embodying these nonconventional inputs replaced farm labor. It costs much less for the nation to increase food output using nonconventional inputs than by using conventional farm labor and land.

Supply can be viewed as an *opportunity cost*. Marginal cost is the value of inputs used to produce another unit of q, or equivalently is the value of production and consumption of other goods sacrificed (called "opportunity cost") to produce another unit of q.[17] That conclusion will be important as we move to welfare analysis in the next section.

---

17 For a market in competitive equilibrium it is well known that

(1) $\Delta q1/\Delta x = px/p1$ and (2) $\Delta q1/\Delta q2 = p2/p1$

where q1 and p1 are respectively the quantity and price of the good in Figure 4.2, q2 and p2 are quantity and price of another good 2, x and px are the quantity and price of input x used to produce q1, and Δ refers to a small change in quantity. Rearranging terms, (1) and (2) respectively can be expressed as

(3) $p1 = \Delta x px/\Delta q1$ and (4) $p1 = \Delta q2 p2/\Delta q1$.

It follows that the supply price p1, the price of q1, is precisely equal to the cost of resource x used to produce another unit of q1 in (3) and also, in (4), is equal to the value foregone of other goods q2 to produce another unit of q1. The two expressions for marginal cost of q1 in (3) and (4) are equal. The conclusion of much significance is that the supply price in Figure 4.2 can be viewed equivalently as the (a) input expense to produce q or (b) the value of the output foregone of other goods (opportunity cost) by producing another unit of q.

The demand curve may be viewed as a marginal revenue curve, and the area beneath the demand curve may be viewed as total revenue. It can be shown from figure 4.2 that a seller who can *fully* discriminate among markets will be able to collect twenty-three dollars from the first unit of q and twenty-one dollars for the second unit of q; these are marginal revenues.[18] The total revenue for the first two units is twenty-three plus twenty-one dollars, or forty-four dollars (see figure 4.2).

Marginal revenue (price) falls to zero by the twelfth unit of q. The reader can verify that the maximum total revenue available from q, the area beneath the demand curve from zero to twelve units, is $144.

People demand q because they derive satisfaction (utility) from its consumption. If they are rational, they will consume q until the satisfaction they receive per dollar spent on it provides no more and no less satisfaction than a dollar spent on something else. Arbitrarily calling that satisfaction from another dollar of spending a "util," the area beneath the demand curve represents the total utility available by consuming q. (The difficult question of whether dollars can be added among people to represent utility is important and has been dealt with by Blue and myself.)

So should society consume twelve units of q to maximize income and utility? The answer is no, because we have not considered foregone production, consumption, and utility of other goods and services as we use more of q. That is, supply as well as demand must be considered in allocating resources to increase income and utility.

Finding Economic Equilibrium

The marginal cost of producing the first unit of q is one dollar and of the second unit is three dollars, where "cost" may be expressed as expenses for labor and other operating inputs, or as the value of other commodities not produced because resources were devoted to q (see footnote 17). The total variable cost of producing these first two units of q is one dollar plus three dollars, or four dollars, as shown in figure 4.2. Non-variable or overhead costs are ignored, because they are considered to be sunk in the length of run considered and do not determine the efficient level of q. In the long run, all costs become variable.

---

18 Each unit of q is assumed to be perfectly divisible for price discrimination along the demand curve. Unlike the earlier example where the "law of one price" held, so the first unit brings $22, in this case of discrimination the first unit along the linear demand curve brings ($24+$22)/2=$23.

Marginal and total costs rise with more output of q. The cost of unit eleven is twenty-one dollars and of unit twelve is twenty-three dollars; the total cost for these two units is forty-four dollars. The entire variable cost for producing twelve units is $144, found by summing the area under the supply curve in figure 4.2. (The fact that this total is the same as the total revenue computed earlier is coincidental and depended on the way the demand and supply curves were drawn.)

Beginning from zero units of q on the left of figure 4.2, marginal benefits of more q, indicated by the demand curve D, exceed marginal cost, as indicated by the supply curve S as we move to the right. Beyond six units of q, however, marginal costs exceed the marginal benefits of producing more q. It is unwise to produce and consume less than six units of q, because producing and con-suming each additional unit provides more benefit than cost. It is unwise to produce and consume more than six units of q, because each additional unit provides higher cost than benefit. Because it is irrational to produce and con-sume more or less than the number of units where marginal cost equals mar-ginal revenue, we call six units the *economic equilibrium quantity* in figure 4.2. The equilibrium price, twelve, clears the market at that quantity.

What is so special about the economic equilibrium price and quantity brought about by supply and demand interacting in a competitive market? For starters, it maximizes the economic surplus, defined as the total revenue less the total variable cost. The reader can verify that the economic surplus from the first two units of q is forty dollars, from the next two is twenty-four dol-lars, from the next two is eight dollars, from the next two is negative eight dol-lars, from the next two is negative twenty-four dollars, and from the next two is negative forty dollars. Thus the maximum economic surplus is seventy-two dollars. Producing more or less than six units of q would have reduced that sur-plus. If we can add the economic surpluses for all goods and services for all par-ticipants in an economy, it follows that pricing and output at the intersection of supply and demand in a competitive economy maximizes the net income of that economy. If a dollar of income has the same utility for everyone, then the economic equilibrium maximizes the utility to society.

Of course, the real world is not that simple. Assumptions listed in Economics 101 textbooks for markets to maximize economic surplus include large num-bers of firms so no one can influence price, perfect information by market par-ticipants, rising costs as output expands, and divisibility and mobility of goods. These assumptions are not met in reality and are often used by market critics to debunk markets. Violations of the strict assumptions do not invalidate the case for markets, however. Experience shows that markets function efficiently with-out large numbers of firms. In fact, in most industries, economies of size are so great that having a large number of firms is inefficient. Even having only one or two firms in an industry in a nation can provide workable competition, if markets are open to competition from abroad. Having perfect information and perfect mobility and divisibility of firms and goods would also be prohibitively costly and inefficient. The conclusion is that the efficiency of markets is robust with respect to these assumptions.

Finally, before leaving figure 4.2, it is important to observe how the equilibrium price divides the economic surplus between a *consumer surplus* going to consumers and a *producer surplus* going to producers. The law of one price prevails in a competitive economy of many buyers and sellers, because it would be irrational for consumers to pay more than the equilibrium price $p=12$ in figure 4.2, and it would be irrational for producers to accept less than that price.

The consumer surplus CS is the sum of the value consumers would be willing to pay in excess of the value they do pay. CS is bounded by the demand curve D on the top, by the market price on the bottom, by the vertical price axis (at $q=0$) on the left, and by the quantity produced and consumed (in this case, $q=6$) on the right in figure 4.2. In figure 4.2, the consumer surplus on the first two units of q is \$22-\$12=\$10, x 2=\$20, on the second two units is \$18-\$12= \$6, x 2=\$12, and on the third two units is \$14-\$12=\$2, x 2=\$4, for a total over six units of thirty-six dollars.

Producer surplus PS is the revenue producers receive in excess of the minimum required of them to bring forth the quantity supplied. PS is bounded by the market price on the top, the marginal cost curve (supply curve S) on the bottom, by the price axis (at $q=0$) on the left, and the market quantity produced on the right in figure 4.2. PS may be called the net return to overhead or fixed resources. Producer surplus for the first two units produced in figure 4.2 is \$12-\$2=\$10, x 2=\$20, for the second two units is \$12-\$6=\$6, x 2=\$12, and for the third set of two units is \$12-\$10=\$2, x 2=\$4. The total is thirty-six dollars, the return to fixed resources. As expected, the sum of the producer surplus PS and the consumer surplus CS, which each just happen to be thirty-six dollars, is seventy-two dollars, the economic surplus. No other output but $q=6$ would produce that large a surplus. The very important conclusion is that economic surplus is maximized with the competitive market outcome. If each member of society derives the same utility from a dollar, then the competitive market outcome also maximizes the utility of society. A monopoly that restricts output to raise price and profit will produce too little q and reduce the economic surplus. A government subsidy raising the price received by firms causes the firms to produce too much and reduces the economic surplus.

It may be noted here that the supply and demand curves apply to a given period of time. In the short run, resources cannot readily be moved among uses to expand output of *q*, so the supply curve tends to be steeply sloped and the producer surplus is large. In the longer run, resources tend to be mobile among uses, and the supply curve becomes much flatter. Hence the producers surplus *PS*, or pure, above-normal profit, disappears—all economic surplus passes to consumers to make *CS* large in figure 4.2.

Adam Smith in *Wealth of Nations*, published in 1776, highlighted the role of *specialization* in shifting supply curves to the right so that real prices of commodities fall and standards of living improve over time. With trade, by having some workers specialize in building carriages and others in supplying food, the workers in both industries live better. David Ricardo (1772–1823) made famous a related concept of *comparative advantage* in trade. With trade, countries can produce the commodities they are relatively best at and lower the cost of consuming their preferred commodity.[19]

Markets also allocate resources and products over time, based on the supply of savings and the demand for investments. Most people prefer to consume now rather than later, so they require compensation in the form of interest to defer consumption and save some of their income. In a poor country, when the alternative to consuming now is to starve, the compensation needed to forego consumption is high; then, only high interest rates will generate saving.

The demand for investment also depends on the interest rate. If the interest rate is low, even low-payoff investments are profitable and the demand quantity of investment is high. At a high interest rate, only a few high-payoff investments are profitable, and the demand quantity of investment is low. The intersection of the upward-sloping supply of savings with the downward-sloping demand for investment in figure 4.2 is at an equilibrium interest rate "price." That interest rate or rate of return clears the market and optimally allocates resources and products over time. The market interest rate also is influenced by money supply, inflation, and risk—topics not treated herein.

---

19 The concept of comparative advantage can be illustrated by how it works. Consider the commodities that a country can produce at international prices arrayed from highest to least rate of return to nontraded resources such as land and buildings. Highest return commodities will be exported. Exchange rates will adjust to change prices and make commodities internationally competitive until the supply of foreign exchange earned by exports just equals the demand for foreign exchange to purchase imports. Thus exchange rates translate absolute advantage into comparative advantage.

Concluding Comments

The conceptual framework outlined above shows that markets work to increase the well-being of people. The chapter makes a case for utilizing the efficiency of markets to promote economic progress. Issues of economic equity are treated in the next chapter.

The framework rests on assumptions that need to be challenged. One of the assumptions is that firms seek profit and individuals pursue their self-interests, preferring more to less. A rich body of economic literature has emerged in recent years, presumably discrediting neoclassical economic presumptions. In particular, some people say they do not prefer more to less. In classroom experiments, for example, many students state that they will accept a lesser economic reward if their competitors simultaneously receive even larger cuts in rewards. Such findings suggest that sometimes *relative* as opposed to *absolute* rewards matter, but they do not invalidate the principle that people predominately make decisions and choose behavior that they perceive will provide benefits in excess of costs.

Historically, much intellectual effort also has gone into the case for the public sector to be the engine of economic progress. The notion that an elite governing body can make the decisions for an economic utopia goes at least back to Plato's *Republic* and continued with Marxism. Modern information and management technologies make that vision even more appealing.

Whether to rely on markets or the public sector as the engine of socioeconomic growth seems to resolve primarily based on the nature of people. Secular humanists have contended that people are basically good and can be depended on to make decisions that improve the lot of society. A contrary view, as asserted by St. Augustine, is that people basically are self-serving. It seems obvious to even unsophisticated observers of human behavior that people are complex, sometimes acting altruistically and at other times selfishly. That conclusion calls for an economic system that is robust, delivering favorable performance whatever the motivation of people. The ability of the market to turn private greed into public good needs to be harnessed. It is also critical to harness the capability for markets to make both buyer and seller better off in a transaction.

No such invisible hand guides government. It can be shown that a "first past the post" (winner take all) political system, as used in the United States, gives rise to a two-party system of government with both parties very close together in the political center (Tweeten, 1979, pp. 545–7). While such an outcome may be reassuring, it does not mean that government will make day-to-day decisions to improve society at the firm and individual level. The tendency among all governments is for rules, regulations, and favored special interests to proliferate over time, creating opportunities for mismanagement and for economic rents, the latter fueling corruption in government.

Governments have the critical role of providing a favorable environment for markets to work. They do the best job of that when checks and balances are built into the public decision-making process. A division of powers among branches of government is but one of several means to improve governance.

Another assumption of figure 4.2 is that the market signals facing market participants also reflect actual costs and benefits to society. Externalities are divergences between private and social costs (or benefits) that if left uncorrected, shrink the real economic surplus. Ways to deal with externalities that distort markets and reduce income are addressed in chapter 6.

References

Barr, Abigail. "Sharing Behavior in Cross Cultural Perspective." *Research Summary 2004*. Oxford, UK: Global Poverty Research Group, 2004.

Blue, E. Neal and Luther Tweeten. "The Estimation of Marginal Utility of Income for Application to Agricultural Policy Analysis." *Agricultural Economics* 16: 155–69, 1997.

Collier, Paul and Anke Hoeffler. "Reducing the Global Incidence of Civil War." Pp. 43–6 in *Research Summary 2004/05*. Oxford, UK: Center for the Study of African Economies, Oxford University, 2005.

Coyle, Diane. *Paradoxes of Prosperity: Why the New Capitalism Benefits All*. New York: Texere, 2001.

Dixon, John and Kirk Hamilton. "Expanding the Measure of Wealth." Pp. 15–17 in *Finance and Development*. Washington DC: IMF and World Bank, December 1996.

Daly, Herman. *Beyond Growth*. Boston: Beacon Press, 1996.

Johnston, Bruce F. "Agriculture and Economic Development." *Food Research Institute Studies* 6: 251–312, 1966.

Krugman, Paul. "Dutch Tulips and Emerging Markets." *Foreign Affairs*, July/August 1995.

Kuran, Timur. "Cultural Obstacles to Economic Development: Often Overstated, Usually Transitory." Chapter 6 in Vijayendra Rao and Michael Walton, eds., *Culture and Public Action*. Stanford, California: Stanford University Press, 2004.

McClelland, David C. *The Achieving Society*. Princeton, New Jersey: Van Norstrand, 1961.

Pritchett, Lant. "The Quest Continues." *Finance and Development*. March 2006, pp. 18-22.

Sachs, Jeffrey. *The End of Poverty*. New York: Penguin Press, 2005.

Sowell, Thomas. *Conquests and Cultures*. New York: Basic Books, 1998.

Tawney, R. H. "Religion and the Rise of Capitalism." In Stanley Coben and Forest Hill, eds., *American Economic History*. New York: Lippincott (reprinted 1966), 1926, pp. 6–17.

Tweeten, Luther. *Foundations of Farm Policy*. Lincoln: University of Nebraska Press, Second edition, 1979.

Tweeten, Luther. "Food Security." Chapter 9 in Luther Tweeten and Donald G. McClelland, eds., *Promoting Third World Development and Food Security*. Westport, Connecticut: Praeger, 1997.

Tweeten, Luther. *Terrorism, Radicalism, and Populism in Agriculture*. Ames: Iowa State Press, 2003.

Tweeten, Luther and Donald G. McClelland, eds. *Promoting Third World Development and Food Security*. Westport, Connecticut: Praeger, 1997.

Weber, Max. *The Protestant Ethic*. London: Allen and Unwin, 1930.

5

Providing Equity

The previous two chapters made a compelling conceptual and empirical case that standard-model policies serve people by providing the means to address hunger, disease, poverty, and environmental degradation. Critics have called attention to problems from reliance on the market component of the standard model: socioeconomic inequality, inadequate provision of public goods, and instability apparent in commodity and business cycles. Critics of the standard model also have noted hardships of economic Darwinism apparent in business failures, unemployment, and the pain of structural adjustments. Some even question the validity of the basic rationality assumption of the standard model—that people prefer more to less, as apparent in firms maximizing profits and consumers maximizing utility.

This chapter addresses the issue of economic equity, and chapter 6 addresses other issues, especially public goods. The chapters propose ways to minimize potential shortcomings of the standard model. The conclusion is that the prescription for economic progress offered by the standard model, however flawed, is far superior to its rivals.

Equity

Much was said about market equilibrium in the previous two chapters. The appealing conceptual conclusion is that market supply and demand interact to determine a price that clears the market and maximizes net economic surplus.[20] In reality, market equilibrium efficiency is only what economists call a *Pareto optimum*, defined as an allocation from which it is not possible to improve the position of one market participant without making someone else worse off. Another way of saying this is that the market equilibrium outcome depends on the initial distribution of assets. Where one ends up depends on where one starts. A market participant who brings nothing to the market brings

---

20 Some critics even reject the concept of "equilibrium," observing that in the ever-changing economic environment, markets never quite catch up. In reality, markets are always in very short-run equilibrium, but never achieve long-run equilibrium.

nothing home. One person may starve while another dies from morbid obesity in Pareto optimum market efficiency. The equity issue must be confronted in applying the standard model.

Economists tend to shy away from questions of economic equity, because the concept is subjective and not amenable to "objective" scientific analysis. Students of economics are told by their professors to avoid value judgments such as whether receiving one hundred dollars adds more to the well-being of a poor person or a rich person.

On the other hand, some forward-looking economists commend efforts to incorporate equity into economic benefit-cost analysis. The 2005 president of the American Agricultural Economics Association, Per Pinstrup-Andersen (p. 1,110), states:

> We should go beyond the new welfare economics [that ignores equity] and take differential marginal utility of income-related weights into account in estimates of the distribution of gains and losses and identify options for how losers should be compensated.

One reason to account for the distribution of income is because judgments about the marginal utility of income can now rest on somewhat more objective grounds. Psychologists and sociologists have devised and validated psycho-sociological scales to measure happiness, trust, anomie, and other dimensions of well-being. Blue and I utilized multivariate statistical procedures to combine these scales into a single scale measuring quality of life, or well-being, We found that well-being in the United States was significantly related to income, age, years of schooling, marriage, gender, region of residence, and selected other variables. The most notable finding for this section on economic equity is that each additional dollar of income adds a great deal to the well-being of a poor person, but successive additions to income give less and less satisfaction to the recipient. Blue and I (p. 167) found that an additional dollar of income on average provides at least fifty percent more satisfaction if received by a poor person than if received by someone with medium income. Someone with four times medium income receives about one-fourth as much satisfaction from another dollar of income as does someone with medium income. Economists call this pattern "diminishing marginal utility of income." If enhancing the well-being of people is the economic objective, then weighting benefits and costs by their respective marginal utilities among income classes can materially change benefit-cost ratios and thus public investment project priorities.

Social scientists give varied reasons—other than being sated with goods—why more income does not add much to the satisfaction of the affluent.

According to Gregg Easterbrook (p. 173), "Sociologists have long assumed that rising income does not necessarily confer rising happiness owing to 'reference anxiety,' a fancy term for keeping up with the Joneses." Affluent people with sumptuous homes can be unhappy because their neighbors are believed to have even finer dwellings. Expectations are critical. A person with low income but expectations of rising income may be happier than a person with a higher income but no perceived opportunity for advancement (Easterbrook, p. 173).

The obvious though incorrect conclusion, given the finding of diminishing marginal utility of income, is that the well-being of a nation is maximized with income equality. There are good reasons why income in a "just" society would be unequal and why the results from the study by Blue and me must be heavily qualified. First, the statistically significant results predict pretty well for groups (where individual variation averages out), but not for any specific individual. That is not a big drawback for application of the standard model, however, because it is about policy for groups—we recognize that the impact of additional income varies even among individuals of equal wealth. Utility is culture-specific. Functions for the United States do not apply to other cultures, but diminishing marginal utility of goods and income seems to be universal.

A second reason to reject equality is to preserve economic incentives. Philosopher John Rawls is famous for a thought experiment regarding inequality. He posed the question of what rules for society one would want if one's position of entry into society were a lottery, with an equal chance of being born into any of the some six billion available slots—the world's population. Most people probably would not favor taking their chances in a world of the current high inequality, nor would they most prefer to land in a world of equality. A happy world does not let dullards pilot airliners, engineer computer hardware or software, perform surgery for appendicitis, research a cure for cancer, or host the *Tonight Show*. Getting the best people into responsible, demanding positions essential for a functioning society requires differential rewards. People favor *equality of opportunity* for education and other means to success (distributive justice) over the unworkable *equality of outcomes*.

Third, unintended consequences argue against full equality. The rule of law essential for a functioning society requires the protection of property. Confiscation and redistribution of property violates the rule of law, reduces incentives, creates poverty, induces violence, and infringes on the concept of *commutative justice*. The latter holds that people are entitled to rewards commensurate with their contribution to society. Flagrant violation of strongly held values can lead to social unrest, which in turn can make everyone worse off. Investors don't build or maintain capital if they arbitrarily stand to lose it.

Blue and I found that income accounts for only a small portion of the variation in quality of life among persons—even after accounting for the indirect impact of income on quality of life through financing health care, education, and other contributors to satisfactions. A person's happiness is determined mainly by his or her temperament or disposition, which to no small degree is a matter of genes inherited from parents (Eveld, p. E3). People tend to return to their predisposed levels of happiness, with a lag of a few months at most, after being subjected to shocks in their lives. It is more important, however, for public policy to attend to income, which can be changed, rather than genes, which can't be changed.

The conclusion remains that the largest and most lasting gains in well-being are possible by improving the incomes of poor people; most of these people reside in developing countries, accounting for eighty-five percent of the global population. Another conclusion is that if the objective is to improve quality of life, then it is unwise for a government to transfer income from poor to rich people. The standard model is for rich or poor countries alike, but this volume emphasizes how standard-model policies can alleviate hunger, poverty, and environmental degradation in poor countries. Rich countries need less attention, because the process of economic development changes attitudes. Among many benefits, the economic education made possible by wealth teaches citizens the advantages of following standard-model policies.

That said, we come back to the proposition from Blue and me that a more equal distribution of income is preferred over a more unequal distribution, *other things being equal.* At issue is whether standard-model policies (as approximated imperfectly by the Economic Freedom Index, or EFI) widen or narrow the distribution of income. A simple static, two-way comparison shows no consistent relationship between the share of income going to the poorest ten percent of population and EFI (Berggren, p. 203). In addition, Berggren (p. 201) reviewed three more sophisticated analyses showing statistically that higher EFIs were associated with greater economic equality. Several other studies reviewed by Berggren that did not include EFI found that the poor benefit from economic growth.

Using a global sample of countries, Gini coefficients (0 = perfect equality of income to 100 for complete inequality) reported by the World Bank (pp. 196–7) range from an average of 40.9 for twenty-seven low-income economies and 39.2 for thirty middle-income countries to 44.9 for eight upper-middle-income countries. (Gini coefficients were not shown for high-income countries.) The proportion of income held by the poorest twenty percent of the population ranged from 6.2 percent for low-income countries and 6.5 percent for middle-income countries to 5.9 percent for upper-middle-income countries. The similarity in distribution coefficients among countries ranked by income is striking.

With countries as the unit of observation, rich countries grew slightly faster on average than did poor countries from 1980 to 2000, so more income seemed to be concentrating in rich countries (Fischer). However, when observations of income per capita by country are weighted by population, the opposite conclusion emerges: income grew faster on average in poor than in rich countries. This latter important conclusion arises mainly because of the rapid growth of China and India. As measured by the Gini coefficient calculated for individuals, the distribution of global income is not becoming more unequal. Slow growth among poor countries is largely because of the dismal economic performance of the many but mostly small nations of Africa. This is another reason why chapter 7 of this volume is devoted to the causes and cures for the poor economic performance of sub-Saharan Africa.

Berry observed that liberalization of Latin American economies widened income distribution in most instances. The widening distribution of income under structural adjustment may be a manifestation of Kuznet's famous hypothesis that economic growth in early stages widens (makes more unequal) and in later stages narrows the distribution of income. Liberalization may initially depress consumer spending, because aggregate demand initially falls when a nation stops living beyond its means under structural adjustment. Also, more open trade often displaces low-wage workers from factory jobs. However, one country, Costa Rica, did not conform to the pattern of widening distribution of income with liberalization, perhaps because of its more equal initial distribution of human capital in the form of education. Other countries investing broadly in human capital eventually are likely to narrow their income distribution, as growth progresses.

Unequal initial distribution of assets, more than unequal income, slows economic growth, according to an analysis by Deininger and Squire (p. 40). They found almost no association between income inequality and growth, but they noted, "Even when inequality has worsened, its negative effect on the poor has been more than outweighed by the positive effect of growth." The prospect of narrowing income distribution with growth in the long term is one reason why Berry (p. 239) concluded that "the best policy to reduce poverty in economies mired in stagnation and underutilization of capacity is to get the economy moving."

The foregoing paragraphs suggest that the tide of economic progress tends to lift most (though not all) boats and that the fruits of economic progress do indeed reach lower-income people, either directly as earnings, or indirectly as transfers from those who earn more. Economic growth tends to widen the *absolute* income gap between rich and poor. Nonetheless, in percentage terms, incomes of the poor increase at about the same rate as incomes of the rich.

In short, empirical evidence supports the concept of *trickle down*, long a contentious issue among social scientists, positing that rising income proportionately lifts all boats. The standard model, with its emphasis on human capital and other investments serving both economic equity and efficiency, can be expected to raise the incomes of poor people and nations proportionately as much or more than the incomes of the wealthy. Even if standard-model policies do not directly shift income shares, those SM policies make redistribution policies feasible, by creating income to redistribute.

Income and Wealth Redistribution Policies

Economic outcomes will be more egalitarian and food security greater if the standard model is applied to countries with more equal initial distributions of asset ownership. Barraclough (p. 130), after reviewing substantial land-reform literature, notes that in countries where rural poverty is widespread and closely associated with power of the landowning class, "land reform becomes the only option for improving rural livelihoods rapidly and substantially." Yet he cautions that land reform "cannot normally be a policy option for governments."

Other redistribution options offer far greater promise.[21] With economic growth, opportunities for redistribution through human resource investments dwarf those from land redistribution. Redistribution through human capital investments also induces less violence.

Table 4.1, depicting wealth levels and forms in an earlier chapter, provided critical insight into the potential for wealth redistribution. One observation is that, compared to rich countries, relatively little wealth is available to redistribute in poor countries. Most notable, however, is that of the less than $30,000 of wealth per capita in sub-Saharan Africa and South Asia, nearly two-thirds is human capital and only one-sixth or less is agricultural land! The potential for wealth distribution through investment in human capital dwarfs that of land reform. Land redistribution also is inefficient; it can cripple an economy when political opportunists replace efficient farmers, as illustrated by "land reform" under President Robert Mugabe in Zimbabwe in the early 2000s.

21 Some (Barraclough) advocate organizing the poor and food-insecure to provide a political bargaining advantage for obtaining more of the public "pie." The problem with this approach is that poor people are notoriously difficult to organize. In the process, the near-poor or wealthy are likely to feel threatened and to organize more effectively, leaving disadvantaged people even more disadvantaged.

Redistribution through human capital investment requires a society open to opportunities for schooling. Some African countries get it wrong. For example, Uganda, prior to the 1990s, charged tuition for attending elementary school while providing tuition-free higher education for students who could qualify. Shifting public funds from the support of higher education to elementary schools increased enrollment in both systems, thereby fostering both equity and efficiency, because rates of return on schooling are high. Enrollment mushroomed in higher education because enrollment was no longer constrained by limited funds from government. Plenty of qualified students were able to pay tuition for college. Tuition allowed the head of my department to get a pay raise above the fourteen dollars per month he had been receiving. Tuition freed up some public scholarships for gifted but poor students who cannot pay. The overall income transfer was progressive, from wealthier college students to poorer elementary students.

Some countries are innovative in capturing the capacity of human resource development programs to serve equity and efficiency. Welfare payments and high dropout rates from schools are facts of life in Mexico and Brazil. Instead of a welfare handout, the countries are making welfare payments to parents contingent on their children staying in school. Other countries use free lunches as inducements for the poor to attend school.

Financing education is a challenge, even in developed countries. The United States has a long tradition of local financing from property taxes. I attended a one-room country school financed by the tax on farmland. An abundant resource, land, was used to finance a high-payoff, scarce resource, education. In the United States today, on average, approximately half of common public-school finance is from local sources, forty percent from state sources, and ten percent from federal sources. Such proportions are inequitable, because many poor school districts see their graduates move to richer places to live, work, and pay taxes. The result is that poor communities transfer capital to rich communities. A related problem is that poor communities lack the economic base or incentives to invest properly in education. As a consequence, inadequately educated migrants from poor communities become social problems plaguing rich communities. More reliance on state and federal funding of schools could alleviate the inequity. Of course, mere money does not necessarily translate into student achievement, but that is a topic for another book.

Property taxes have been used for a century or more in developed countries—for example, Japan initiated a three-percent tax on farm property in 1873. Even today, property taxes are little used in developing countries. If rates are graduated, such taxes could be a more effective and nonthreatening tool than land reform for equity in countries committed to asset redistribution;

however, a sense of trust and public administrative capability are required for such asset redistribution. As such, devolution of government to local communities is long overdue in many countries. Smaller political-administrative entities have propinquity, affording a sense of community and obvious connection between taxes and services; hence, they have a greater capacity than central governments to tax property to fund local schools and roads.

Land reform does more than affront the rule of law and respect for property. Reformers rarely get farm structure right. In East Asia, land reform in the late 1940s and 1950s gets credit for diminishing social grievances fueling Marxism, but it left countries with farms much too small to compete in the international marketplace or to provide a decent living standard without large subsidies from government or consumers. At the other extreme, central planners in the former Soviet Union created farms too large and too poorly managed to produce food efficiently.

Other than following sound macroeconomic, infrastructure, and human resource development policies of the standard model outlined in chapter 2, what is a country to do to address income inequality? Because the issue is so laden with value judgments, not much can be said with certainty; however, I offer some suggestions. One is to utilize a tax structure that at least does not favor the rich. A proportional tax system allows taxation at the source, rather than taxation tailored to each individual or family, so it diminishes tax avoidance. With modern computer software readily available in developed countries, asset values can be deflated for inflation. Then, unlike current procedures, taxes can be imposed only on real capital gains as ordinary income, and not also on nominal capital gains that represent no increase in buying power.

In addition, much can be said for a tax system that taxes corporate earnings only once, in contrast to the U.S. system, which taxes corporate income once as earnings by the corporation and again as dividends received by individuals. Taxing of equity capital (dividends) but not debt capital (interest) also biases business toward debt financing, raising the risk on equity capital. Higher risk demands higher returns and diminishes the supply of equity capital. Double taxation on dividends is one reason why corporate income taxes sacrifice nearly fifty cents of national income per dollar of tax collected, making it one of the most inefficient taxes devised by man (Ballard et al., p. 13). The problem is compounded because reinvested corporate earnings are the major domestic sources of saving in America—households save little, and the federal government destroys savings through massive budget deficits. In contrast, federal income taxes, on average, cost the nation approximately sixteen dollars of national income for every one hundred dollars collected.

An alternative to immediate taxation to cover public spending is to "spend and borrow," or what some people might label "Reaganomics" or "supply-side economics." The standard-model rule is that government operating account deficits are unjustified in a full-employment economy. Because some of the unemployed take time to find the best job or are otherwise in the normal "pipeline" between jobs, in the United States, noninflationary "full employment" is perhaps on average five-percent unemployment. Economists widely support a Keynesian central government budget deficit stimulus if the economy is at less than full employment. A problem is that political decision makers too often label almost any unemployment rate as less than full employment. Their short tenure in office means they can reap the benefits of deficit spending now and defer the pain of servicing the debt until they have left office.

Furthermore, fiscal irresponsibility is endemic because the U.S. Congress is a *non-encompassing* institution. Thus, a congressperson from an average district in the U.S. House obtaining $1 million in pork barrel for his or her district pays only 1/435 of the cost. With a nominal local benefit-cost ratio of $435, the congressperson has every reason to spend federal money, even on frivolous projects, in the home district. Another way to look at the incentive is to recognize that a "bridge to nowhere" that produces only one dollar of benefit for $435 spent on it will have a local benefit-cost ratio of one dollar if the nation's taxpayers are paying the other $434. Self-serving behavior by each congressperson acting individually sums over the entire Congress to a national fiscal debacle. Government budget deficits accrue perennially, and accumulated debt is not paid off, but must be serviced—inequitably—by future generations, who did not vote for the largess.

Perennial public deficits absorb savings. The government budget deficit spending is not called investment but is called "negative saving," because funds are mostly devoted to consumption rather than to building productive capital. The shorting of savings supply relative to investment demand generates perennial budget deficits, pushing up real interest rates and slowing investment and economic growth.

Borrowing funds for public investments is justified if the return on investment exceeds the cost of capital. The cost may be more than just the interest rate on government bonds. The U.S. Congressional Budget Office calculates that each dollar of federal borrowing reduces investment in the economy by up to thirty-six cents ("The Budget Deficit," p. 23). Few public investments made with borrowed funds yield that high rate of return.

Keeping marginal tax rates low by means such as broadening the tax base enhances economic incentives. A flat tax on consumption, income, or value added may be judged unacceptable, because it taxes poor people at a high rate.

On the other hand, a flat-rate value-added tax (VAT) has high tax efficiency, with approximately ten cents of lost national income or deadweight cost per dollar collected. VAT is like a national sales tax but is collected on value added at each stage of the production process. It tends to self-correct for errors. Underreporting of sales by firms in the lower link raises the observed value added and taxes of firms at the next link in the value chain. The latter have incentives to report errors in the lower link.

In many countries, VAT is the main source of revenue in a broad-based tax system.[22] A VAT can tax consumption while minimally interfering with resource allocation; hence, it is more consistent than are most taxes with economic efficiency. VAT can be made more equitable to consumers by including services while exempting food and medicine, and more acceptable to businesses by exempting exports.

To serve economic equity, increase savings, and tax consumption while minimizing subsidies to the wealthy, mortgage interest could be taxed in the United States, as is currently the practice in many countries. Home ownership is socially commendable, but mortgage interest payments could be made income-tax deductible only up to (say) $10,000 annually—in keeping with the principle of taxing consumption and the wealthy.

Another means to correct for externalities and broaden the tax base is to increase the tax on gasoline and/or carbon. Parry (p. 31) of Resources for the Future, a respected environmental think tank, estimates that externalities such as traffic congestion, air pollution, urban sprawl, and outlays for protection of precarious foreign oil sources warrant doubling or tripling the gasoline tax in the United States. This would still leave the unit tax on gasoline half or less of that charged in the United Kingdom, France, Germany, and Japan. Higher taxes on fuel for trucks could encourage more freight to move on fuel-efficient railroads, thereby reducing pollution, road congestion, and energy consumption. Parry (p. 32) contends that trucks do not pay taxes proportional to the damage done to highways, noting that "road damage increases exponentially with a vehicle's axle weight so that a truck weighing 10 times as much as a car does 1,000 times the damage." In addition, Americans would benefit from ending the indefensible practice of providing billions of dollars of tax breaks to "synfuel-producing" firms that do little more than spray diesel fuel over coal.

Several European countries with approximately half of their economies in the public sector provide some lessons on how to tax and regulate with minimum damage to economic efficiency and living standards. Sweden provides

---

22 Some fiscal conservatives oppose the VAT because it raises so much revenue with so little cost in personal discomfort and lost national income that opponents of big government are lulled into acceptance.

a generous safety net by taxing consumption while encouraging investment with some of the lowest tax rates in the industrial world on corporate earnings. It provides generous unemployment benefits (a disincentive to work), but accompanies payments with strong pressures to obtain job training and employment.

In contrast, France and Germany make it very expensive for firms to dismiss workers. If employers can't afford to release workers, they don't hire. The countries also provide generous payments to the unemployed. The combination of disincentives to hire and generous payments to the unemployed has kept unemployment rates in France and Germany near double-digit levels for years. In France, thousands of Muslim young men (mostly sons of migrants) with inadequate schooling and work experience have been chronically unemployed. Those marginal workers became a major source of civil violence in 2005. The lesson is that policies undertaken to promote equity for blue-collar workers, such as high minimum wages and payroll taxes coupled with penalties for releasing workers, actually leave marginal workers unemployed and disaffected.

Economic growth has not had much global impact on the distribution of income among individuals, but it has affected the United States more than most other industrial countries. In the past quarter-century, the share of the nation's income going to the poorest fifth of the population fell from 5.4 percent to 4.4 percent (Parker, p. 12). Meanwhile, the share going to the richest fifth went from 40.9 percent to 46.5 percent. With VAT, the share going to the wealthy could rise further. Many Americans think the rich are entitled to their success but want each generation to earn its own success. Of concern is the failure of blue-collar incomes to grow since 2000 while the United States has enjoyed one of the fastest rates of economic growth among industrial nations. The benefits of growth are accruing to capital and management, and not to laborers.

Several options are available to narrow the income distribution without retarding economic growth. The slowing of illegal immigration, through stiffer penalties on firms and individuals who hire illegals (enforceable with a reliable bioidentification system), would open jobs to American minority and other blue-collar workers. The standard retort that "illegal workers take only jobs that American workers won't take" needs to be relegated to the pantheon of "big lies"—American workers will take the jobs *if the pay is attractive*. Ending the corporate business practice of allowing CEOs to appoint their own board members, who in turn reward the CEO with outsized pay, perks, and (golden) parachutes, would free some funds to reward blue-collar workers. But investment in human capital is the most effective means to improve the earnings of currently disadvantaged workers in the United States. That means restructuring schools to create incentives for excellence. With public funds provided to students as education vouchers to be used at the school of choice, schools would be required to compete for students to survive. Schools would need to reward teaching and program merit to survive.

Safety Nets

Data from Edward Lazear, chairman of the Council of Economic Advisors, highlight the importance of human resource investments in advanced global economies. In the United States since 1980, real hourly earnings of college-educated workers increased twenty-two percent, while real hourly earnings of high school graduates remained nearly unchanged and earnings of high school dropouts fell three percent (p. 7). Changing technology and demand favored growth in hourly earnings in American industries such as professional and technical services with comparative advantage, while hourly compensation fell in declining occupations such as administrative (*e.g.,* secretarial) support and manufacturing. From 2001 to 2005, hourly earnings in the fast-growing industries averaged $30.14 and in the slow-growing industries averaged $21.24 (Lazear, p. 5). College graduates, prominent in high-income occupations, earn 2.5 times as much as high school dropouts. Unemployment rates average 2.2 percent for college graduates but fully seven percent for high school dropouts. The conclusion is that human resource investments are highly rewarding in advanced global economies.

At issue in such economies is how to raise the earnings of those lacking the will or ability to complete college. It is important to recognize that full implementation (if that were possible) of human resource investments in broad-based development under the market-oriented standard model would leave considerable socioeconomic inequality; that is, achieving meritocracy would leave a bell-shaped income distribution paralleling the bell-shaped distribution of ability and ambition in the population. The "deserving poor," who are severely handicapped and hence cannot earn their own way, likely would receive transfers from government. More troublesome is how to provide equity to able-bodied adults who have low earnings even after being given opportunities to raise their competence. The challenge is to raise their incomes without reducing real national income and distorting incentives to work.

Beyond schooling and health services serving equity and efficiency, what safety net programs are appropriate? Much depends on the stage of development. A poor country can afford little beyond programs of food distribution carried out in conjunction with charitable organizations, such as churches. As a nation grows in wealth and administrative skills, it may be able to fund a food stamp program accessible to anyone with low income. A family may be required to pay (say) thirty percent of its income for food stamps whose monetary value can be applied to food-only purchases deemed adequate for a minimal nutritious diet. Such a program is self-targeting, because it is irrational for richer families that spend less than thirty percent of their income for food to purchase stamps.

As countries become more developed, safety nets in the form of a demogrant, a negative income tax, or a wage supplement become feasible. The demogrant proposed by James Tobin features an annual cash grant for every individual. The demogrant remains unchanged whether an individual is rich or poor, employed or unemployed, so it is presumed to minimally influence employment and real national income while guaranteeing at least a minimal level of living. Earning another dollar does not reduce the payment to the individual, so the incentive to earn is retained. The demogrant has minimal stigma, because everyone receives payments, but it is expensive to taxpayers. National income is lost, because taxes to finance the demogrant diminish national income.

Nobel laureate Milton Friedman proposed the negative income tax (NIT) to replace all other welfare programs. He reasoned that if a positive income tax was appropriate for persons with high incomes, then a negative tax (payment to the "taxpayer") was appropriate for persons with low or no incomes. The proposed plan had two key parameters: the guaranteed payment to a person or family with no earnings, and a negative tax rate applied to additional earnings until the guarantee is exhausted. If the guarantee is (say) $20,000 for a family of four, then such a family with no earnings would receive a payment of $20,000 spread over a year. If the negative tax rate is fifty percent, then each dollar earned subtracts fifty cents from the guarantee until the guarantee is exhausted. A family of four earning $10,000 annually would receive $15,000 ($20,000-[0.5 x $10,000]) annually from the government, for a total income of $25,000. The break-even level is $40,000 of income, at which the tax of $20,000 ($40,000 x 0.5) is equal to the guarantee. In contrast to some welfare programs that reduce payments by one dollar for each dollar earned, this program would only tax fifty cents, so work incentives would remain. Still, controlled experiments in the 1970s found sizable lost national income from disincentives in the negative income tax (see Tweeten and Brinkman, chapter 6). The NIT was never adopted on a national scale. However, the NIT-like Earned Income Tax Credit currently available under the U.S. income tax law provides a modest cash income supplement to those with low income.

Omission of raw labor from figure 4.1 does not absolve the resource from standard-model reforms. Numerous countries pursue policies discriminating against labor, particularly against less-skilled and young workers. Examples include high minimum wages, high payroll taxes, and high severance allowances that firms must pay their discharged workers. Combined with generous unemployment insurance, such policies leave marginal workers unemployed, because it doesn't pay firms to hire them. The wage supplement can promote equity by encouraging rather than discouraging employment of marginal workers.

The wage supplement would especially target the working poor, while encouraging employment and competitiveness in industries hard hit by competition from low-wage countries. Under the wage supplement, the government would establish a target wage of (say) twelve dollars per hour and pay a wage supplement of (say) sixty percent of the shortfall of the actual wage below the target wage. The worker would negotiate for the highest wage attainable from an employer. An unskilled worker worth only two dollars per hour to the employer would receive a supplement of 0.6 x ($12-$2), or six dollars per hour. For a forty-hour week, the worker would receive eighty from the employer and $240 from the government, for a total of $320. Workers would seek the highest possible wages from employers, because sacrificing wages to obtain a higher supplement would reduce their total hourly earnings. In other words, the supplement would not fully replace fewer dollars received from the employer. To hire, firms would have to compete among themselves with higher wages for employees, hence raising wages and restraining the size of the supplement. Employment would increase (if the tax to pay the supplement did not come at a high cost in lost jobs), workers would receive a living wage, and workers and firms would be competitive in markets. Because the wage supplement would offset or replace some current market distortions such as the minimum wage, real national income could increase, making the program both equitable and efficient. Poor countries possess neither the administrative expertise nor the public budget to provide a wage supplement, but they can build that capability over time by following standard-model policies.

The wage supplement is proportional to hours worked, so it does more to encourage employment than does the Earned Income Tax Credit that supplements low incomes under the U.S. income tax code. Unlike the wage supplement, the credit does not require wage employment.

Employers do not hire disadvantaged, entry-level, or low-skilled workers if they contribute less to their employer's earnings than the minimum wage. An alternative to a high minimum wage, for governments that can afford it, is instituting programs of job training, search information, and relocation assistance to workers who have low skills or have been displaced by imports or technological change.

A Tax Reform Proposal to Serve Equity

How would the nation pay for school vouchers and safety net programs such as a wage supplement? America's standard-model score is quite high; however, several options are available to finance equitable and efficient reforms of policies. Terminating farm price and income support programs that serve special interests but no public purpose could save some $20 billion annually. A limit on mortgage interest payment write-off from taxes, coupled with a tax on petroleum and an end to the ethanol subsidy, could raise billions to pay for health care, school vouchers, and a wage supplement. An end to pork barrel spending by Congress would free additional billions of dollars.

One means to promote equity and avoid creating a hereditary aristocracy is to accompany the VAT with a progressive tax on unearned income. The United States currently taxes earned income more heavily than unearned income. It seems patently unfair that one who exerts much physical and mental labor to earn money is taxed, while one receiving income as a gift need not pay taxes. The proposal is not to tax estates (that could be labeled a "death tax"), but to tax inheritance as ordinary income to the recipient. With a progressive income tax, a poor recipient in a low tax bracket would pay no tax, and a rich recipient in a high tax bracket would pay considerable tax. Income would not be taxed twice to the recipient—a criticism of the current estate tax—but would be taxed only once, just as earned income is taxed only once to the recipient. Inheritance might be taxed as part of an overall tax on the sum of all gifts received by persons. Gifts made directly to charitable or other organizations might be taxed at a flat rate of (say) twenty-five percent. Exemptions might be provided to minors and on gifts totaling less than (say) $15,000 annually per person.

Conclusions

Achieving economic efficiency and equity are thought to be desirable although competitive goals in a market economy. The system, it is argued, rewards those who bring the most resources to the market; hence, markets are not equitable. However, data indicate that benefits of markets indeed "trickle down"—economic growth tends to "lift all boats," but it does not much change the shares of income going to the rich and the poor.

Analysis cited in this chapter indicates that the rate of return (measured by utility gain) on redistribution of income can be sizable, rivaling the rate of return on conventional investments; however, government interventions to level income have a mixed record of success. Persons possessing human and material wealth tend to be as successful at accruing largess from government as from the market. Funds, regulations, and agencies intended to help the poor have an all too common pattern of being hijacked to serve higher-income people. Farm commodity programs in the United States and the European Community are "Exhibit A" of this pattern.

It has long been as fashionable as it is erroneous to argue that the poor are poor because the rich are rich. Paul Farmer is an eloquent proponent today of the view that poverty and the hunger, disease, and misery attending it can best be addressed by redistribution of the world's resources from the rich to the poor. Farmer (pp. 243, 244) and those he cites with approval condemn "neoliberal policies" of globalization, the North American Free Trade Agreement and other free trade efforts, privatization, deregulation, expanded entrepreneurship, and structural adjustment programs. The hitch is that those who reject such standard-model policies in favor of wealth redistribution are making a false choice: they will achieve neither economic efficiency nor equity. That sharp left turn leads down a dead end. Even as we rightly applaud the generosity of rich persons and nations, we must recognize that even major wealth transfers by the relatively few people and nations in the rich world will be woefully inadequate to perennially provide a decent living for the world's poor. It is said that a nation can't change what it doesn't acknowledge. Poor countries must recognize what is wrong with their policies and institutions and be eager participants in pursuing standard-model policies essential to long-term success.

Sad to say, the economic development policies advocated by antiglobalists, Luddites, liberation theologians, dependency theorists, and postmodernists would only make the "patient" worse. Unlike lawyers who get upset by laypersons who "practice law without a license," I am flattered that non-economists such as Paul Farmer are so eager to practice economic policy. But such "intellectuals" implicitly make a compelling case that economics should not be practiced "without a license."

My good and wise friend, Professor Peter Dorner, then (1981) director of the Land Tenure Center at the University of Wisconsin with extensive experience in land reform, said in a candid moment over a beer in Mexico City, "The problem with land reform is that it takes too many AK-47s." Violent revolution brings a perverse equality, not by redistribution that lifts the income of the poor, but by making most everyone in the nation poor.

It follows that pro-poor policies need to be pursued with care. A good place to begin is with human resource and infrastructure investments serving both equity and efficiency. Beyond that, it makes sense to transfer income to the poor in a manner minimizing economic distortions. This chapter laid out several options for collecting taxes and transferring income in ways that serve equity without retarding real national income. Many of the proposals are not now politically expedient or affordable, but they can be in the future as nations strive for economic growth with equity under standard-model policies.

References

Ballard, C. L., J. B. Shoven, and J. Whalley. "General Equilibrium and Computations of the Marginal Welfare Costs of Taxes in the United States." *American Economic Review*. 75:128–38, 1985.

Barraclough, Solon. *An End to Hunger*. London: Zed Books, 1991.

Berggren, Niclas. "The Benefits of Economic Freedom." *The Independent Review*. 8(2): 193–211, Fall 2003.

Berry, Albert. "The Social Challenge of the New Economic Era in Latin America." Pp. 199–264 in Constanza Valdes and Terry Roe, eds., *Economic Integration of the Western Hemisphere*. St. Paul, Minnesota: Department of Applied Economics, International Agricultural Trade Consortium, University of Minnesota, 1997.

Blue, E. Neal and Luther Tweeten. "The Estimation of Marginal Utility of Income for Application to Agricultural Policy Analysis." *Agricultural Economics* 16: 155–169, 1997.

"The Budget Deficit." *The Economist*. August 20, 2005, pp. 22, 23.

Deininger, Klaus and Lyn Squire. "Income Growth and Income Inequality." Pp. 38–41 in *Finance and Development*. Washington DC: IMF and the World Bank, March 1997.

Easterbrook, Gregg. *The Progress Paradox*. New York: Random House, 2003.

Eveld, Edward M. "You Can't Buy Happiness." *Orlando Sentinel*. February 12, 2005, pp. E1, E3.

Farmer, Paul. *Pathologies of Power.* Los Angeles: University of California Press, 2005.

Fischer, Stanley. "Economic Focus." *The Economist.* August 23, 2003, p. 62.

Lazear, Edward. "The State of the U.S. Economy and Labor Market." (Paper presented at Hudson Institute, May 2, 2006) Washington DC: Council of Economic Advisors, http://www.hudson.org/index.cfm?fuseaction=publication_details&id=3997&pubType=HI_Speeches, 2006.

Parker, John. "Degrees of Separation." *The Economist.* July 16, 2005, pp. 3–20.

Parry, Ian. "Is Gasoline Undertaxed in the United States?" *Resources.* Washington DC: Resources for the Future. 148: 28–33, Summer 2002.

Pinstrup-Andersen, Per. "Ethics and Economic Policy for the Food System." *American Journal of Agricultural Economics.* 87: 1097–1112, December 2005.

Rawls, John. *A Theory of Justice.* Cambridge, Massachusetts: The Belknap Press of Harvard University Press, 1971.

Tobin, James. "Raising the Incomes of the Poor." In *Agenda for the Nation.* Washington DC: Brookings Institution, 1968, pp. 77–116.

Tweeten, Luther and George Brinkman. *Micropolitan Development.* Ames: Iowa State University Press, 1976.

World Bank. *From Plan to Market: World Development Report 1996.* New York: Oxford University Press, 1996.

6

Providing Public Goods

Standard-model policies are designed to increase real income from resources. Ideally, the term "real income" refers to nominal income corrected for inflation, instability, externalities, and utility of income. The market-centered standard model is especially subject to criticism for inadequately accounting for two issues: economic equity and externalities. The previous chapter addressed equity. This chapter treats externalities and the related issue of public goods and services.

Public Goods

In chapter 4, we learned that the standard model maximizes net economic benefits only under specific conditions. A central proposition of neoclassical economic theory is the normative concept that if the goal of any socioeconomic system is to improve the well-being of people, then society needs to pursue policies and activities that provide *social* benefits in excess of *social* costs.

This proposition raises a host of questions, including how to measure social costs and benefits, where "social" refers to society as a whole. Firms and consumers ordinarily respond only to private costs and benefits: those accruing only to their own financial accounts. In the case of a concentrated animal factory farm emitting odors, flies, and wastes and polluting downstream or downwind neighbors, the social cost to society as a whole is greater than the private costs reflected in the financial account of the polluting firm.

Economists call the difference between social and private cost (or benefit), the part that a firm passes to others, an *externality*. Firms base decisions on private costs (benefits), so if S and D in figure 4.2 include only private costs (benefits) that differ from social costs (benefits), the market equilibrium will not be efficient for society. The profit-maximizing firm will produce at a socially optimal output level (where incremental social costs equal incremental social benefits) if the cost of emissions (the externality) is added to the private cost to the firm. This can be accomplished by public policies such as taxes on emissions, limits on inputs or outputs, or subsidies to environmentally friendly technologies. The same concept applies to consumers. The dissatisfactions imposed by second-hand smoke from cigarettes are called negative externalities. Various forms of public policy can internalize externalities, but they are not equally effective.

The value of goods and services foregone by economic distortions causing output to deviate from the competitive market equilibrium (six units in figures 4.2 and 6.1) with supply curve S and demand curve D is called the *deadweight cost*. Because national income is the sum of all economic surpluses, deadweight cost is loss of national income from market distortions. The deadweight cost A from producing three rather than the equilibrium of six units in figure 6.1 is the triangle bounded by S and D from three units to six units. The deadweight cost B of producing and consuming in excess of equilibrium is the triangle bounded by S and D from six units to nine units. Deadweight cost is sometimes called the *Harberger triangle*. Figure 6.1 indicates that producing three rather than six units of q or nine rather than six units of q would lose eighteen dollars. The reader can verify that the deadweight cost grows exponentially larger as actual output diverges ever farther from equilibrium.

Figure 6.1. Demand **D** and Supply **S** for Quantity **q** (price of **q** in dollars) with Deviation of Social Supply **S** from Private Supply **S_1** and **S_2**

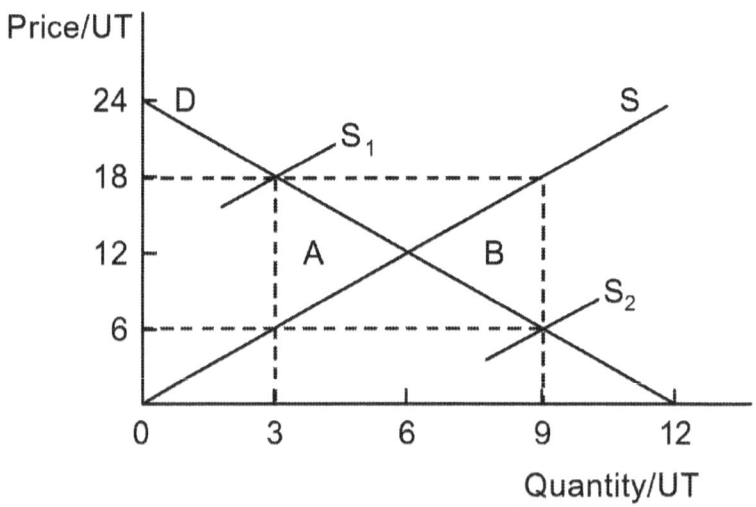

Deadweight costs stem from numerous sources, but one of the most common is when private cost and hence supply (such as at S_1 or S_2) differs from the social cost to society represented by the supply curve S. Before observing how market distortions sacrifice economic surplus or national income, definitions of several terms are reviewed below:

- *Private costs (benefits)* accrue to the private accounts of firms and individuals who produce and consume a good q. Firms are assumed to be rational and supply additional output if their incremental cost is covered, so the marginal cost curve is also the supply curve.
- *Social costs (benefits)* accrue to society and hence to those involved and not involved in market decisions regarding the allocation of q. The social cost includes public and private costs.
- An *externality* is the difference between the private cost (benefit) and the social cost (benefit). Externalities may be positive or negative, as noted below. Whatever the source, they cause market distortions in the form of output deviating from the efficient market outcome q=6 units in figure 6.1. In other words, externalities cause deadweight costs.

Two important principles must be kept in mind in the following analysis of externalities, their cost, and appropriate policies to achieve efficient markets:

- Market participants establish market price and quantity by equating *private* marginal cost or supply with *private* marginal benefit or demand.
- Economic surplus is measured by the difference between *social* marginal cost or supply S and *social* marginal benefit or demand D.

The possibility for either negative or positive externalities associated with demand or supply make for four possible cases in figure 6.1:

1. *Positive supply externality.* Positive supply externalities are illustrated by the private supply curve S_1, above and to the left of the social supply curve S in figure 6.1. At any price, private firms supply less than would a well-functioning market. Assuming no externalities in demand, so that D is the social and private demand curve, with the private cost S_1 in figure 6.1, the uncorrected market equilibrium price at eighteen dollars is above the efficient market price of twelve dollars, the quantity produced and consumed is three, and the deadweight cost is A= $18. A public subsidy of S_1-S per unit of q can lower the private supply

curve to the social supply curve to raise the quantity from $q=3$ before the subsidy to $q=6$ after the subsidy. This subsidy eliminates the dead-weight cost A.

An example is the holding of food buffer stocks. The risk is large for private stockholders (speculators) because of unpredictable weather, pests, government action, and other factors. Stockholding takes lots of financial capital, and due to default risk, creditors will extend credit to stockholders only at high interest rates. The interest rate may be less for a public lender because of scale, which allows risks to average out and because the public has access to many sources of funds. The private supply curve lies above and to the left of the social supply curve, so the private firm will supply less than the socially optimal level of buffer stock q in figure 6.1.

A related example is music. Once it is written and recorded, distribution is virtually costless with today's technology. The marginal cost is zero and lies along the horizontal axis in figure 6.1. The competitive market price is zero. That "optimal" price for society of zero would appeal to music lovers, but it would decimate the music industry, to the detriment of society. One option, widely used in eighteenth-century Europe, is for government or another benefactor to underwrite composers and publishers. Another option in wider use today is for governments to bestow copyrights. Without a copyright providing market power, private firms would lack the means to recoup the considerable development expense to get their products on the market. Granting market power is only a second-best solution—an externality (inefficiency) remains in that the firm is charging a supply price in excess of the social marginal cost.

2.   *Negative supply externality.* A negative supply externality means that the social marginal cost S exceeds the private marginal cost S_2 to firms in figure 6.1. Examples are plentiful from environmental factors in food production. In the case of soil erosion, much of the cost of soil erosion occurring on a farm is borne by "downstream" firms, municipalities, and individuals, who must deal with sediment and perhaps chemical residues from fertilizers and pesticides. Because the farmer whose soil is eroding only bears the cost accruing on his farm, but not the downstream costs, the offending farm lacks incentives to properly control the erosion.

To illustrate the outcome in figure 6.1, the demand D is assumed to have no externalities, hence the private demand curve is also the social demand curve. Firms maximizing profits and consumers maximizing satisfaction in a competitive economy with social supply curve S and private supply curve S_2 will produce and consume $q=9$. Price $p=6$ is half that of an efficient market, but producers are not bearing the full cost of producing q. The deadweight triangle B is the economic surplus sacrificed by this output $q=9$, rather than the socially efficient output $q=6$. Note that the deadweight cost is a function of quantity rather than of price; however, price and subsidies or taxes affect the distribution of costs and benefits.

A *Pigouvian tax* on soil erosion would raise the private supply curve up to the social supply curve, bringing market equilibrium at $q=6$. The unit tax of S-S_2 eliminates the deadweight cost. It may be noted that the tax on producers raises the price of q to consumers while benefiting taxpayers, perhaps other than those who produce q. The incidence of the redistribution of income depends on how the policy is implemented, but the elimination of the deadweight loss means that in principle, society as a whole is better off. Assuming heroically that losers are compensated in a manner that does not affect output, no one need be worse off as others are made better off.

3. *Negative demand externality.* In the case of a negative demand externality, private benefits fall short of social benefits. Heroin produced from poppies and cocaine from coca plants are examples of negative demand externalities. These hard drugs presumably benefit the users more than they benefit society as a whole, as addicts make life difficult for nonusers.

In figure 6.1, the private demand curve will lie above and to the right of the social demand curve D. (Private demand curves are not shown in figure 6.1 to simplify the graph.) Assuming no divergence between social and private supply S, too much q will be produced and consumed and the deadweight cost will be of type B. A Pigouvian tax bringing the private demand down to the social demand D would eliminate the deadweight cost.

4. *Positive demand externality.* In the case of a positive demand externality, the private demand curve lies below and to the left of the social demand curve D. The presence of such externalities implies that a good will be underproduced and consumed because the suppliers of a good will not be able to appropriate enough monetary benefits from sales to cover their costs. In figure 6.1, if private demand cuts the supply curve S at $p=6$ and $q=3$, then firms will underproduce and incur a deadweight cost of eighteen dollars when social demand is D.

A firm may invest millions of dollars in a new seed variety, only to sell it for a few hundred dollars to a few farmers, who then reproduce the seed and sell it to other farmers, with no payment to the seed developer. The benefit to society of the new variety may be huge, but the developer is unable to appropriate enough monetary benefits to enter the industry or survive after entry. Possible policy corrections include the granting of intellectual property rights in the form of patents, copyrights, and trademarks, bestowing enough market power for the firm to raise prices and cover costs. Another option is for the public to perform research or subsidize private firms to do it; however, limited public funds often preclude that option.

Efficient Means to Correct Externalities

The second law of welfare economics (see annex to chapter 2) is that government intervention is appropriate only if the intervention costs less in administration, mismanagement, and the like than the cost of ignoring the externality. Thus, lowering the cost of correcting an externality strengthens the economic case for correcting the externality. This section explores some ways to reduce the cost.

Much progress has been made in the design of innovative ways to correct externalities in previously nonexistent markets for air, water, and soil. Many of these techniques draw on the Coase Theorem, named after Nobel prizewinner Ronald Coase. That theorem holds that externalities arise from a lack of property rights. The term "tragedy of the commons" refers to excessive exploitation of open-access property. What is optimal behavior for each actor operating independently is disadvantageous for actors as a group, or for society. The air is polluted because it is an open resource, accessible to all but owned by none. Individuals and firms dump emissions into that common property, because each user is not charged the cost of foul air imposed on society by the user's action. Ranchers overgraze open-access grassland. Fishermen overfish the open-access ocean. Each boat catches all the fish it can "before the hoarders get them," until fish stocks are depleted, perhaps to extinction. Erosion is excessive on farmland, because downstream parties do not charge offending farmers for residues entering their land and water supply. An obvious solution to externality problems is to create property rights. The "cap and trade" method described below is a form of that approach.

Cap and trade policies have gained favor by successfully addressing environmental problems at low cost, relative to other methods of control. The cap and trade method establishes a market for an externality, hence it is a market-government hybrid solution. One technique is for a government to grant emission permits to each source based on each firm's history or to auction off permits. If the goal is to reduce emissions forty percent, each emission source is provided an emission permit set at three-fifths of its historic emission level. After initial permits are allocated, firms are allowed to trade emission permits in a market. A firm that derives little monetary value from products it produces from emission-producing inputs foregoes little profit by reducing emissions. It can sell some or all of its emissions permit. The buyer is likely to be a firm that derives high value from producing goods, but has a high cost of controlling emissions. In recent years, the cap and trade method has been employed with great success to reduce at low cost the sulfur dioxide emitted, especially by coal-burning power plants. In the absence of controls, sulfuric acid generated by airborne sulfur dioxide falls to the ground as acid rain, damaging limestone buildings and killing fish by building acidity in lakes.

In another example of cap and trade, fishermen are awarded (based on their past share) or may purchase (in auction from the government) the property right to catch an allotment of fish that in aggregate will ensure a sustainable fish population. Allotments, once awarded, can be bought and sold, so they end up in the hands of low-cost, high-revenue fisherman.

Markets can be used in other ways to efficiently correct for externalities. The United States offers a bewildering, cost-ineffective, politically motivated set of programs to protect the environment in agriculture. The programs are not well tailored to local needs. An attractive alternative is to provide environmental block grants to states. States would be held accountable for achieving environmental protection goals established in conjunction with the federal government, technical experts, and other interested parties. Farmers then would bid for compensation for performing measures to protect the environment, and the most cost-effective bids would be funded. This approach promises to accomplish more environmental protection at less cost than do current programs.

Externalities can be positive. A farm providing a scenic view or preserving biodiversity cannot capture (appropriate) enough benefits to cover incremental costs. In this case of a positive externality, the uncorrected market produces too little to best serve the public. Another example is education that has benefits (*e.g.*, wise voting, reduced crime, and a skilled military) accruing to society in excess of benefits to the individual. A subsidy to the private firm or outright public provision of the public good may be appropriate.

Contagious diseases such as malaria entail externalities, as the infection of one person increases the likelihood of others becoming infected. Easterly (pp. 13, 14) relates how markets were used to address the malaria problem in Malawi. Planners had been unsuccessful in getting the people of Malawi to use bed nets to avoid malaria-spreading mosquito bites. Although the bed nets were low in cost, potential distributors lacked incentives to place bed nets in the hands of the poor. By using market incentives for nurses in health clinics to provide bed nets to pregnant women and children, the proportion of children under five sleeping with bed nets went from eight percent in 2000 to fifty-five percent in 2004. Higher prices paid by persons of means for nets were used to subsidize nets for the poor. The use of bed nets was almost universal among those who paid for them, and nurses were allowed to keep a portion of the payment as an incentive to stock and distribute the nets. In contrast, a program providing free nets in Zambia found that seventy percent of recipients didn't use them.

In summary, externalities are ubiquitous and constitute a major stumbling block for a laissez-faire economy attempting to serve the public interest. It is cautioned that Coase's assumption of no transaction cost for establishing property rights is not realistic. The challenge of establishing property rights to air and oceans is obvious. Correcting externalities must face the same test faced by other uses of scarce resources: remediation is pursued only as long as the incremental benefit of correction exceeds the cost. Because costs of administration and mismanagement are positive, externalities optimally are not fully corrected.

Some environmentalists object to the cap and trade market for pollutants, because it seems to be a license to pollute. On the other hand, by sharply lowering the cost of reaching whatever environmental target is chosen by society, the cap and trade market solution allows society to do a better job of protecting the environment, because it can do so at an acceptable cost. Indeed, cap and trade may be the only mechanism that can reduce greenhouse gas emissions at a politically acceptable cost in lost economic activity. And some poor countries could benefit by selling emission permits to affluent countries.

Impact of Rising Income on the Environment

The case for the standard model is weakened if it fails the environmental preservation test. The test is challenging indeed, because at least since the birth of agriculture about 11,000 years ago, humanity has been messing with Mother Nature. Forests and grasslands were converted to cultivated land, bringing soil erosion, water pollution, and loss of habitat for wildlife. The process accelerated with the industrial revolution that began in about 1750. Won't standard-model policies raising per capita income place unacceptable demands on the environment?

Yes and no. To be sure, rising income is spent partly for material things and energy that degrade and deplete natural resources. When poor people earn a little more income, they spend it mostly for food and other necessities that have high natural-resource content per unit of income. In contrast, when richer people earn a little more income, they spend it mostly for services, such as health care and entertainment, that have low natural-resource content per unit of income. Furthermore, as people gain affluence, they can afford to support governments that protect the environment. The affluent know those environmental protection policies will raise taxes, but presumably they reckon that the benefits of collectively protecting the environment will outweigh the costs.

Keeping people poor will not save the environment. The worst environmental degradation I have observed is in poor countries with dense and growing populations. Chapter 9 elaborates on the impact of standard-model policies on population growth. Having sufficient income to favor and afford protection of natural resources and biodiversity, coupled with reduced birth rates, makes the standard model a boon to the environment.

That conclusion is affirmed by the Environmental Performance Index (EPI) published in 2006 (Esty et al.), the most comprehensive measure to date. The EPI is comprised of 16 indicators divided into six categories: environmental health, air quality, water resources, biodiversity and habitat, productive natural resources, and sustainable energy. The single EPI made up of the six components was positively correlated with per capita income (r=0.73) and the Economic Freedom Index (r=0.66) contained in tables 3.1 and 3.2. Nordic, Anglo-Saxon, and Western European countries topped the rankings whereas sub-Saharan African countries were at the bottom of the 133 countries considered. Perhaps the principal outlier was the United States, which ranked only 28*th* from the top—below much poorer countries such as Malaysia and Columbia. The U.S ranked high in drinking water quality and other categories but ranked poorly in greenhouse gas emissions. Performance was measured against international standards that of necessity must be subjective. The problem of greenhouse gas emissions contributing to global warming is palpable, but the United States has the technology and wealth to address the problem if the political stars align properly.

A large number of studies estimate the relationship between income and environmental variables (table 6.1). The so-called Environmental Kuznets Curves (EKCs), relating per capita income to environmental degradation, with few exceptions display a turning point. Rising per capita income worsens environmental variables to a point, after which more income reduces environmental "bads" per capita. Many of the estimates in table 6.1 from Hervani and Tweeten, and from a large number of studies summarized by Yandle *et al.*, indicate turning points in the $20,000–30,000 range (year 2003 U.S. dollars) of income per capita.[23] Turning points differ considerably among studies because of different samples, methodologies, quality of data, and other factors.

Table 6.1. Environmental Kuznets Curve Turning Points Based on International Data

Environmental variable	Turning point ($2003/capita)	
	Yandle *et al.*	Hervani and Tweeten
Air pollutant		
Carbon dioxide	18,680–50,000	25,806
Methane	—	31,302
Nitrogen oxides	18,750–29,700	22,086
Sulfur dioxide	9,600–18,700	20,596
Particulates	12,300–30,400	2,264
Land and water		
Organic water pollution	—	28,770–29,108
Water for irrigation	6,108–18,578	—
Phosphate fertilizer	—	19,540–23,574
Deforestation	1,300–11,823	—
Other		
Oil	—	25,177–26,033
Energy	—	29,106–29,684
Total materials	28,100	—

Source: Hervani and Tweeten; Yandle et al.

Particulates, mostly tiny carbon particles in the air from engine and power-plant exhausts, seem to turn around at lower income per capita than the range listed above. Evidence suggests that deforestation per capita also reaches a turning point at lower per capita income. A turning point is consistent with the rising area in forests in the United States and Western Europe. Agricultural no-till and conservation tillage, coupled with high-yield varieties and other advanced farming technologies made possible by massive public and private investments in science, reduced the need for cropland and cut erosion while freeing millions of hectares of cropland for forests, recreation, and urban development.

The numerous studies summarized by Yandle *et al.* largely ignored the impact of economic growth on population. Hervani and Tweeten (pp. 220–8)

23   Early estimates by Grossman and Krueger are generally consistent with Table 6.1 results after adjustment for inflation.

estimated that the effect of rising income on population growth was small at low income levels. But a one-percent increase in per capita income from a base of $16,000 annually reduced population 1.2 percent and from a base of $32,000 reduced population by 2.5 percent. These estimates accounted for direct and indirect effects of income on population. Indirect effects included the impact of higher incomes on female education and labor force participation, infant mortality, and urbanization that in turn influence birth rates and population growth. Combining the population response with the per capita response of environmental variables to income, as shown in table 6.1, Hervani and Tweeten (p. 227) estimated that rising income per capita not only improved environmental variables *per capita* but also *in total* for nations, once per capita income exceeded approximately $15,000.

This felicitous conclusion supporting the merits of economic growth under the standard model warrants at least two caveats. The first concern is how many nations are affluent enough to protect the environment. Fifteen of the seventeen countries in the top half of EFI scores in table 3.2 had per capita income of $15,000 or more in 2003. Only eight countries in the lower half of high EFI countries in the table had per capita income of $15,000 or more. Income in countries with high EFI scores tends to grow rapidly, however, and in the near future, several nations will reach income levels that can support successful environmental efforts.

A second, more worrisome caveat is that countries such as China and India with low incomes per capita and rapid growth rates will do vast environmental damage before reaching the environment-saving income level. One optimistic note here is that Environmental Kuznets Curves appear to be shifting to the left over time, so that environmental degradation is less at each income level and the turning point is being reached at ever-lower income levels. The related point is that the technology being developed to address the environment in industrial countries can be utilized in developing countries to reduce environmental damage.

The Case of Energy

Before concluding, this chapter briefly examines two issues—energy and instability—important to the world economy and at least tangentially involving externalities. High and unstable energy prices have raised fears of running out of energy if reliance is placed on markets to allocate energy. Economics emphasizes that the world will never run out of oil; however, oil at some very distant time will become uneconomic to produce in volume.

Proven oil and gas reserves will last perhaps sixty years, but close substitutes such as tar sands, shale, and coal reserves are sufficient to last for scores if not hundreds of years. Environmental consequences, particularly in the form of greenhouse gases generating global warming, are a divisive issue and a road-block to the use of some energy sources.

Fortunately, alternatives to fossil fuels are available, although considerable capital investment is required. The Royal Academy of Engineers estimates that fossil fuel energy costs 4.2 to 6.11 cent per kilowatt hour (kwh), wind energy costs 7.1 cents per kwh, and nuclear energy costs 4.4 cents per kwh ("The Atomic Elephant," p. 53). Solar energy costs an estimated eighteen to twenty cents per kwh ("Sunrise for Renewable Energy," p. 18). Wind energy costs only a little more than fossil fuels but has reliability problems. Energy generated by new nuclear power technology generates only one-tenth as much waste as did generation with the old technology. Today's nuclear power plants are safer and cleaner than fossil fuel power plants. Still, a major impediment to nuclear power is fear, not just of meltdown of reactors, but also of being in proximity to stored spent fuel. That fear may be unjustified, but it raises costs over the estimate shown above.

Sound energy policy calls for governments to avoid subsidizing energy use troubled by negative externalities such as air pollution, traffic congestion, urban sprawl, and military forces to protect foreign sources of oil. A controver-sial issue in the United States is whether ethanol should be subsidized. Whether or not to subsidize depends heavily on two issues: the impact of ethanol on the environment and on the nation's dependence on foreign oil.

Ethanol can reduce dependence on fossil fuel imports if a unit of fossil fuel energy produces more than one unit of ethanol energy to power motor vehicles. The United States Department of Energy (p. 2) summarized studies of energy, five indicating that a unit of fossil fuel energy produced less than a unit of corn ethanol energy and 10 studies indicating a net energy gain producing ethanol from corn. The current "best" estimate included in that summary, one from Argonne National Laboratory, is that a unit of fossil fuel energy produces 1.3 units of corn ethanol energy. This small net positive energy balance is hardly a ringing endorsement for reliance on domestic corn ethanol production to sever addiction to foreign oil. Furthermore, ethanol poses problems of stor-age and transportation. It cannot be transported by pipeline, is corrosive, and degrades in storage as it absorbs water.

Biofuel's environmental credentials also are mixed. A given volume of corn ethanol reduces greenhouse gas emissions 18 to 29 percent compared to the same volume of gasoline, but that advantage for ethanol is small indeed if expressed per unit of energy because a gallon of ethanol has one-third less energy than a gallon of gasoline (U.S. Department of Energy, p. 3). Ethanol reduces sulfur and carbon monoxide emissions but may contribute to smog ("Semi-Respectable Ethanol", p. A18). Producing biofuels from corn or soybeans depletes organic matter in the soil, contributes to soil erosion, and diminishes water quality. Using all U.S. land currently in corn, soybeans, and sugar crops to produce ethanol would supply only one-third of the nation's motor fuel needs. Thus production of biofuels clearly will add to food costs and increase dependence on imports of food.

Ethanol's lack of clear positive externalities erodes the economic case to subsidize it or to tax it less than fossil fuels. Currently, ethanol is heavily favored by government policy. As of March 2006 ethanol imports into the U.S. faced *a 2.5 percent ad valorem tariff plus a specific duty of 54 cents per gallon. This import tax was designed to keep especially Brazil from taking advantage of the 51 cents per gallon tax credit the United States provides for blending 10 percent ethanol into gasoline.* A danger is that the ethanol lobby, like the farm commodity program lobby, will become institutionalized to continue subsidies long after the justification for handouts has passed.

The better part of discretion with the current state of technology is for the United States to end domestic tax exemptions and the stiff tariff on ethanol imports from Brazil, and let the market determine the appropriate level of biofuels use. Extending gasoline taxes to ethanol will finance desperately needed infrastructure improvements in the dangerously overcrowded highways found in many parts of the nation. With high petroleum prices expected in the future, unsubsidized ethanol and biodiesel can compete with other energy sources. Finding biological agents that will turn cellulose from crop biomass, trees, or switchgrass into ethanol—perhaps using recombinant DNA bioengineered organisms—could lower the cost and improve the energy yield from biofuels. Chapter 9 shows costs of alternative energy sources, including biofuels to power vehicles.

The appropriate general public policy is support for basic and applied research to improve energy conservation and energy-producing technology while continuing taxes on fossil fuels that degrade the environment. The world's coal, tar sands, and shale energy resources are plentiful but unduly contaminate the environment when supplying energy. Consequently, technology to provide clean-burning coal and safe nuclear power will be critical components of future energy provision.

Irrational Expectations

One perennial shortcoming of market economies, and hence of the standard model, has not been overcome: business and commodity cycles. A rigidly controlled economy is not the answer. Too much efficiency is lost in an economy unwilling or unable to change. Following standard-model policies diminishes but does not eliminate cycles.

An economic concept called "rational expectations" became fashionable in the 1970s. It held that people and firms do not make systematic errors; that is, they do not repeat mistakes over and over. That theory is flawed; people do make systematic errors. Instability from business and commodity cycles remains endemic to market economies. Examples for the United States are ubiquitous and go back a long way. The English settlers who first arrived in the Jamestown, Virginia colony found tobacco to be a highly profitable export. That profitability led to oversupply of tobacco in the market, Europe. Consequently, prices fell in Virginia. In 1630, the colonists reacted by rioting—burning tobacco barns in protest over low prices. Commodity cycles continued. Nearly all farm commodities exhibit cyclical behavior. Commodity cycles have dampened but still average approximately four years for hogs and ten years for cattle.

Cycles arise from time lags, fixed assets, and imperfect expectations. In farming, the cycle may begin with a shock in the form of drought. The resulting short crop brings a high price. Farmers, who tend to base future price expectations on present prices, buy inputs and expand production, anticipating that the high crop price will continue. Such behavior by many farmers brings market glut and low price. An expectation by farmers that that low price will persist motivates them to produce less than the long-term equilibrium output, bringing a high price. The cycle persists.

Other notable examples of cycles include the Great Depression of the 1930s and the "dot com" bubble of the 1990s. The Japanese economy took fifteen years to recover from the asset speculation bubble that burst in 1990. Business cycles are fueled by speculation. Rising housing prices bring speculative gains. Investors bid housing prices up further as they compete to buy houses for speculative gain. Eventually, perhaps after several years, investors realize that high housing prices have generated excess housing supply and that other assets offer better rates of return. The demand falls for housing. The collapse of housing prices as the market is saturated with new houses, speculators exit, and mortgage loans are foreclosed leaves a wake of bankruptcy and misery. Builders and investors leave the market until housing prices improve.

The public and private sectors provide many tools to diminish cycles and to reduce risk and uncertainty in general. Public agencies gather and disseminate information and analysis. Analysis is of special importance, because changing prices and quantities are part of any healthy, dynamic economy. Outlook information thus must separate normal market change essential for efficient resource allocation from irrational exuberance. Private-sector tools include insurance, forward markets (contracts, futures, and options), storage, and outlook information. Futures markets allow entities to be speculators or hedgers. By hedging his commodity, the hedger can "lock in" a price for some specified future time. The speculator (the other side of the hedge) makes or loses money depending on whether the market moves in the direction he anticipated. The futures market enhances welfare, because risk-averse persons can hedge, and risk-seeking persons can speculate.

A critical issue is whether risk has public goods properties that justify government intervention. The answer is that risk exhibits few externalities warranting public intervention in markets; however, public subsidies may be a helpful safety net when disaster strikes. Farmers, at least in developed countries, are remarkably good at self-insurance through saving, diversification, flexible enterprises, storage, contracting, and the use of private risk-management markets such as insurance and futures. Although risk-management subsidies are hard to justify for farmers in rich or poor countries, governments of poor countries may wish to purchase insurance in international markets. The purpose is to protect against inadequate foreign exchange to purchase food in international markets when facing systemic domestic food production failures.

Concluding Comments

Public choice economics holds that the government has a role to make markets work better by correcting externalities and maintaining competition. Public choice economics also holds that public intervention is warranted in markets only if the administrative and other public costs of intervening are less than the deadweight cost of market failures being corrected.

It is tempting to write off the standard model, with its emphasis on markets, as unsuited for today's environmental problems. One of the exciting new developments in economics is to adapt markets for supplying public goods and correcting externalities. Environmentalists can embrace cap and trade "market" solutions to provide public goods, because externalities are corrected at less cost. Thus, more cases satisfy the second law of welfare economics: that externalities be corrected at less cost than allowing them to continue. It is not easy to extend property rights and markets to natural resources such as the earth's oceans and air. Even here, clever adaptation of markets, such as cap and trade systems, shows promise.

Environmental protection is a public good that will not be properly provided by laissez-faire markets alone. The extreme solution, socialism, is not the answer. Socialism has an abysmal record of protecting the environment. Making the state both policeman and polluter is a formula for failure.

Developing countries in general have a poor environmental record, in part because it takes money and administrative competence to monitor and protect rainforests, soil, rangeland, wildlife, biodiversity, and scenic attractions. Following standard-model policies can help such countries build the administrative competence and finances essential to supply public goods.

References

"The Atomic Elephant." *The Economist*. April 30, 2005, p. 53.

Coase, Ronald. "The Problem of Social Cost." *Journal of Law and Economics*. Vol. 3, 1960. Reprinted in Robert Stavins, *Economics of the Environment: Selected Readings*. edition. New York: Norton, 2000.

Easterly, William. *White Man's Burden: Why the West's Efforts to Aid the Rest Have Done So Much Ill and So Little Good*. New York: Penguin Press, 2006.

Esty, Daniel C., Marc A. Levy, Tanja Srebotnjak, Alexander de Sherbinin, Christine H. Kim, and Bridget Anderson. *Pilot 2006 Environmental Performance Index*. New Haven: Yale Center for Environmental Law and Policy, 2006.

Grossman, Gene and Alan Krueger. "Environmental Impact of the North American Free Trade Agreement." Working Paper 3914. Cambridge, Massachusetts: National Bureau of Economic Research, 1991.

Hervani, Aref and Luther Tweeten. "Kuznets Curves for Environmental Degradation and Resource Depletion." Chapter 11 in L. Tweeten and S. Thompson, eds., *Agricultural Policy for the 21st Century*. Ames: Iowa State Press, 2002.

"Semi-Respectable Ethanol." *Washington Post*, May 23, 2005, p. A18.

"Sunrise for Renewable Energy." *The Economist.* December 10, 2005, pp. 18–21.

U.S. Department of Energy. *Argonne National Laboratory Energy Study: Key Points.* Washington DC: Office of Energy Efficiency and Renewable Energy, USDE, 2006.

Yandle, Bruce, Madhusadan Bhattarai, and Maya Vijayaraghavan. "Environmental Kuznets Curves: A Review of Findings, Methods, and Policy Implications." PERC Research Study 02-1. http://www.perc.org/pdf/rs02 1a.pdf, April 2004.

7

Economic Development Emphasizing Sub-Saharan Africa

With exceptions such as Haiti, poor countries outside of Africa are making impressive economic gains while reducing poverty, hunger, disease, and birth rates. Developing countries outside of Africa show signs of progressing through the demographic transition to slow population growth that will allow continued economic growth and more attention to protecting the environment.

In the 1960s and 1970s, some development "experts" called for triage; that is, for abandoning assistance of rich countries to "hopeless" cases such as Bangladesh that were judged too poor to save from chronic hunger and poverty. Rather, it was said that aid assistance should focus on countries with more promise. That notion that some countries were beyond repair was wrong in the 1960s and 1970s, and it continues to be wrong in the twenty-first century. Fortunately, the notion was not heeded. Per capita income in Bangladesh was $1,553 in 2003 and grew 2.81 percent annually on average in the previous decade. With an EFI (see table 3.1) of only 5.9 in 2002, the country has considerable room to improve its policies for more impressive economic progress. Especially important for this densely populated nation, the total fertility rate per woman averaged only 3.1 children in 2000, down from 6.6 children in 1975.

Doomsayers were wrong about Bangladesh, but how about Africa? Sub-Saharan Africa has faced and will continue to face unusual pestilence. Sub-Saharan Africa (SSA) is the only major region of the world falling seriously short of the Millennium Development Goal of cutting abject poverty in half between 1990 and 2015. The World Bank (see Berg and Qureshi, p. 21) reports that abject poverty in sub-Saharan Africa was 46.4 percent of the population in 2002 versus an already devastating 44.6 percent in 1990. Africa, with 12.4 percent of the world's population, has only 3.2 percent of the world's purchasing power and 2.1 percent of the world's international trade (*The Economist*, p. 27). Africa is the poorest world region, averaging only $560 per capita GDP in 2003.

Of the eighteen nations of the world that experienced food emergencies more than half of the years in the 1986–2004 period, eleven were in Africa

(FAO, p. 17). The FAO estimated that of the sixteen cases of chronic food emergency in Africa, eleven were caused by armed conflict (and hence man-made) and five were caused by weather. The region would have experienced massive fatalities from hunger in the absence of food aid from abroad.

Malaria, other parasitic diseases, and AIDS are taking so many lives that life expectancy and population are falling in many countries of Africa, despite continued high birth rates. Africa is not blessed with rich soils, dependable rainfall, navigable rivers, and convenient access to ports. Less than one-quarter of the region's people live within 100 kilometers from the coast. Nonetheless, these shortcomings only partly explain why Africa is poor.

Explaining Pathologies of Africa

Africa's ubiquitous pathologies are inseparable from the region's rejection of the standard model, as is apparent in chapter 3. With nearly half its population in abject poverty (see table 1.2), it comes as no surprise that Africa is the most hostile region to do business in the world. *The Economist* ("Doing Business in Africa," p. 61) summarizes:

> According to the World Bank's "Doing Business" report, Africa is, on average, the most difficult place to do business in the world when it comes to red tape. The report examines regulatory obstacles and ranks performance using criteria such as ease of starting and closing a business, hiring and firing of workers, enforcing contracts, getting credit, and protecting investors....As a result, over 40 percent of the region's economy is informal—the highest proportion in the world....And firms of all types must contend with the severe problems of political upheaval, war, corruption, and an HIV/AIDS pandemic.

Compared to costs in well-run regions, importing goods into Africa loses seventeen days to dilapidated roads and forty-three days to customs and other paperwork (World Bank). In Burkina Faso, anyone ambitious enough to start a legal business must deposit five times the country's per capita average annual income with authorities. Firing an employee will cost the firm fifty-seven weeks of wages.

One or two procedures are sufficient to start a business in well-run countries; in Uganda, it takes seventeen procedures, and in Chad it takes nineteen. The cost of starting a business in a well-run country is nominal, but in Sierra Leone it is 825 times and in Zimbabwe it is 1,442 times the average per capita income. In Sierra Leone, taxes average 164 percent of gross profits. Thus, Africans are driven to operate as informal black-market businesses.

The informal market sector operates outside the law, thereby avoiding taxes and regulations. But entrepreneurship so evident in the innovative informal sector cannot flourish, because of the hostile environment for business. Achieving economies of size would lower production costs but raise the informal-sector firm's profile. That high profile would bring heavy taxation and regulation. Informal businesses lack critical support systems, such as protection by law enforcement and judicial systems. The law is unable to enforce contracts and debt repayments. Laws requiring firms to protect the environment will not be enforced if environmental protection agencies don't know the firms exist. Workers in the informal sector lack protections that are commonplace in the rest of the world. In short, Africa could unleash a powerful force for economic development by creating an institutional environment facilitating the creation and expansion of private firms in the formal sector.

Africa is sometimes commended for its widely used system of allocating land by local authorities, often the tribal chief. That has resulted in a more equitable system of land access than the highly unequal ownership structure inhibiting development in some regions, notably Latin America. The lack of secure property rights in the African system creates formidable problems, however. One is that it is susceptible to favoritism. Another is that lack of secure property rights inhibits farm operators from investing in real estate improvements such as buildings, irrigation, or soil fertility. Such improvements remain with the land transferred to a new operator. For similar reasons land and improvements cannot be used as collateral for loans to improve resource productivity or living standards. Much land in Africa needs to remain fallow for several years to restore fertility between croppings. The fallow period is unduly shortened because operators lacking clear title fear losing their land as the deciding authority reallocates "unused" fallow land to someone ready to crop it.

William Easterly, a former World Bank economist, estimates that the West has spent $450 billion on foreign aid to Africa over the past forty years ("Special Report on Aid to Africa," p. 25). Much of the aid has been wasted, falling into the hands of corrupt African officials or invested in infrastructure, such as roads, that Africans have allowed to become dilapidated.

Tsetse fly infestation is another scourge of Africa. The bite of the fly transmits a parasite that causes debilitation or death to productive breeds of cattle and horses. The parasite, if not treated, causes deadly sleeping sickness (trypanosomiasis) in humans. The tsetse fly renders millions of hectares in central Africa uninhabited or underutilized by humans as well as by productive breeds of cattle and horses. Effective, affordable control of the fly would provide cattle grazing, food, and a humanly habitable area for large numbers of Africans.

Some 1.1 million persons die of malaria each year, nearly 90 percent of them in tropical Africa ("Special Report on Aid to Africa," p. 24). Malaria, like sleeping sickness and riverblindness, is caused by a parasite but is spread by the mosquito. Science has yet to find a way to give people immunity to malaria, but some cheap and somewhat effective preventatives are available. Mosquito bed nets, impregnated with insecticide, can cost less than four dollars and cut the risk of infants dying from malaria by as much as sixty-three percent ("Special Report on Aid to Africa," p. 26). Efforts of foreign donors to provide bed nets and medications to Africans unfortunately have often been thwarted by government tariffs on imports and by siphoning off of benefits by corrupt officials.

The most recent and devastating disease scourge of sub-Saharan Africa is HIV/AIDS. Africa accounted for some seventy-five percent of the 3.1 million deaths from AIDS in 2004 ("Special Report on Aid to Africa," p. 24). In Botswana and South Africa, where over twenty percent of adults are HIV positive, the population by 2020 is projected to be falling at an annual rate of 2.1 percent and 1.4 percent respectively (Jayne *et al.*, p. 2). In the seven hardest-hit countries of Africa (Botswana, Lesotho, Namibia, South Africa, Swaziland, Zambia, and Zimbabwe), the female population by 2020 is projected to be down by twenty-nine percent for women aged less than twenty years, forty-five percent for ages twenty to fifty-nine years, and thirty-five percent for women aged over fifty-nine compared to what population would have been in the absence of AIDS (Jayne *et al.*, p. 3). The male population fares only a little better. The working-age male and female population will be especially devastated. Death rates are markedly high among better-educated and skilled Africans, hence much wisdom and expertise will be lost.

Several factors could mildly mitigate the severe hardship implied by the foregoing numbers. One is that underemployment, especially in the non-farm informal economy, is currently huge, providing a labor reserve to fill productive but vacated farm and non-farm jobs. Second, low-cost anti-retroviral medication is increasingly available and will extend lives. Third, infection rates are lower in some countries than in the worst cases listed above, in part because leaders (as in Uganda) have aggressively campaigned to provide prophylactics and to change the risky sexual behavior causing venereal diseases. Nonetheless, AIDS inevitably will further devastate an already troubled region of the world. Despite help from donors in rich countries, medications will not seem cheap to Africans.

Africa, with some outside help, can turn itself around. Humanitarian aid of food and selected medicines has saved the lives of many Africans. For example, the pharmaceutical giant Merck donated worm-killing drugs that saved the sight of an estimated 600,000 people afflicted with parasites causing riverblindness. Aerial spraying of breeding grounds for the parasite's host, blackfly, has opened twenty-five million hectares of fertile land along rivers to settlement and food production.

The high cost of addressing the plagues of Africa heightens the urgency of reforms called for by the standard model. Africans will be unable to generate essential buying power without major economic reforms that only the countries themselves can make.

In 1988, I was sent with a team of three American social scientists coupled with three Tanzanian social scientists "to ascertain the root causes of third world socioeconomic injustice" (Kidd *et al.*). The African from a nongovernment organization who was responsible for the scope of the study asked us to test three hypotheses: that socioeconomic injustice was the result of (1) declining terms of trade, whereby Tanzania was receiving lower prices for exports while paying higher prices for imports from the West; (2) neocolonialism, whereby the economic problems of Tanzania were the result of exploitative past and continuing interference by Western countries, apparent in inadequate access to rich world markets, finances, and technology; and (3) exploitation by multinational firms. It is notable that none of these hypotheses recognized that Tanzania's problems could have internal origins.

The American team members responded to these hypotheses. Hypothesis 1 draws from the Paul Prebisch-Hans Singer thesis, first advanced in 1949, that prices for primary products were declining over time, relative to prices of manufacturing products. Thus, benefits of trade were distributed "unjustly" from poor countries producing primary agricultural products to rich countries producing manufactured products. That thesis and related dependency theory have since been discredited. World prices of agricultural products fell because of especially rapid improvements in agricultural productivity, made possible by investments in science and education. Also, agriculture was especially suited to mechanization, made possible by the internal combustion engine with accompanying technologies, including the tractor and combine. Adequate-sized, reasonably well-managed farms achieved high resource returns and living standards, even as food prices fell. There was no conspiracy justifying redress. As net food importers of temperate food products, consumers in poor countries benefited from advances in agricultural productivity.

Addressing Hypothesis 1, the team noted that Tanzania's terms of trade had not changed much over the years, but any drop in terms of trade could be explained by the innovations raising the productivity of agriculture throughout much of the world. Farmers in Tanzania suffered because the government neglected agricultural technology and infrastructure while taxing farm exports heavily. A nation is left behind when it fails to raise its productivity while other nations move forward.[24] The economic pain suffered by Tanzania's farmers came from bad decisions by the Tanzanian government, and not from the malevolence of rich countries or shortcomings of local farmers.

Regarding Hypothesis 2, team members viewed colonialism as an abomination, but they noted no systematic association in Africa or elsewhere between being under colonial rule and economic prosperity. In world perspective, some rich countries, such as Australia, Canada, the United States, South Korea, and Taiwan, were once under colonial rule, while some of today's poorest countries, such as Ethiopia and Liberia, have been independent.[25] Considerable road, rail, agricultural research, and governmental infrastructure in Africa was assembled in the colonial era; progress has been meager since the early 1960s, when many African countries became independent. As for neocolonialism in the form of former masters interfering in today's life of African countries, European countries have been especially supportive in giving research and development funds, higher education, preferential trade access, and food aid. For many years, Tanzania was the largest per capita recipient of economic aid from rich countries. To those who contend that Africa is poor because the West is rich, the team noted that African countries rely heavily on markets in Europe. That is a major reason why African markets expand and economies perk up when economies of the West perk up. In 1984, Peter Bauer (pp. 31–2) contested the myth that poverty in Africa is the product of cash export cropping and trade with the West:

> Throughout the less developed world the materially most advanced societies and regions are those with the most commercial contacts with the West, as for instance the cash-crop producing areas in the Far East, West Africa, and Latin America; the mineral producing areas of Africa and the Middle East; and the cities and ports throughout the less developed world. This is not surprising. The spread of material progress from more advanced to less advanced areas is a commonplace of economic history.

---

24 The dumping of agricultural products on markets by the West was reprehensible. At the time of the study, the net effect of ending rich-country farm support programs would have lowered farm prices as idled land was returned to production. An exception is cotton. Ending U.S. cotton supports would have opened some markets for Tanzania's farmers. Its principal export, coffee, was not affected.

25 Ethiopia was under Italian domination from 1933 to 1938.

Regarding Hypothesis 3, it was difficult to blame multinational corporations for the economic travails of Tanzania when such corporations were nowhere to be found. Tanzania desperately needed management, technology, capital, job creation, and access to first world markets offered by multinational corporations. Multinational corporations do not go where they are unwelcome and unable to make a profit.

The incorruptibility of Julius Nyerere (1922–1999), leader of Tanzania, was only exceeded by his disdain for sound economics. His African Marxist economic policy called *Ujama* brought people together into village communes and placed the government in charge of food distribution. The government had only a few trucks to bring food from the country to hundreds of thousands of urban consumers. Laws prohibiting marketing by private individuals were widely violated; if they had not been, a great many people could have starved. The American team (Kidd *et al.*, p. ix) concluded by stating that impoverishment of Tanzania is:

- The result more of internal policy decisions of Tanzania, rather than transnationals, declining terms of trade, or of the North;
- The result of the political-economic *system* in Tanzania, rather than of malevolent leaders, unenterprising or slothful citizens, or perverse economic behavior;
- The result of market distortions by the state (government failure), rather than poor performance by private firms (market failure);
- The result of government attempting too much central planning and direction, rather than focusing on a few critical needs for the provision of public goods;
- The result of too little emphasis on export cropping and agriculture and too much emphasis on food self-sufficiency and industrial development; and
- The result more of low productivity due to inadequate human, material, and technological capital formation, rather than failure of world markets or terms of trade.

The above conclusion, which applies generally and not just to Tanzania, that hunger and poverty are caused by unfortunate policy choices by poor countries rather than caused by rich countries, is not a reason to abandon assistance to poor countries.

Policy Example

It is more than coincidence that Africa is at once the poorest and most over-regulated region of the world. But practices in Africa that defy the standard model can be reformed, as indicated by the example below of educational institutions.

From my desk in an office at Makerere University in Uganda in 1990, I could see a puzzling new development: rows of students peering from outside windows into a lecture auditorium. I was informed that these were an overflow of students caused by a change in enrollment policy. The traditional policy was for the state to pay for higher education at Makerere University but for parents to pay for elementary and secondary schooling. Public financing of Makerere had been justified in the name of giving access to all students, not just those with rich parents who could afford to send their children to school. One result was few students in higher education, mostly from privileged families, because public funds were very limited, and children of more wealthy families had the best credentials. They had attended the best elementary and secondary schools.

Student enrollment increased fivefold, with fees charged and used to hire more university instructors. Fee revenues provided several stipends to support attendance by able students of limited financial means. Monies received from food services, alumni, and other sources supplemented student fees to serve educational needs. Less reliance on government funding of higher education released some public funds for the support of elementary and secondary schools.

Prioritizing

The standard model calls for investments offering high rates of return. Markets, of course, seek out high-payoff activities. Getting priorities right is harder for governments, as observed earlier in chapter 2. Analytical economic expertise within governments can help to establish priorities. Unfortunately, it is difficult for governments in developing countries to employ the best analysts for such positions, in part because of problems with the level and continuity of pay. I have helped to establish centers of economic expertise in African countries, only to see those centers devastated by a change of regime or funding due to armed conflict, political intervention, or exhaustion of support funds from donors.

Whether to give priority to public-or private-sector investments for the development of poor countries poses a "chicken-egg" dilemma. Sachs (p. 3) states:

> When the preconditions of basic infrastructure (roads, power, and ports) and human capital (health and education) are in place, markets are powerful engines of development. Without those preconditions, markets can cruelly bypass large parts of the world, leaving them impoverished and suffering without respite. Collective action, through efficient government provision of health, education, infrastructure, as well as foreign assistance when needed, underpins economic success.

Who will pay for those public goods? Marxist Mengistu Haile Mariam, dictator of Ethiopia from 1974 to 1991, offered the citizenry a commendable cocktail of free vaccinations, veterinary clinics for livestock, and improved feeder roads. Those promised offerings could not be delivered, because he ignored sound economic policies essential to generate the tax base that could finance social programs.

The economic law of variable proportions predicts that the high ratio of labor to capital in Africa will be manifest in high rates of return on investment. The high return will attract investment from at home and abroad, generating capital and income growth. That prediction has not held. Capital flight from Africa indicates that investment returns have been low relative to risk. Paul Collier and his colleagues (Collier *et al.*, p. 55) in the World Bank point out that Africans hold forty percent of their wealth outside Africa. This contrasts sharply with the four-percent capital flight in South Asia.

Ian Taylor (p. 4) of the School of International Relations, University of St. Andrews, Scotland, noted in a letter to the editor of *Foreign Policy* that in thirty out of fifty-three African countries, capital flight from 1970 to 1996 (including interest earnings) totaled $274 billion. That was equal to 145 percent of Africa's foreign debts. He went on to note that more than 100,000 African millionaires on the continent alone held $600 billion in wealth (in and outside their countries). These numbers belie the fashionable "expert wisdom" that there are major opportunities for high-payoff investments in Africa for capital in African hands, a good part of which is held abroad.

Massive capital flight indicates a toxic local investment climate. That Africans themselves choose to invest outside rather than inside Africa is a red flag, casting serious doubt whether more developmental aid to Africa—as championed by Jeffery Sachs, U2 singer Bono, and many others—will be well used unless preceded and attended by standard-model policies.

These observations raise the related issue of whether public or private capital is better for development. As noted above, *private-sector* wealth is diverted abroad, because the local investment climate ignores or sabotages the standard model. But public-sector aid going from foreign governments (or quasi-government bodies such as the World Bank) to recipient governments and non-government organizations suffers from mismanagement. Funds too often end up in the hands of corrupt agencies and individuals that either use funds for private consumption or divert funds to foreign assets. The bottom line is that lack of effective standard-model policies and institutions thwarts the ability of developmental foreign aid to promote the general welfare.

John Mellor, the celebrated development economist, used to say (personal communication) that the geography of Africa dictated three development priorities: "roads, roads, and roads." Rich countries hesitate to provide extensive infrastructure in Africa, because poor countries do not provide essential maintenance.[26] On humanitarian grounds, rich nations will provide food and medicine needed by the poor and hungry. While commendable, humanitarian aid too will be woefully inadequate.

Private and public sectors must develop synergistically. With three-fourths of people in poor countries employed in agriculture, the long road to development begins with the farm sector. Improved agricultural technology, such as disease-, pest-, and stress-resistant varieties from public and private research, will raise crop and animal yields. Recombinant DNA technology offers promising new advances. With improved technology, farm families formerly living at subsistence levels, consuming all they produced, can generate at least meager savings. Some of the surplus generated by improved technology can be used to improve farm family living standards and production capital, and some can be used to improve schools and infrastructure.

In the semi-arid savannah of SSA today, a typical family can cultivate only about two hectares of land with its fifty dollars of production capital invested in hoes and sickles. The soil is low in nutrients and unsuited to intensive cultivation—even in a well-functioning economy. Families on these farms currently are near subsistence living, because they produce so little, despite long hours of labor.

---

26 There is more to the road problem. Donors are unwilling to pay for adequate roads, so asphalt blacktop is spread only three inches thick on a dirt base. Weights are not controlled, so overloaded trucks quickly destroy what little hard surface is laid down. Solutions to the problem include building gravel roads that require less maintenance, providing donor funds for continuing maintenance as well as construction, or working in countries adopting sound economic policies that will generate income, so that recipient countries can build and maintain their own roads.

Contrast the African example with a typical Midwest American cash-grain commercial farm. The American farm has $500,000 invested in machinery alone. It operates over 500 hectares of land, much of it rented, and the farm operator's family net income is approximately $50,000 per year. The total production cost of a bushel of corn is similar on the African and the American farms, because the cheap labor on the African farm is offset by labor-saving, cost-reducing capital on the American farm.

A later generation of the African family farms may achieve a satisfactory income by producing (say) grain sorghum and other crops on an extensive scale with a combine harvester and other machinery. To be economic, such a farm will need to occupy hundreds of hectares. As capital accumulates, budgets indicate that the first step beyond subsistence is oxen draft power to reduce unit production costs and raise output per worker. For various reasons, many African farmers wish to skip that step and move to tractor power. Other less-productive African lands will be able to provide a decent living for families if utilized as extensive ranches or intensive crop irrigation.

Under the best of circumstances, with a generous assumed ten-percent annual return on investment poured back into the African farm, ninety-seven years would be required to go from fifty dollars to $500,000 of capital investment per farm. For such size, farm consolidation must occur. Many farm people will need to move to jobs in other sectors over the years. The synergy apparent in that process requires economic and job growth properly balanced between the farm and non-farm sectors. The conclusion is that an economic-sized farming unit in Africa cannot be achieved in a reasonable period of time by the traditional reliance on internal savings. Time and patience will be required to build the African financial infrastructure and return-enhancing technologies essential to attract much-needed outside financial capital to African agriculture.

In short, the intensification (higher yields) and extensification (more cropland) essential for economic progress in Africa will require considerable capital accumulation and balanced growth among sectors, made possible only by standard-model policies and decades of time. Numerous farm people will need off-farm employment. Patience with the slow but essential process will surely wear thin, and leaders will be tempted to take shortcuts offered by populist demagogues. Shortcuts will be setbacks. Sound development policies as outlined in chapter 2, if followed, will attract foreign direct investment to speed development. That development will provide the wherewithal to attack HIV/AIDS, poverty, and the other scourges of Africa.

Reform Attempts

Recent African reform attempts have a mixed record of success. The New Partnership for African Development (NEPAD) exemplifies the current stage of development policy in SSA. The rhetoric is exemplary; the execution is disappointing. The NEPAD strategic framework document arises from a mandate given to the five initiating heads of state (Algeria, Egypt, Nigeria, Senegal, and South Africa) by the Organization of African Unity (OAU). The 37th Summit of the OAU in July 2001 formally adopted the strategic framework document. Commendable primary objectives of NEPAD are:

1. To eradicate poverty;
2. To place African countries, both individually and collectively, on a path of sustainable growth and development;
3. To halt the marginalization of Africa in the globalization process and enhance its full and beneficial integration into the global economy; and
4. To accelerate the empowerment of women.

Priorities are to establish the conditions for sustainable development by ensuring peace and security; democracy and good political, economic, and corporate governance; regional co-operation and integration; and capacity building. The priorities are appealing.

As of 2006, NEPAD remained mostly rhetoric. A cynical view is that the effort was more about a commitment to obtain funds from rich countries, rather than about genuine collaboration among rich and poor countries for promoting socioeconomic development. That suspicion is supported by one of NEPAD's statements of principle: "Increased levels of official development assistance to the continent."

It is easy to become confused between proper economic policies for the household, firm, or village versus for a nation. That confusion is apparent in the voluble development economist Jeffrey Sachs' set of priorities for development in a poor village in Kenya. He (2005, p. 74) calls for "clinical economics," much as clinical psychology is the application of psychology to individual and family problems as opposed to theoretical or adolescent fields of psychology. He (p. 56) dismisses the simplistic notion that "poverty is the result of corrupt leadership and retrograde cultures that impede modern development," despite having spent time in Zimbabwe and other countries of Africa that have been devastated by incompetent, malevolent leaders, and/or civil violence.

How does Sachs explain poverty in Africa? One source of poverty in Africa, according to Sachs (pp. 56–8), is "the poverty trap": people have too little income to forego consumption, to save, and to invest in capital that would raise their income. Sachs contends that "When poverty is very extreme, the poor do not have the ability—by themselves—to get out of the mess." Are African farms and firms in fact caught in a poverty trap, with firms so poor that they cannot afford to forego current consumption to save, invest, and build human and material capital essential for economic progress? Are African countries so poor that they cannot afford to build or maintain the infrastructure, schooling, agricultural research and extension, and the rule of law critical for markets to work for economic progress?

The answer is that African countries and most firms are not caught in a poverty trap. Data from the World Bank reported by Sachs (p. 57) show savings rates of ten percent of income for the least-developed countries, nineteen percent for low-income countries, and twenty-five to twenty-eight percent for middle-income countries. If these rates apply to Africa, then the poor of Africa save relatively much more than do Americans, whose personal savings rates averaged only two percent of income from 1999 to 2005.

Farmers and countries throughout the world once were poorer than those in Africa today. In the early 1950s, South Korea was as poor as are countries of Africa today. Now, South Korea enjoys a higher income per capita than do several countries in Western Europe. To be sure, South Korea had invested more in human resources (education) and institutions such as agricultural research prior to its takeoff than has Africa. That observation tells African countries that they must attend to such investments to stimulate economic progress.

I have been on tea plantations in East Africa that prospered under East Indian ownership and operation, but grew up to weeds after the Indians were forced to leave and locals gained control of the land. White farmers in Zimbabwe, South Africa, and elsewhere have shown that African farms can be operated efficiently and profitably. In spite of often inadequate roads and other infrastructure, such farms compete favorably with farmers from around the world and earn much-needed foreign exchange in international markets. White and Indian farmers have been successful in undeveloped nations not because of their race, but because they bring management capabilities and a "can do" mindset. They and other farmers in Africa would be far more successful if their governments followed standard-model policies.

Lack of a supportive institutional environment for firms has been instrumental in Africa's decline to two percent of world trade in 2005 from six percent in the 1980s. Thaker (p. 58) estimates that even a one-percentage-point increase in trade share would add $70 billion in export receipts. Such earnings could finance many food and medical necessities in short supply in Africa.

Poverty in Africa also is explained by geography and pathogens, according to Sachs (p. 192). Large areas of Africa are indeed subject to sparse and intermittent rainfall, but so are relatively wealthy vast areas of the United States, Australia, and Canada. Landlocked Botswana and Uganda, located far from navigable rivers, are doing better than Ethiopia, Kenya, Liberia, Somalia, and Tanzania, which are located on the coast. Poverty in Africa is widespread, reaching from the rich volcanic soils around Urusha, Tanzania, to the depleted soils of the Sahel, and from the savanna of the central highlands to the rainforests of Central Africa and West Africa. No single explanation for poverty suffices, but corruption, tribalism, and poor policy explain much. The HIV/AIDS epidemic came much too recently to explain perennial poverty in Africa, but it severely intensifies an already-difficult economic situation.

Sachs' economic prescription to alleviate poverty in a village of 5,000 residents in Sauri, Kenya reveals his priorities for development. His proposal detailed in chapter 2 called for spending of an estimated seventy dollars per person in the village on fertilizers, a health clinic staffed by a doctor and nurse, a village truck, modern cooking fuel for schools, a few cell phones, a grain storage facility, electricity for the school and clinic, water wells and storage for the community, plus various outlays to improve community management and deliver services.

One potential problem with this proposal is that considerable funds could leak to corrupt officials and administrators. The community and donor administrative capacity could be inadequate to properly allocate funding. Sachs (p. 236) estimated that such a program for Kenya would require donor support totaling $1.5 billion, compared to current donor support of $100 million, or one-fifteenth of the needed amount.

Most serious of all, the proposal, if implemented, would not bring sustainable development. It fails to address the institutional and cultural environment that has kept Kenya from building capital and income to address its problems of hunger, disease, and poverty. Sub-Saharan Africa desperately needs improved agricultural research development and technology transfer to raise productivity and conserve soil. It needs investments in infrastructure such as farm-to-market roads and irrigation systems to make commercial fertilizer and commodity marketing economically feasible. It needs more training for teachers to improve education, better training of civil servants to reduce corruption, and better-informed voters and politicians to improve governance. Community improvements will not be sustained and roads will fall into disrepair if Kenya and other countries in Africa continue their current policies.[27]

An alternative that would cost Kenya and international donors nothing would be for Kenya to adopt standard-model policies to raise income that in turn could perennially finance worthy projects such as those identified by Sachs. Based on the quadratic equation relating EFI to income in chapter 3, raising the EFI by one point (on a scale of one to ten) adds $2,698 to per capita income of the poorest countries. Raising the current index level of 6.4 to 6.5 would generate more than the seventy dollars per capita Sachs considers necessary for Sauri. Due to lagged response, more than one year would be required to generate the desired income, but needed improvements in policies—and hence in income—are well within the reach of Kenya and other countries in sub-Saharan Africa. Donors can help countries to develop essential policy-making capacity and delivery.

Concluding Comments

Africa can be an economic and social success. That success will depend not on the United States and other rich countries, but on the decisions made by poor countries themselves. Success will depend on man, and not on nature. Africans will need to change some attitudes, including their tolerance for auto-cratic, incompetent, corrupt rulers. Africans will need to examine their own policies and not reflexively blame others for their countries' failings. They will need to be patient with standard-model policies, adhering to them along the challenging road to success and not digressing into dead-end populist policies. A stance that such advice "blames the victim" will be counterproductive to correcting institutions and policies.

A recurring theme of this volume is that for sustainable economic progress, microeconomic policies applicable at the firm and household level need supportive macroeconomic policies at the national and international level. Of necessity, due to space limitations, this chapter cannot devote proper detail to the local policies required for sustainable development that has so long eluded Africa. The International Food Policy Research Institute, from its extensive

---

27 I have noted recurring instances in Africa of donors, after observing the decrepit state of agricultural research in a country, agreeing to fund the building of research facilities and training of scientific personnel for say five to ten years, after which the recipient country is to continue funding and control. Often, however, the research effort collapses as donor support ends.

background of incisive insights into the economic problems of Africa, provides a useful summary of economic advice (Heidhues *et al.*, p. 35):

> Since the root causes of poverty and hunger vary from country to country, highly context-specific policies and strategies are required. Recommendations for African governments and other agencies with respect to alleviation should therefore be based on the particular features of the subregion or country in question.

Heidhues *et al.* (p. 36) rate governance in eastern and southern Africa as "poor" and go on (p. 38) to elaborate:

> Good governance, the rule of law, and a reliable and independent judicial system are preconditions for decentralization, community empowerment, and privatization. Private sector initiatives, entrepreneurial activity, and ownership by local people cannot be expected in an environment of arbitrariness, corruption, lawlessness, and insecurity.

These conclusions are consistent with standard-model prescriptions, including the recommendation that "Agriculture needs to be returned to the top of the development agenda" (Heidhues *et al.*, p. 39). Rosegrant *et al.* (p. 27) spell out the potential for irrigation, genetically modified organisms, and "low external input sustainable agriculture" in SSA in some detail. That study concludes that prospects for diminishing poverty and hunger in SSA are bright if sound policies are followed.

References

Bauer, Peter T. *Reality and Rhetoric: Studies in the Economics of Development.* Cambridge, Massachusetts: Harvard University Press, 1984.

Berg, Andy, and Zia Qureshi. "The MGDs: Building Momentum." *Finance and Development.* Washington DC: International Monetary Fund, September 2005, pp. 21–3.

Collier, Paul, Anke Hoefler, and Catherine Patillo. "Capital Flight as Portfolio Choice." *World Bank Economic Review* 15(1): 55–80, 2001.

"Doing Business in Africa." *The Economist.* July 2, 2005, p. 61.

FAO. *The State of Food Insecurity in the World 2004*. Rome: Food and Agriculture Organization of the United Nations, 2004.

Heidhues, Franz, Achi Atsain, Hezron Nyangito, Martine Padilla, Gerard Ghersi, and Jean-Charles Le Vallee. *Development Strategies and Food and Nutrition Security in Africa*. 2020 Discussion Paper 38. Washington DC: International Food Policy Research Institute, December 2004.

Jayne, T. S., Marcella Villarreal, Prabhu Pingali, and Gunter Hemrich. *HIV/ AIDS and the Agricultural Sector in Eastern and Southern Africa: Anticipating the Consequences*. Rome: Food and Agriculture Organization, 2005.

Kidd, Katherine, Mark Lund, and Luther Tweeten. *Tanzanian-U.S. Roundtable on Development and Justice*. Geneva: Lutheran World Federation, 1989.

Rosegrant, Mark, Sarah Cline, Weibo Li, Timothy Sulser, and Rowena Valmonte-Santo. *Looking Ahead: Long-Term Prospects for Africa's Agricultural Development and Food Security*. 2020 Discussion Paper 41. Washington DC: International Food Policy Research Institute, August 2005.

Sachs, Jeffrey D. *The End of Poverty*. New York: Penguin Press, 2005.

"Special Report on Aid to Africa." *The Economist*. July 2, 2005, pp. 24–6.

Taylor, Ian. *Foreign Policy*. Nov./Dec. 2005, p. 4.

Thaker, Pratibha. "Africa: Hope or Hype?" *The World in 2006*. London: The Economist, 2005.

The Economist. *Pocket World in Figures*. London: Profile Books, 2005.

World Bank. "Global Outlook and the Developing Countries." In *Global Economic Outlook 2004*. Washington DC, 2004.

8

International Trade and Aid Policy

Open international trade encourages goods and services to be produced where fewest resources are required, thereby raising income while reducing hunger and poverty. This chapter documents the idea that freer trade, a cornerstone of the standard model, is "low-hanging fruit." Trade, like improved technology, raises productivity—output per unit of input. Trade offers massive economic gains to rich and poor countries alike. Affluent countries can enrich poor countries by opening markets to products of poor countries, ending unfair competition such as farm subsidies, and encouraging poor countries to open their own markets.

Agriculture is the principal obstruction to multilateral free trade. Agricultural trade protectionism is largely a by-product of domestic farm commodity price and income support policies, especially of those in rich countries. All forms of farm price and income supports do not equally disrupt trade. Soil conservation and direct payment programs, decoupled from current farm prices and production, have a minor impact on trade. Export subsidies, used especially by the European Union, disrupt markets but are being phased out. The most pernicious government intervention in trade is tariffs and quotas, because they limit market access. This chapter measures impacts on national income of ending trade barriers. It also includes sections on food aid and on domestic agricultural price and income supports.

The case for aiding poor countries rests broadly on (1) humanitarian and (2) developmental grounds. In the following discussion, donations to provide food and health care are classified as humanitarian assistance. Humanitarian assistance is justified as the right thing to do because the recipient is poor and hungry or sick, and regardless of whether the recipient is worthy or whether the donor benefits.

In contrast, assistance to promote economic development is a choice. Ideally, trade and technology transfer and institution building benefit both donor and recipient. An important conclusion from theory and empirical evidence is that "*The major losers from market interventions are the countries that practice them.*"(Tweeten, 1992, p. 279, emphasis in original). Exporters and importers alike gain from freer trade. Neither the United States nor any other country benefits from having more failed, semi-autarkic states such as Haiti, North Korea, or Zimbabwe. Of course, aid for development is unjustified if it is wasted.

The Tortuous Path to Trade Liberalization

Prior to the Doha Round of multilateral international trade negotiations (named after the capital of Qatar, where talks were launched in 2001), liberalization was largely a preoccupation of rich countries led by the European Union and the United States. Motivated by the "mutually assured destruction" of trade and economic prosperity wrought by the protectionism that energized the Great Depression, industrial nations were keen to disarm their trade barriers multilaterally. Eight rounds of multilateral trade negotiations since the 1940s achieved great success. They reduced the world's industrial tariffs on average from forty percent to a nearly insignificant four percent of trade value by 2006. Freer industrial-product trade energized the global economy.

Trade negotiators had much less success reducing barriers to agricultural, textile, apparel, and services trade. In 2001, applied actual tariffs on agricultural commodities and processed foods averaged 16.7 percent, on textiles and clothing averaged 10.2 percent, on manufactured goods averaged 3.5 percent, and on all goods averaged 5.2 percent (table 8.1). According to table 8.1 (Anderson *et al.,* p. 343), import tariffs averaged 2.9 percent in rich countries but 9.9 percent in developing countries in 2001. By 2005, following Uruguay Round implementation, the accession of China to the World Trade Organization, and the addition of ten new members to the European Union, tariffs in developing countries dropped to 8.4 percent—still well above tariffs in rich countries. Tariffs in the lowest-income countries averaged an appalling 15.9 percent in 2001, exceeding tariffs in all other income-grouped countries in each industry classification.

The eighth, or Uruguay Round, of multilateral trade negotiations, completed in 1994, accomplished very little trade liberalization either in rich or poor countries. The round's most important contribution was converting to tariffs many nontariff trade barriers, such as quotas and sanitary and phytosanitary (plant health) regulations. Tariffs reductions are easier to negotiate downward and police than are a cacophony of discordant nontariff barriers, hence the Uruguay Round essentially set the stage for the liberalization of world trade in the Doha "development" Round of multilateral trade negotiations. Dispute settlement and rule enforcement procedures originating in the Uruguay Round also set the stage for the policing of subsequent agreements.

Table 8.1. Import-Weighted Average Applied Tariffs, by Sector and Region, 2001

Importing region	Agriculture, processed food	Textiles, clothing	Other manufacturing	All goods
	(Percent)			
High-income countries	16.0	7.5	1.3	2.9
Developing countries	17.7	17.0	8.3	9.9
(As of 2005[1])	(14.2)	(14.3)	(7.1)	(8.4)
Middle income	16.5	16.8	7.3	8.9
Low income	22.2	17.9	14.5	15.9
Developing countries				
East Asia and Pacific	26.3	17.8	8.6	10.5
(China)	37.6	19.4	11.3	13.6
South Asia	33.9	20.1	22.2	23.5
Europe and Central Asia	14.8	10.7	4.1	6.0
Middle East and N. Africa	14.1	27.1	7.2	9.8
Sub-Saharan Africa	18.2	23.7	10.5	12.6
Latin Amer. and Caribbean	10.3	11.3	7.1	7.7
World total	16.7	10.2	3.5	5.2

Source: Anderson et al., p. 343.

[1]Numbers in parenthesis are averages as of 2005 following accessions including China to the World Trade Organization, the Uruguay Round implementation, the end of the Multifiber Arrangement and attendant textile quotas, and enlargement of the European Union to 25 members.

The Uruguay Round was characterized by much "dirty tariffication," replacing nontariff barriers by tariffs that were bound (with maximums set by World Trade Organization negotiations) at high levels that distort trade as much or more than the nontariff barriers they replaced. By 2005, agricultural tariffs averaged sixty-two percent and textile and apparel tariffs averaged twelve percent (Cline, p. 23). Actual applied tariffs were much lower, as observed in table 8.1. Of note is that a major negotiated reduction in *bound* tariffs in the Doha Round might only take up overhang, or slack. Countries could reduce bound tariffs considerably without reducing their *applied* tariffs and without thereby liberalizing trade.

Poor countries in multilateral trade negotiations were so busy seeking protection for their producers from imports and so engrossed in seeking trade-opening concessions into rich country markets that they overlooked the economic plague that their own protectionist trade policies inflicted on their people. It is tragic that the highest tariffs in the world in 2001 were in the region of South Asia, with historically the largest numbers of people experiencing poverty and chronic hunger (table 8.1). And the second largest tariff rates in 2001 were in sub-Saharan Africa—the region destined in the future to have the greatest numbers of poor and underfed people. Given that agriculture is the largest single source of income and employment in poor countries, it is tragic that eight rounds of multilateral agreements to reduce trade barriers have mostly bypassed poor countries where most people make their meager living in farming.

Anderson and Martin (pp. 12–13), summarizing data from various analysts, provide two important conclusions regarding projected free-trade welfare (income) gains in 2015 over year 2001: (1) sixty-three percent of global welfare gains come from agriculture, compared to only fourteen percent from textiles and clothing and twenty-three percent from other merchandise; and (2) ninety-three percent of global welfare gains in agriculture come from market access, such as the removal of import tariffs and quotas, compared to only two percent of gains from removing export subsidies (widely used by the European Union) and five percent from ending domestic supports such as direct payments, used extensively by the United States. The case for agricultural trade reform is clear.

Development begins but does not end with agriculture. Given that lack of buying power is the principal impediment to food and health security in poor countries, we must look for industries in addition to agriculture to generate income in these countries. The structure of international trade has undergone a radical transformation in recent decades, and this transformation is most notable for developing countries. In 1965, agriculture accounted for forty-five percent and manufacturing for only twenty-four percent of exports from poor countries (Hertel *et al.,* p. 119). By 2000, the agricultural export share had fallen to ten percent and the manufacturing share had increased to seventy-five percent. Thus, to generate more earnings from agriculture and manufacturing, poor countries must have broad access to markets in rich and poor countries alike. And trade is a two-way street: poor countries will need to open their protected markets for their own benefit as well as to ensure that richer countries will continue to open theirs.

Calling the Doha Round officially the "Doha Development Agenda" perhaps was a moment of hubris, generating unwarranted expectations by poor countries for access to the markets of rich countries. Dominating the numbers of the 149 countries participating in the Doha Round, poor countries made themselves heard early as international leaders assembled in Seattle in late 1999 to organize the new round of multilateral trade negotiations. The meeting disbanded in disarray, in no small part because developing countries opposed environmental and social (labor) provisions (dictating minimum standards of all signatories to a trade agreement) being promoted for the WTO by the United States and the European Union. Poor countries, having little more than cheap labor to attract foreign direct investment and jobs for their workers, opposed the loss of that advantage. A typical wage in China, $140 per month for a textile plant worker, may not appear to be an acceptable, living wage to a Western labor union member but is a godsend to the Chinese laborer whose alternative is a job at half that wage.

The Dhaka Declaration of 2003 outlined the objectives of thirty-nine less-developed countries (LDCs) for the Doha Round. The declaration called for free and secure access of LDCs to markets in more developed countries and an end to export subsidies. The declaration also called for an end to the anti-dumping, countervailing, and safeguard measures frequently invoked by rich countries to limit imports from poorer countries.[28] The declaration also called for more technical and financial assistance to LDCs, for freer movement of labor among countries, and for permission of LDCs to protect their markets from international competition until their "infant" industry becomes more globally competitive.

The Doha Round suffered another severe setback in September 2003, when a meeting of world trade ministers in Cancun, Mexico broke up. The breakup followed the rejection by a group of twenty developing countries with a strong interest in agricultural markets (the so called G20, led by Brazil and India) of a vague and modest proposal from the European Union and the United States to reform their agricultural policies by cutting tariffs, export subsidies, and trade-distorting domestic agricultural subsidies. The poor-country/rich-country conflict was further exacerbated when poor countries of the African Sahel

---

28 Countervailing and safeguard measures "temporarily" protect financially troubled domestic industries from imports (usually from developing countries) until the industries have a chance to recover.

complained strongly about unfair competition from subsidized U.S. cotton producers. In 2004, a World Trade Organization panel ruled for Brazil, charging that the United States'"Step 2" subsidies on American cotton violated WTO rules. Four African cotton producers, namely Benin, Burkina Faso, Chad, and Mali, have incurred losses averaging nearly $100 million annually since 2001 due to U.S. policies—according to the Food and Agricultural Policy Research Institute (see Good, p. 1).

Poor countries complain that they often are excluded from regional free trade agreements that include a rich country. Furthermore, extant preferential trade arrangements that include rich and poor countries often omit the exports of developing countries that count most—agricultural commodities, processed foods, and labor-intensive manufactured products. In 2001, tariffs by developed countries on the labor-intensive industrial exports prominent from developing countries averaged double or triple the rich-country average industrial rate of four percent (Hertel *et al.,* p. 123). These labor-intensive industrial goods are of special importance; along with agricultural commodities, they constitute nearly three-quarters of exports from developing countries.

Doha Round trade negotiations were suspended indefinitely July 24, 2006 in a flurry of finger pointing blame for the failure. No one country was to blame but one industry was to blame—agriculture. The United States offered to reduce its trade distorting farm subsidies from the existing $19.1 billion to $7.6 billion. That was the maximum offer politically powerful U.S. farm interests would accept but the European Union and other countries were unwilling to offer market access to make even that proposal politically acceptable. The Doha Round may not be revived for years because essential U.S. Trade Negotiating Authority (featuring an up or down vote of congressional approval without amendments) expires in July 2007 and may not be revived by a free-trade averse new Congress.

It is apparent that prominent issues in global food and fiber trade upset rich and poor countries alike. Still, some helpful trade provisions already exist for poor countries. (Ironically, the reluctance of poor countries to abandon these historic preferential provisions, especially those protecting local manufacturing, contributed to delays in Doha Round negotiations.) In 1971, the General Agreement on Tariffs and Trade (predecessor to the World Trade Organization) adopted a waiver authorizing rich countries to give unilateral tariff preferences to poor countries for ten years without violating the WTO's "most-favored-nation" principle. That principle holds that the most generous trade restrictions given to any one nation must be extended to all. Under the Generalized System of Tariff Preferences established by the Trade Act of 1974, the United States quickly eliminated duties on over 2,700 items imported from developing countries. The Lomé Convention initiated in 1975 and the "Everything but Arms" policy originating in 2001 gave numerous low-income countries preferential access to European Union markets. The end in 2005 to quotas on clothing and textile imports into rich countries also provides major benefits to poor countries.[29]

The African Growth and Opportunity Act (AGOA, signed into law by President George Bush on May 18, 2000) granted duty-free access to the U.S. market for substantially all products of thirty-seven AGOA-eligible countries. The act, extended in June 2004, continues to probe ways to increase trade and investment between the United States and sub-Saharan Africa. Sub-Saharan Africa also is a principal target of the United Nations' Millennium Development Goal, which pledged to reduce by half the number of people who suffer from hunger and poverty by the year 2015. G8 (seven rich countries plus Russia) leaders meeting in Scotland in mid-2005 pledged to increase development aid by $50 billion and agreed to an ambitious debt cancellation package for heavily indebted poor countries. In referring to the ongoing Doha Round of trade negotiations, President George Bush and other leaders of rich countries stated in Scotland, "We are committed to eliminating all forms of agricultural export subsidies." However, there is little indication that in fact either rich or poor nations are willing to give up their considerable protection of agricultural markets. Progress in opening markets will be slow and grudging.

Estimating Gains from Freer Trade

Opening markets in rich and poor countries to trade and investment is arguably the single most important policy instrument in fostering international development. Poor countries have a comparative advantage in exporting labor-intensive products produced by lower-income, lower-skilled workers. The export of labor-intensive manufactured goods from poor countries raises income in their farm and non-farm sectors as underemployed agricultural workers move to better-paying jobs in export industries; thus, free trade is pro-poor.

Table 8.1 earlier summarized the degree of protection from markets, as evidenced by tariff rates in selected countries and regions. Table 8.2 shows additions to real income with an end to the tariffs shown in table 8.1. The results

29 Some poor countries have been made worse off because low-cost Chinese producers have captured an inordinate share of the new rich-country market at the expense of other developing countries. The benefits have been restrained by safeguard agreements with China to slow exports to protect textile and clothing production jobs in the United States and the European Union.

are from the World Bank's dynamic computable general equilibrium model, which accounts for the feedback of freer trade in sectors to overall national saving, investment, and capital accumulation. Exposure to international markets imparts dynamism to domestic markets, raising productivity. Because that productivity effect is not easily measured and hence is not included in table 8.1 results, the model may underestimate the gains from freer trade.

Table 8.2. Impacts on Total Real Income and on Agricultural Exports and Agricultural Output from Full Trade Liberalization by 2015 over 2001 Baseline

Country/region	Total real income		Agri. exports	Agri. output
	(Bil. U.S.2001$)	(% incr.)	(Bil. U.S.2001$)	
High-income countries	201.6	0.6	115.8	-204.7
EU25 and EFTA	65.2	0.6	21.7	-185.8
United States	16.1	0.1	18.4	30.7
Japan	54.6	1.1	2.8	-91.7
S. Korea and Taiwan	44.6	3.5	33.2	-0.4
Developing countries	141.5	1.2	191.9	66.8
Middle income	69.5	0.8	156.1	88.2
Low income	16.2	0.8	35.8	-21.4
East Asia & Pacific	23.5	0.7	34.8	5.2
South Asia	4.5	0.4	8.9	-27.8
Europe & Cent. Asia	7.0	0.7	14.2	-30.0
Middle E. & N. A.	14.0	1.2	13.2	-7.8
Sub-Saharan Africa	4.8	1.1	16.4	2.6
Latin Am. & Carib.	28.7	1.0	96.3	121.8
World total	287.3	0.7	307.7	-137.8

Source: Anderson *et al.*, pp. 346, 351, and 352.

The free trade assumed in table 8.2 assumes nearly undistorted domestic commodity markets, eliminating export subsidies, import quotas, antidumping duties, and "coupled" (to production or market price) price and income supports. The model predicts income with and without liberalization each year from 2001 to 2015. Results for liberalization include the reduction of trade barriers beyond 2001 to which countries have committed themselves. Results in table 8.2 show a snapshot of the difference in 2015 alone between income with and without trade liberalization assumed to begin in 2001. Keep in mind that given the complexity of world trade and the ways that economies operate across the world, no model of trade is exact.

Based on data presented earlier in this chapter, of concern is whether ending the expensive, trade-distorting aspects of farm commodity programs in rich countries provides more benefits than ending the high tariffs characterizing poor countries. Results in table 8.2 provide some clues:

- Worldwide economic benefits of freer trade are enormous: $287 billion in 2015, according to table 8.2. Annual benefits grow with time, being below $287 billion annually before 2015 and above that level after 2015. Arbitrarily assuming an average of $287 billion annually in perpetuity and discounting at a 5 percent rate, the present value of all future benefits is $5.7 trillion!
- Global income benefits are greater in high-income countries ($201.6 billion) than in developing countries ($141.5 billion) in *absolute* value in 2015, because rich countries' economies are large and have had major trade interventions. In *relative* terms, however, developing countries gain twice as much as high-income countries; that is, in 2015, national income in developing countries is up 1.2 percent, but in high-income countries, it is up only 0.6 percent with liberalization.
- Agricultural trade, as measured by exports, is $308 billion greater in 2015 due to trade liberalization (table 8.2). Gains in middle-income countries such as Brazil and Argentina in Latin America and the Caribbean region are especially large.
- Without market distortions, world agricultural output falls by $138 billion. As expected, the cutbacks in production are in regions such as Western Europe and in countries such as Japan that have used subsidies to induce farm commodity production at costs and prices well in excess of what the commodities are worth, as measured by world prices.
- Anderson *et al.* (p. 349) estimate that LDC's share of global agricultural output goes from seventy percent in 2001 to seventy-five percent

in 2015. With trade liberalization, LDC's share of agricultural exports goes from forty-seven percent to sixty-two percent in the same period. Free trade turns developing countries from net agricultural importers who benefit from dumping by rich countries that lower food prices (consumers gain more than farmers lose) to net exporters who gain from higher agricultural-product prices.

An earlier World Bank study (2004, chapter 1) contained additional insights. The benefits of liberalizing manufactured-goods trade in rich countries are modest for high-income and low-income countries. The reason is that manufactured-goods tariffs in rich countries are already low, as noted in table 8.1. It follows that rich countries are not able to offer much income benefit to poor countries by lowering manufactured-goods tariffs. Global income gains are greater for liberalizing international trade in agriculture than in manufactured goods.

More of the economic gain from liberalizing trade in poor countries accrues to poor countries than to rich countries. More of the economic gain from liberalizing trade in high-income countries accrues to these rich countries rather than to poor countries. The World Bank results highlight the importance of reducing trade barriers in all countries. The results reaffirm the conclusion that the countries that most distort trade also pay the highest cost in lost income from protectionism.

Counted over several years, the numbers removed from poverty are large from trade liberalization. The World Bank study (Anderson *et al.*, p. 381) underlying tables 8.1 and 8.2 estimates that abject poverty would afflict thirty-two million fewer persons, a five-percent drop of overall numbers, in 2015 due to free trade. Poverty in Africa is estimated to fall relatively more: six percent by 2015, due to free trade. William Cline (p. 22) contends that free trade could lift an estimated 500 million persons out of poverty over fifteen years, or thirty-three million per year, most of them in poor countries. He estimates that developing countries could gain an estimated $200 billion of income annually from trade liberalization, half of that attributed to the removal of barriers to their exports to industrial countries. These and numbers in table 8.2 dwarf the $90 billion of official development assistance provided annually to poor countries by rich-country governments and quasi-government agencies such as the World Bank.

The Congressional Budget Office (CBO, December 2005, p. 3), summarizing numerous studies of gains from trade liberalization, places the World Bank numbers in table 8.2 at the upper bound of alternative estimates of potential gains. Still, the 2005 CBO summary concludes that agricultural trade distortions account for two-thirds of the costs of all policies that distort global merchandise trade. The CBO further concludes that agricultural-product tariffs and import quotas (as opposed to domestic subsidies, export subsidies, and production controls) account for eighty to ninety percent of the national income lost because of agricultural policies. East Asian food importers (such as Japan and South Korea) and the European Union especially rely on the most trade-distorting types of policies.

The foregoing numbers, albeit inexact, seriously challenge the wisdom of the bargaining stance of poor countries in the Doha Round of multilateral trade negotiations. Several poor countries have threatened to scuttle negotiations if rich countries do not first commit to eliminating or at least sharply reducing their trade-distorting policies. At the same time, poor countries would retain their own market protections.

Poor countries have every right to ask for an end to the trade-distorting policies of rich countries, but poor countries "cut off their nose to spite their face" when they hold multilateral trade liberalization hostage to ending trade distortions by rich countries. Data from the World Bank (chapter 1) indicate that poor countries would benefit hugely from unilaterally ending their own trade distortions, even if rich countries persist in distorting trade. Better yet, rich and poor countries will benefit by jointly ending all trade-distorting policies.

Developing countries could especially benefit from the removal of tariffs and subsidies used by rich countries to protect their sugar, cotton, and rice producers. Anderson *et al.* (p. 354) estimate that liberalization of all merchandise trade would reduce rich-country self-sufficiency (the ratio of domestic production to consumption) by 2015 (compared to 2001) from ninety-eight to ninety-three percent for agriculture and food, seventy-four to seventy percent for textiles and apparel, and no change from ninety-eight percent for manufacturing. But self-sufficiency in rice would fall from ninety-seven percent to forty-nine percent and in sugar from ninety-two to forty-seven percent. With liberalization, by 2015, the share of the world's cotton exports accounted for by developing countries is predicted to rise to 85 percent from 56 percent (Anderson *et al.*, p. 352). Producers in rich countries will exert much political power to resist such losses in markets for rice, sugar, and cotton. Loss of self sufficiency in these commodities in rich countries in no way will threaten food security, although America and other rich-country producers will make that claim in order to retain market distortions.

Prodded by the World Trade Organization, the United States ended cotton export and domestic mill use (so-called Step 2) subsidies in August 2006, the European Union has signaled willingness to end export subsidies and shift from commodity price supports to direct payments, and the Australians and

Canadians may terminate their wheat boards, which have been faulted for practicing price discrimination. A major achievement would be to end the practice in rich countries of placing higher duties on imports of processed than of raw materials—a practice that has retarded the development of food processing industries and employment in poor countries.

Such reform will not necessarily benefit Africa. An end to restraints on clothing and textile imports into rich countries in January 2005 mainly benefited China. Other poor countries, formerly operating under quotas giving their textiles and clothing preferential access to developed country markets, had not developed the efficiency required to compete with China in liberalized world markets. This illustrates the point that most poor countries will need more than concessions from rich countries to reap the full benefits of freer trade. Poor countries require comprehensive standard-model domestic policies to be prosperous and competitive in world markets.

Why Trade Distortions Persist

If trade barriers serve neither rich nor poor countries, why do these barriers persist and—at times—grow? The well-known answer lies in the political system. Typically, freer trade benefits millions of consumers and hurts a few producers. Although overall economic gains to consumers far outweigh losses to producers, the benefits per consumer are less than the loss per producer. Of course, some producers will benefit handsomely from freer trade, but they are not a vocal free-trade lobby, because markets do not reveal who are the gainers until trade is freed. In the political arena, millions of benefiting consumers, not one of whom finds it worthwhile to organize and lobby for freer trade, are no match for a few determined big-producer and labor-union losers.

An obvious solution, collective action by consumers to overwhelm the producer lobby and obtain free trade, suffers from the "free rider" problem. Each consumer refrains from paying the price of political involvement, reckoning to get a free ride by participating in the free trade made possible by those consumers who do band together in paying dues and spending time lobbying to achieve free trade for all. Collective action by consumers is thwarted, because every consumer wants to be a free rider.

Nowhere is political paralysis in search of open trade more apparent than in agriculture. A few French farmers who lose from free trade threaten to veto a multilateral world freer trade agreement worth hundreds of billions of dollars to rich and poor nations alike. The European Union, cowed by the threatened veto by France of a generous trade liberalization proposal, offers too modest a farm-product access proposal to entice developing countries to give up their considerable protection of domestic markets for industrial products. A successful Doha Round also remains elusive, because although the United States would benefit handsomely from freer trade, a relatively few high-income U.S. farmers who receive the lion's share of farm commodity subsidies demand greater access to European markets than the EU is willing to offer. To paraphrase Winston Churchill, never have so few farmers gained so much at so great loss to so many poorer consumers and taxpayers at home and abroad. Freer trade comes slowly and grudgingly indeed, despite compelling evidence of its benefits.

The inability of the Doha Round of multilateral trade negotiations to deliver much of the potential gains from trade shown in table 8.1 causes more nations to sign bilateral and regional free-trade agreements; however, bilateral and regional agreements are only partial substitutes for global free trade. In August 2005, President George Bush signed the U.S.-Central American Free Trade Agreement, or CAFTA, with Costa Rica, El Salvador, Guatemala, Honduras, Nicaragua, and the Dominican Republic, after a bitter fight with Congress over the direction of American trade policy. The free-trade pact narrowly won passage in the House of Representatives (in a 217 to 215 vote) following a huge lobbying and "horse trading" blitz by Bush and his top aides. The agreement eliminates tariffs on billions of dollars of U.S. exports to Central America and the Dominican Republic. It also locks in the duty-free status and expands the access those countries already have to U.S. markets. The narrow margin of support in Congress for a very modest-sized agreement bodes ill for approval of the far more ambitious proposed Free Trade Area of the Americas (encompassing the Western Hemisphere) and the Doha Round (encompassing the 149 countries in the World Trade Organization).

Outsourcing

Few globalization topics have generated more negative publicity than the outsourcing of service jobs in rich countries to poor countries. The conventional wisdom among many vocal groups in the United States is that the outsourcing of jobs in telemarketing and information technology to India and elsewhere has generated unemployment at home.

Outsourcing, like other forms of trade, is a two-way street. The United States is a major net exporter of business services, in contrast to being a massive net importer of goods. Amiti and Wei (p. 39) report that in 2003, the U.S. net surplus in outsourcing was $18 billion, second only to the United Kingdom.

The authors went on to conclude, "In the final analysis, outsourcing does not lead to net job losses." They find that cost-cutting by the outsourcing of jobs allows domestic firms to form, grow, and hire domestic workers in higher-skill, higher-pay occupations.

Amiti and Wei noted that most service trade is among more developed nations. Poor countries are net importers of services. Given the need for more jobs and earnings in poor countries, attention is warranted on how to generate more service jobs there to earn additional income from domestic and foreign sources.

Trade or Aid for Development

Tables 8.3, 8.4, and 8.5 help us to see the relationship of trade and foreign aid to economic development. Trade openness in table 8.3 is exports plus imports as a percent of gross domestic product (GDP) by major region and for China. China's openness was only 12 percent in 1980, but increased to 48 percent in 2000. No region of the world came close to the quadrupling of trade opening of China in the twenty years from 1980 to 2000. (It should be remembered that a larger country tends to be more self-contained in its diversity of domestic production and resources; hence openness normally will be larger for a small country or region than for a large country or region.) The *change* in trade openness is of particular interest. Whereas China quadrupled its openness, sub-Saharan Africa tied with East Asia (excluding China) for the least opening of trade.

Table 8.3. Trade Openness (Exports+Imports as Percent of GDP)

Country/region	1980	1990	2000	% change, 1980–2000
China	12	25	48	300
East Asia (excluding China)	92	85	113	23
Latin America	32	33	43	34
South Asia	19	20	32	68
Southeast Asia	61	66	96	57
Sub-Saharan Africa (excl. South Africa)	49	51	61	24

Source: PENN World Tables presented by Teal, p. 24

It is difficult to find a positive link between foreign aid and subsequent economic progress, even among countries and regions starting from similar per capita income (see also Easterly, chapter 2). Foreign aid per capita was highest and rising for SSA among regions from 1980 to 1995 (table 8.4). Aid to China was miniscule. Aid to regions other than sub-Saharan Africa was too low to have much impact on economic development, but served humanitarian purposes at crucial times.

Table 8.4. Foreign Aid per Capita in Constant 1996 U.S. Dollars

Country/region	1980	1990	1995	% change, 1980–1995
China	0.07	0.85	0.46	557
East Asia (excluding China)	3.05	7.44	0.05	-98
Latin America	3.37	5.42	3.59	7
South Asia	6.46	4.65	3.11	-52
Southeast Asia	4.96	8.67	4.74	-4
Sub-Saharan Africa (excl. South Africa)	18.3	32.64	30.23	65

Source: PENN World Tables presented by Teal, p. 24

Per capita income data in table 8.5 show that China began with the lowest income, but more than doubled its income between 1980 and 2000. South Asia's per capita income, only $1,146 in 1980, more than doubled to $2,346 in 2000. Both of these entities had lower income than sub-Saharan Africa in 1980. Africa's income increased only 10 percent from 1980 to 2000. Because of economic stagnation in SSA, income in China and other parts of Asia had far outpaced that of SSA by 2000. Income gains were also disappointing in Latin America. Fortunately, Latin America, on average, had achieved middle-income status by 1980 and faced less severe poverty than SSA.

The economic success of Asia was apparent in opening to trade and falling foreign aid (tables 8.3–8.5). No doubt trade is an effect as well as a cause of economic progress. But a lesson of the foregoing tables is that even very poor countries and poor regions can experience explosive economic progress without much foreign aid if they make use of international markets and if people and leaders are committed to success.

Table 8.5. Income (GDP) per Capita in Constant 1996 U.S. Dollars

Country/region	1980	1990	2000	% change, 1980–2000
China	1,069	1,787	3,747	251
East Asia (excluding China)	5,748	11,156	17,236	200
Latin America	6,431	5,929	7,074	10
South Asia	1,146	1,645	2,346	105
Southeast Asia	2,559	3,576	4,520	77
Sub-Saharan Africa (excl. South Africa)	1,499	1,510	1,646	10

Source: PENN World Tables presented by Teal, p. 24

Reforming Farm Policy

Among all goods industries, agriculture is most protected by governments and the most egregious violator of the standard model. Market interventions in agriculture are justified in the name of food self-sufficiency and preserving family farms. Farm commodity prices held above world levels in domestic markets must be protected from imports by quotas and tariffs. High-support prices and subsidies expand domestic production, crowding out food imports or dumping surpluses in foreign markets. Rich countries hurt poor countries more by failure to open their markets than by subsidizing exports. In fact, aside from exceptions such as Argentina, Brazil, and Thailand, export subsidies by rich countries tend to benefit poor countries, because consumers gain more than producers lose from "dumping" of temperate-zone foods on international markets.

A common pattern is for rich nations to subsidize agriculture and poor nations to tax agriculture. Domestic farm economic supports of all types, including for conservation and research, averaged $87 billion in the EU, $71 billion in the United States, and $29 billion in Japan annually from 1998 to 2001 (CBO, August 2005, p. 22). These three large spenders accounted for 84 percent of global economic support for agriculture. "Only" $75 billion of the $222 billion, or 34 percent of global support, was considered to be production- and trade-distorting. The remainder was direct payments, outlays for conservation and research, and the like, which minimally distorted global markets.

Together, the United States, the EU, and Japan accounted for 87 percent of the trade-distorting outlays, with the principal culprit being the EU. Only one-fifth of U.S. and Japanese farm supports were trade-distorting, versus half in the EU. Japanese farmers depended on the government for 56 percent of their gross farm receipts in 2004 (CBO, August 2005, p. 47). This was well in excess of the 33 percent by EU farmers and the 18 percent share by U.S. farmers of their gross receipts from government.

In rich countries in 2004, government supports accounted for 75 percent of receipts from rice and 58 percent from sugar. Data are not available for cotton, but it also is heavily subsidized, especially by the United States. Poor countries have a comparative advantage in these tropical or subtropical commodities. To compete, rich countries heavily subsidize these commodities. The United States and the EU are making major reforms so that their farm supports will less distort markets.[30]

The EU and the United States have shifted much of the support for agriculture from price and export subsidies to direct payments in recent years. Payments are based on historic rather than on current area and yield, hence are said to be "decoupled" from incentives to distort production and export markets; however, no program is fully decoupled (Tweeten 2002, pp. 9–14). Nearly all farmers have capital and credit constraints. Some of the income and financial credit made available by "decoupled" lump-sum payments is spent on production inputs that raise output. The historic crop area and yield used to determine payments are updated periodically, thus operators are wise to maintain their production, and with it, their payment base. Still, direct payments distort markets less than do other means of government farm-income support. Rich and poor countries would be well served if multilateral global trade negotiations made direct payments (decoupled from current production and prices) the only acceptable farm-income support.

It is difficult to justify even direct payments except in a short to intermediate run transition program. The $115 billion to $222 billion that rich countries

---

30   In 2003, the European Union reformed its Common Agricultural Policy, replacing a plethora of price supports with a Single Farm Payment scheme. Lower price supports reduced the need for export subsidies. Direct payments were at least somewhat decoupled from current market prices and output, hence they distorted incentives less than previous programs. Payment was contingent on farmers following socially desirable practices for public and animal health and for land management. Price support dropped from eighty percent above world market prices in the 1980s to one-third above world prices. Overall subsidies fell from two-fifths of farm receipts in the 1980s to one-third of receipts in 2004. Requirements for farmers to divert land from crop production also reduced dumping in international markets.

spend on farm-income support each year have higher returns elsewhere. The payments are inefficient (reducing national income) and inequitable (transfers to persons of high income and wealth). The benefits of government programs raise rents and are capitalized into land values. The benefits are quickly lost by renters and by new landowners paying inflated land prices. Landowners, who probably are wealthier than farm operators or taxpayers, receive the monetary gains from inflated rents and land values. Because the benefits of subsidies accrue to landowners and not to farm operators, farm support programs do not raise farm operator income, except in the short to intermediate run.

Meanwhile, inflated land prices and rents generate a cash-flow squeeze, deterring the entry of young, new farm operators. Effective political proposals for payment limitations—confining subsidies to small, low-income family farms—consistently have been rejected by policymakers. "Green payments" for preservation of the environment can be justified as public goods, but will not effectively target either farm income or environmental problems if such payments are made a "Trojan horse" to lift farm income.

A useful rule of thumb for governments of poor countries is to pursue policies that raise rather than lower real (externality corrected) national income. Taxes on farm exports are collectable and thus expedient—but pernicious, because they are paid by domestic producers rather than by rich foreign consumers. Governments of poor countries supporting farm prices and incomes impose undue burdens on their taxpayers and consumers.

Some poor countries impose pan-seasonal and pan-territorial pricing. Pan-territorial pricing offers the same price to producers in all regions of a country. Such uniform pricing sounds fair but is inefficient. It provides the same encouragement to producers near or far from markets. A well-functioning market provides the same price, *less transportation cost* to producers; hence producers near markets get higher effective prices and produce more. Producing close to markets conserves resources.

Pan-seasonal pricing—paying the same price each season—is inefficient, because it provides the same encouragement to market when demand is great or small. A well-functioning market provides higher prices to encourage farmers to store commodities and deliver them when demand is high and supply is low.

What public policies are appropriate for farmers? As outlined in chapter 4, the appropriate role of government is to provide public goods. Farm commodities are market goods, not public goods; thus markets, for the most part, work well in agriculture to determine what, when, where, and how to produce (Tweeten 2002, pp. 4–25). The public sector can assist markets by helping with price reporting, outlook information, grades, standards, basic research, education, infrastructure, and environmental protection. That is a tall order. Poor countries must begin such programs at modest levels indeed, and it is inappropriate for them to detract from such efforts by supplying national-income-reducing farm subsidies, price supports, and controls. A food safety net is appropriate in dire circumstances, but there is no justification for it being a "farm" program available only to people in agriculture.

Farmers in rich and poor countries alike face much instability; however, instability is not a prima facie case for government intervention. The Las Vegas gambler, futures market speculator, and Wall Street plunger are taxed, not subsidized. Farmers in rich countries have income and access to institutions such as savings, insurance, futures and options markets, outlook expertise, and storage to deal with risk in a manner consistent with the standard model. Farmers perform well indeed in maintaining consumption from year to year in the face of unstable production. Such self-insurance behavior helps to explain why farmers worldwide do not appear to be very risk-averse. Nowhere in the world are farmers willing to pay for all-purpose crop or revenue insurance—unless, of course, it is heavily subsidized by taxpayers.

Farmers in poor countries have fewer tools than do farmers in rich countries to cope with uncertainty, and the government is inevitably called upon for help. Poor countries often exhaust budgets supporting farm prices. When funding stops, the drop in prices destabilizes the very markets that the government was trying to stabilize.

International trade is the cheapest source of buffer stocks for small, poor countries to use to stabilize domestic food markets and prices. Nonetheless, some provision may be needed for modest domestic buffer stocks, to provide food until imports arrive after local crops fail. One low-cost option used by several countries is for government to stabilize domestic food prices with a variable import duty (see Knutson and Nash, p. 4). The procedure is to tax food imports, in years of domestic food abundance, by the shortfall of the current domestic price below the (say) five-year moving average world price. The tax is placed in a stabilization fund and used to subsidize the excess of the current domestic price over the moving average world price, in years of short domestic food supply.

To simplify administration, the above interventions would apply to only a major staple and would not take place until the current price deviates (say) 20 percent or more from the moving average price of the commodity being stabilized. A reverse procedure would be used for exports. The procedure would help stabilize domestic prices at low net cost, but it is not recommended unless a government feels compelled to "do something." Even this modest program tends to unduly challenge the integrity and administrative expertise of many poor countries.

Foreign Direct Investment

Foreign direct investment complements trade to foster economic progress. Poor countries adopting standard-model policies speed economic growth by attracting foreign direct investment (FDI) from rich countries. In theory, the high ratio of labor and natural resources to capital in developing countries should create high returns to capital and attract massive domestic and foreign private investment. Low-cost labor attracts FDI. In reality, aside from exceptions such as China in recent years, poor countries have pursued policies and politics keeping capital returns low and repelling FDI.

Foreign direct investment fluctuates considerably from year to year due to world business conditions, and it fell from $1.4 trillion in 2000 to $560 billion in 2003 (data from UNCTAD, reported in "Foreign Direct Investment," p. 122). Whatever the total, FDI originates largely in rich countries, and approximately four-fifths of it flows to rich countries.

Even the modest share of FDI going to developing countries dwarfed the $90 billion of official development assistance provided by the public sectors of developed countries to developing countries in 2003 (IMF, p. 14). Of the ODA, $60 billion was bilateral aid from one country to another; $20 billion was through multilateral agencies, such as the World Bank, the International Monetary Fund, and the United Nations; and nearly $10 billion was from nongovernment organizations, such as religious groups. Among regions, sub-Saharan Africa was the dominant aid recipient, receiving over $16 billion per year, or thirty-five dollars per capita, for the 2000–2003 period. In that same period, South Asia and Central Asia received $7 billion each year, although as shown in table 1.1, undernutrition is much more extensive in Asia.

Sound economic policies in poor countries could attract massive FDI to alleviate poverty and the ills that attend it. Foreign direct investment, multinational corporate activity, and trade are inseparable. This volume repeatedly emphasizes the importance of multinational firms to the development of poor countries. Without trade, multinational firms cannot recover their investments.

Food and Other Humanitarian Aid

Food aid supplements commercial trade and foreign investment to improve well-being in poor countries. Cereal food aid, the major form of international food aid, has averaged approximately twelve million tons per year since the mid-1980s (figure 8.1). Food aid has saved the lives of many hungry people, although its volume is dwarfed by commercial grain exports, annually averaging over 230 million tons in recent years.

Food aid has been criticized for being poorly managed and for being a disguised export subsidy for building commercial markets in defiance of the spirit of World Trade Organization rules. *For example, the* U.S. Public Law 480 Title I program dating back to 1954 provides concessional loans to purchasers of U.S. agriculture commodities in developing countries *as a form of export promotion.* Other U.S. export subsidy programs guarantee the repayment of loans extended to purchasers of American farm exports, thereby reducing interest rates.

**Figure 8.1. Targeted and Program Cereal Food Aid
1978 - 2000**

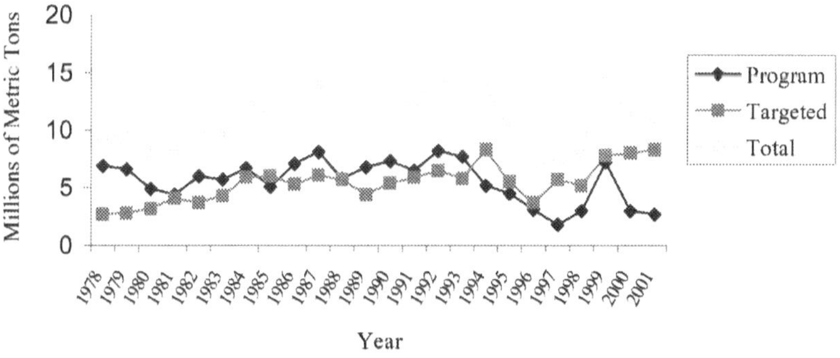

Source: World Food Program

At issue is the place of food aid in the world food system. To address this issue, it is useful to consider the various types of food aid. Aid may be targeted or nontargeted food assistance (figure 8.1). Targeted food aid for humanitarian purposes is distributed to hungry people mostly by nongovernment organizations (NGOs) for little or no charge, or targeted food aid may be used to promote development through food-for-work or school feeding programs in developing countries. Nontargeted or "program" food aid is given to poor countries to market commercially, and the receipts are used to fund agricultural research, cooperatives, or other development programs. These official classifications boil down to essentially two aid categories—humanitarian assistance given to people to alleviate transitory lack of food, and development assistance to promote economic progress. The case for humanitarian food aid is much stronger than the case for development food aid.

Because affluent nations cannot remain idle while people starve, there is little controversy regarding the case for humanitarian aid donated to feed the hungry, regardless of their ability to pay. The proper form and method of aid is controversial. Given that food is often available even in regions of famine, it may be argued that the basic problem is lack of buying power, which would best be addressed by giving vouchers that can be redeemed to purchase food, kerosene, soap, medicine, or other high-priority needs. A problem with giving food from donors' stocks rather than giving vouchers is that it takes four to five months to send food from industrial nations to Africa. The food crisis may be over by the time food arrives. Meanwhile, people have starved. The food aid may be whatever is in surplus (*e.g.*, California raisins in 2003) rather than what recipients need and find palatable.[31]

Another shortcoming of food assistance is that free or concessional food imports added to commercial food imports lower food prices in recipient countries, thereby diminishing incentives for local farmers to expand or store food production. An option is to provide food assistance only to food-importing countries. That way, donations will save aid recipients' foreign exchange and only replace commercial food imports, without affecting local prices. The dilemma is that only "additional" aid increases consumption in poor coun-

31 Sometimes recipient governments act foolishly toward food aid. Zambia and Zimbabwe turned down transgenic corn donated by the United States for their starving people. The governments contended that such corn was unsafe to eat (although millions of people and animals have consumed it for years without ill effects), could transfer genes to local corn varieties (not if ground into meal), or might destroy exports of corn-fed livestock products to the transgenic-gene-averse European Union. *A World Trade Organization dispute settlement panel ruled on February 7, 2006 that the European Union had illegally banned some genetically modified crops.* That finding against the EU sends an important warning to other parts of the world—particularly nations in Africa and Asia—against following the Europeans in banning genetically modified crops. The case was launched in 2003 by the United States, Canada, and Argentina, then the world's biggest growers and exporters of genetically modified crops.

tries, but the farm lobby in donor countries, providing critical political backing for food assistance, is reluctant to support food aid that displaces commercial exports.

Nongovernment organizations that distribute food to needy people abroad, such as CARE, finance their relief efforts by selling some of the food aid from America. Approximately half the value of food aid distributed by NGOs goes toward commercial sales to purchase administration, transport, and storage of food aid. The value of food aid for a given aid budget also is reduced, because the law requires certain types of food aid to be shipped in American flag vessels, which have high costs.

One consequence is that NGOs dependent on commercial sales of food aid join an "iron triangle" with the American farm lobby and American shippers to require that food aid be produced in America, when in reality, purchasing food abroad with American cash or food vouchers would better serve hungry people and food producers abroad, as well as taxpayers in the United States. Notions that NGOs operate solely from altruism were dispelled by their successful opposition to a proposal by President George Bush in 2005 to provide one-fourth of "food" aid in voucher form, which could be used to purchase food in the time, place, and form that best meets local needs.

One case for aid as food rather than as cash or vouchers is that nations are more generous about providing aid in kind rather than in cash. Donors fear that cash or vouchers are more likely to be misused than food aid.

Beyond humanitarian food aid, the case for international food assistance has shortcomings. Development food aid, typically donated to recipient country governments that in turn market the food to consumers, is especially vulnerable to corruption. Receipts from food sales, intended for agricultural research or for infrastructure development, often end up in the pockets of politicians and bureaucrats. Nongovernment organizations can help to administer food-for-work and food-for-school-lunch programs in poor countries with less loss to mismanagement and corruption. Nonetheless, development aid, including food-for-work and school-feeding programs, ordinarily is not the most effective type of aid for promoting economic development and food security.

As in the case of humanitarian aid, the best case for development food aid is that donors will provide it in excess of other types of assistance. Another reason to confine food aid to humanitarian hunger situations, rather than to promote development, is that poor people and nations are wary of becoming dependent on food donations that are subject to the political whims of affluent nations. For example, cereal food aid fluctuated widely from over thirteen million tons in 1994–1995 to less than seven million tons in 1996–1997 to fifteen million tons in 1999–2000. This variation was due more to the changing harvests and prices in donor countries than to the need in recipient countries (figure 8.1).

Standard-model policies fostering food self-reliance (not self-sufficiency!) take on added priority in poor countries given the expected decline in future food aid.[32] Rich-country governments have a history of accumulating surpluses generated by price support programs. However, under prodding from the World Trade Organization, nations that insist on financially supporting their farmers are shifting from price supports, which generate surplus production, to cash payments, which are somewhat decoupled from production incentives. With less surplus stock reserves held by governments, a higher proportion of food aid seems destined for humanitarian rather than surplus disposal purposes. Some forms of development food assistance are being condemned in international trade forums as disguised export subsidies. Finally, an ever-rising share of world food production converted to biofuels for powering internal combustion engines raises food prices and diminishes the grain and vegetable oil available for food aid.

The foregoing case for targeted humanitarian food and health aid does not diminish the case for foreign development assistance. However, beyond humanitarian food and health aid, assistance to developing countries may take varied forms to best help the poor without distorting markets. Such forms include skills and technology development and transfer, infrastructure investment, and opening markets to trade.

Conclusions

Farm commodity programs do more than violate the standard model. They and the trade distortions inseparable from them constitute plenty of contradictions. Rich countries are asking poor countries to give up protectionist policies that mostly hurt poor countries and which rational minds would expect poor countries to be eager to end without any quid pro quo. Poor countries are asking rich countries to give up commodity-program and trade policies which

---

32 Food self-reliance emphasizes building productivity to produce food at home or to be able to purchase it abroad. It contrasts sharply with food self-sufficiency, a reckless policy if it compromises buying power so that a nation cannot afford to purchase food abroad when local production fails, as it is prone to do. No one loses sleep over the low food self-sufficiency of Japan, Hong Kong, and Singapore, because they have food self-reliance, in part from the wealth generated by efficiently producing and exporting nonfood products.

mostly hurt rich countries and which rational minds would expect rich countries to end without a quid pro quo from poor countries.

Efforts by rich countries to subsidize their farmers underlie crop subsidies that dump production on world markets at well below the cost of production. Outrage by the general public in rich countries, over the idea that commodity programs and their accompanying trade distortions were hurting poor countries, became the rallying cry for commodity-program reform during trade negotiations in the Doha Round. Reasons abound to remove distortions in farm commodity and trade markets, but poor countries will not necessarily gain unless they open their own markets. Panagariya of the IMF estimates that if rich countries liberalized agricultural trade, Brazil and Argentina would gain, but the rest of Latin America would lose $559 million per year, sub-Saharan Africa would lose $420 million, and North Africa and the Middle East would lose $2.9 billion per year.

The standard model emphasizes the critical role of the public sector in providing public goods, such as protection of the environment, and providing a safety net for those who cannot provide for themselves from their own resources or those of others; however, that is not what farm commodity and trade market interventions are about. Poor people will especially pay in lost opportunities if the world continues to forego gains from economies of size and specialization afforded by more open trade.

References

Amiti, Mary and Shang-Jin Wei. "Demystifying Outsourcing." *Finance and Development,* December 2004, pp. 36–39.

Anderson, Kym, Will Martin, and Dominique van der Mensbrugghe. "Market and Welfare Implications of Doha Reform Scenarios." Chapter 12 in Kym Anderson and Will Martin, eds., *Agricultural Trade Reform and the Doha Development Agenda*. Report No. 34206. Washington DC: World Bank, 2006.

Anderson, Kym and Will Martin. "Agriculture, Trade Reform, and the Doha Agenda." Chapter 1 in Kym Anderson and Will Martin, eds., *Agricultural Trade Reform and the Doha Development Agenda*. Washington DC: The World Bank, 2006.

CBO. *Policies that Distort World Agricultural Trade: Prevalence and Magnitude.* Washington DC: Congressional Budget Office, August 2005.

CBO. *The Effects of Liberalizing World Agricultural Trade: A Survey.* Washington DC: Congressional Budget Office, December 2005.

Cline, William R. "Doha Can Achieve Much More than Skeptics Expect." *Finance and Development.* 42: 22–23, March 2005.

Easterly, William. *White Man's Burden: Why the West's Efforts to Aid the Rest Have Done So Much Ill and So Little Good.* New York: Penguin Press, 2006.

"Foreign Direct Investment." *The Economist.* September 25, 2004, p. 122.

Good, Keith. *The Farm Policy News Summary.* www.FarmPolicy.com, August 25, 2005.

Hertel, Thomas, Bernard Hoekman, and Will Martin. "Developing Countries and a New Round of WTO Negotiations." *The World Research Observer.* 17: 113–140, Spring 2002.

IMF. "Aiding Development: Tracking the Flows." *Finance and Development.* Washington DC: International Monetary Fund, September 2005, pp. 14–15.

Knutson, Odin and John Nash. "Agricultural Price Stabilization and Risk Reduction in Developing Countries." (Mimeo.) Washington DC: World Bank, May 1988.

Panagariya, Arvind. "Agricultural Liberalization and the Developing Countries." http://www.columbia.edu/-ap2231/, 2005.

Teal, Francis. "The Commission for Africa and Economic Research on Growth." Pp. 19–24 in *Research Summary 2004/05.* Oxford, UK: Center for the Study of African Economies, Oxford University, 2005.

Tweeten, Luther. *Agricultural Trade: Principles and Policies.* Boulder, Colorado: Westview Press, 1992.

Tweeten, Luther. "Farm Commodity Programs: Essential Safety Net or Corporate Welfare?" Chapter 1 in L. Tweeten and S. Thompson, eds., *Agricultural Policy for the 21st Century.* Ames: Iowa State Press, 2002.

World Bank. *Global Economic Prospects 2004: Realizing the Development Promise of the Doha Round Agenda*. Washington DC: World Bank, 2004, chapter 1.

World Food Program. INTERFAIS (International Food Aid Information System). Rome, 2003.

9

Coping with a World of Falling Population

The term "megatrends" refers to trajectories of critical variables determining the future human condition. This chapter reviews key megatrends regarding food and population. I make a case that seminal demographic, economic, and environmental variables follow distinct temporal phases that help to trace their path over time. Standard-model policies and institutions affect the way these phases unfold.

Perhaps the best know megatrend is Parson Thomas Malthus' prediction, just over two centuries ago, that the world's food supply increases arithmetically (1, 2, 3, 4, etc.), whereas population increases exponentially (1, 2, 4, 8, etc.). If Malthus is correct, population inevitably will outrun food supply. Then wars, pestilence, and famine will need to bring food supply into balance with food demand.

Despite overall food abundance since World War II, the Malthusian specter looms just below the surface in the minds of many. In October 1999, the earth's human population passed six billion, a milestone greeted by a doomsday symphony. For example, ecologist David Pimentel warned that by 2100, "12 billion miserable humans will suffer a difficult life on earth" (see Crenson, p. 1).

The musings of Cassandras are placed in perspective in this chapter by reviewing two megatrends—global food supply and demand. Data on food supply trends since World War II are downright Malthusian. Global crop and livestock yields have been increasing on average at a linear (straight line) rate since the 1950s (Tweeten, 1998, pp. 16-23). With annual yield additions nearly constant and yields on average about doubling since the 1950s, the annual *percentage* increase in yields has been halved. In 2006, the trend percentage increase in global food yields was near the rate of increase in population, 1.3 percent per year. With irrigated area and total cropland area nearly static since 1990, the Malthusian portents, at first blush, seem clear.

A very different picture emerges when the second megatrend, food demand, is placed beside supply to depict the global food balance. The evidence of a momentous demographic reversal is apparent. After growing exponentially for centuries, global population in the twenty-first century seems destined to grow at a decreasing rate until the rate of population growth reaches zero and even becomes negative. The thesis of this chapter is that this demographic transition is part of an interconnected set of socioeconomic transitions. Standard-model economic policies are an important driver of these transitions, having profound environmental, social, and political as well as economic implications.

Interrelated Demographic and Economic Transitions

The transformation of human society is multi-dimensional, but the economic and demographic transitions provide useful and clear stages for categorizing the broader transformations. These two transitions are not exactly alike, but they are portrayed together stylistically in figure 9.1 (see Shiptsova; Tweeten and Zulauf, p. 55). Stages I to III are briefly addressed; I will pay principal attention to Stage IV.

Stage I is a traditional society with low population density and growth. Population grows slowly, because high birth rates are offset by high death rates. Not until year 1800 did global population reach one billion. Primitive technology contributes to low income and living standards in Stage I.

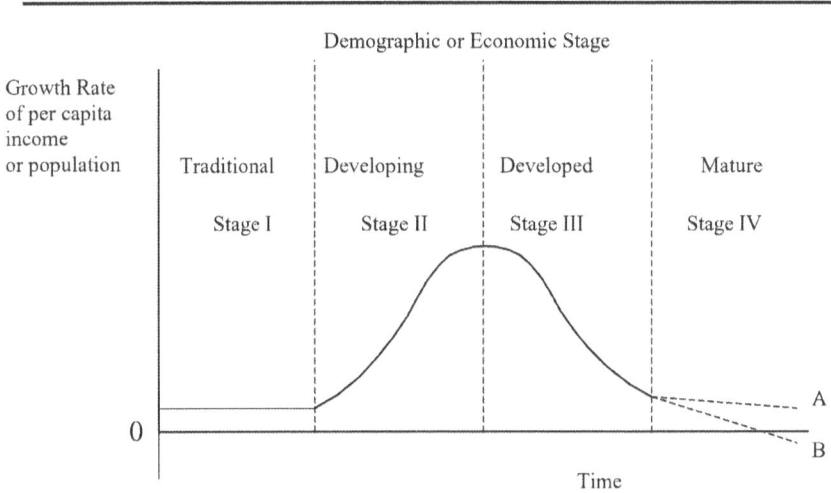

Figure 9.1. Hypothetical Demographic and Economic Transitions

Human society exits the hunter-gatherer traditional Stage I and enters the developing Stage II, characterized by agriculture. That process began about 11,000 years ago. Domestication of plants and animals was central to the development of agriculture (Diamond). A more plentiful food supply feeds population growth in Stage II. Increases in agricultural productivity and food production bring economic surpluses that enable growth in capital and per capita income. The ability of people to remain in one place while cultivating improved plants and feeding improved livestock freed some people to work in other occupations, such as governance and health care. Technological change beyond agriculture (especially in public health) accelerates the decline in death rates.

For any one country, the onset and speed of the reduction in death rates depends on whether agricultural and medical technology is developed internally or imported from more advanced countries. Change can occur faster in countries that are able to adapt technology from elsewhere rather than create it. That fact helps to explain why demographic, economic, and technological change has been especially rapid in countries that belatedly entered Stages II and III.

Population growth accelerates in much of Stage II, because birth rates, which are determined by very slowly changing cultural norms, decline more slowly than death rates from the high rate of Stage I. Death rates respond quickly to improved medical technology. Industrial growth and urbanization, though modest in Stage II, are beginning to induce major demographic change. When combined with continued rapid population and food-production growth, these two forces give rise to the natural-resource exploitation and environmental degradation in Stage II.

Economic growth, near zero in Stage I, is positive in Stage II. The rate of economic growth increases first at an increasing rate and later at a decreasing rate in Stage II. It is emphasized, however, that the demographic and economic transitions do not move in lockstep and are not as smooth as portrayed in figure 9.1.

Birth rates fall faster than death rates, ushering in Stage III. The population growth rate falls, partly because the socioeconomic status and role of women change. Women in most countries in Stage III receive more schooling, rights, and job opportunities. Smaller proportions of people live on farms and thus derive less economic value or social security from children. Emerging birth-control technology allows adults to have no more children than they desire.

Technology and income continue to improve, but generally at a slowing rate in Stage III. Many technological breakthroughs in Stage II came from innovative laypersons; breakthroughs in Stage III tend to require scarce, highly trained, experienced, and costly technicians and scientists, which not many countries can afford. Many readily accessible raw materials have been exploited by Stage III. Obsolescence of current technology requires investment in maintenance science. The productivity of service activities, which grow in importance, is harder to increase than that of agriculture and manufacturing. Countries may decide to accept less economic growth in order to achieve greater economic equity in Stage III.

The transition from demographic Stage II to Stage III varies by country, but for the world as a whole, it was in 1990, when it added ninety million inhabitants, the most ever before or since that year (CBO, p. 7). The general trend is to add fewer people each year. Rapid productivity gains continue for agriculture in Stage III, as investments in education and science made in Stage II produce long-term payoffs. At the same time, declining rates of income growth and population growth, coupled with a falling response of food demand to income (income elasticity), slow food-demand growth. Food self-sufficiency increases in some countries after falling in Stage II; however, agricultural trade grows on average, as more affluent consumers demand a variety of foods sourced around the world, and as economies of size in food supply cause specialization and shipments of differentiated intra-industry products among countries. An example of the latter is simultaneously shipping cars made in Germany to Japan and those made in Japan to Germany.

Stage IV of the Demographic Transition

The main focus of this chapter is Stage IV, the future of the world's inhabitants and thus the least-charted of the transition stages in figure 9.1. Many developed countries have recently entered or will soon enter this stage. The seminal attribute of Stage IV is negative global population growth (NPG), as indicated by trajectory *B* in figure 9.1. NPG is at variance with the long-held view that global population growth will slow to the low but positive trajectory designated by *A*. The case for NPG is strong, however, and its implications are enormous. Standard-model policies will hasten NPG. Whether that outcome is positive or negative for the well-being of humanity is controversial and not resolved in this volume.

Global Population Growth

Since the 1950s, the total fertility rate (TFR, the expected number of children a woman bears throughout her life) has fallen in every region of the world. From an average of near six children per woman in 1950–1955, TFR by 1990–1995 fell to 3.0 in Latin America, 3.4 in India, and 3.5 in "other Asia" (UN, 1998, p. 11). Rates continue to fall. TFRs in the 1990–1995 period were below the 2.1 average children per woman needed to sustain population over the long run in Europe (1.57), China (1.92), and North America (US and Canada, 2.02).

North America is the only major exception to the sustained downtrend in TFRs. However, its increasing TFR during recent years may be a transitory phenomenon associated with immigration and a large "baby boom" cohort of females deciding to have children relatively late during their childbearing years.

The TFR has fallen in Africa as elsewhere, but because TFRs have been higher in Africa than in other regions for several decades, the continent's TFR remained at a higher rate, near six, in the 1990–1995 period (UN, 1998, p. 11). The AIDS epidemic will especially slow Africa's population growth, as noted in chapter 7. The impact would be even greater, except that many adults bear their children before succumbing to AIDS.

The medium UN population projection is a widely used demographic forecast, but it appears to unrealistically assume that TFRs will converge to 2.1 in both developed and developing countries. That assumption overestimates future population, according to Lutz *et al.* (p. 365):

> The United Nations and other institutions preparing population forecasts assumed that fertility would increase to replacement level and that subreplacement fertility was only a transitory phenomenon....It is difficult, however, to find many researchers who support this view. Too much evidence points toward low fertility. Many significant arguments support an assumption of further declining fertility levels. They range from the weakening of the family in terms of both declining marriage rates and high divorce rates, to the increasing independence and career orientation of women, and to a value change toward materialism and consumerism.
>
> These factors, together with increasing demands and personal expectations for attention, time, and also money to be given to children, are likely to result in fewer couples having more than one or two children and an increasing number of childless women. Also, the proportion of

unplanned pregnancies is still high, and future improvements in contraceptive methods are possible. The bulk of evidence suggests that fertility will remain low or further decline in today's industrialized societies.

The UN's low/medium scenario could be more realistic. It presumes a continuation of TFR trends, but converging to 1.9 TFR for all regions by the year 2025. This scenario projects a peak world population of 8.0 billion people in 2050, declining to 6.4 billion by 2150 (UN, 1998, p. 14).

Several peak population projections are summarized as follows:

	Peak Global PopulationNumbers (billion)	Year
World Bank (Bos *et al.*)[33]	11.3	2128
Int. Inst. for Applied Systems Anal. (Lutz *et al.*, p. 376)	10.8	2080
United Nations (UN, 1998), low/medium scenario	8.0	2050
Dennis Avery	Under 9.0	2040
David Seckler and Michael Rock	8.0	2040
Steven Mosher	7.0	2030

Steven Mosher, president of the Population Research Institute, along with David Seckler of the International Irrigation Management Institute, Michael Rock of Winrock International, and Dennis Avery of the Hudson Institute, all project that global population will peak by the year 2040 or earlier. Most projections point to peak global population in less than a century, followed by NPG. Thus, the global demographic transition seems destined to reach Stage IV in the twenty-first century. Today's population is not expected to double before global population peaks.

The medium UN projection may overestimate future TFRs (2.1) in developed countries, but the low/medium UN projection may underestimate future TFRs (1.9) in developing countries. Alternative scenarios are employed herein in projecting food demand. However, it is useful first to examine population growth differences by region and age.

---

33 Tweeten (1998) extended the World Bank projection to ZPG using a quadratic equation.

Regional Population Distribution

The regional differences in population growth rates under the low/medium total-fertility-rate scenario of the United Nations portend large demographic realignments. Especially notable is the decline in total and global share of population in Western countries—the first three rows, or group I of table 9.1. Their combined share of 29 percent in 1950 is projected to be only 10 percent by 2150.

Demographics in Japan help to describe what is happening in other rich countries. The country's population, 128 million in 2005, is projected to fall to 86–100 million by 2050 (see Emmott, pp. 14–15). That observation prompts recall of the Heisenberg Uncertainty Principle—the act of observing something changes its behavior. Japan and other wealthy countries observing marked population decline can afford and likely will undertake strong measures to change demographics. To raise birth rates, governments already are providing child cash allowances, tax breaks, free public services, and generous parental leave and job security policies. Following standard-model policies provides countries with more means and options to promote population growth—if they so choose. If these inducements are generous enough, they can generate new demographic trajectories quite unlike those in this chapter.

Under the low/medium UN scenario, even assuming that Europe's TFR recovers from its current level of 1.6 to 1.9, Europe's population declines to 368 million by 2150—half its current level. Europe's share of world population falls to 6 percent. North America's population peaks at 310 million in 2050, but its global share falls consistently and by 2150 is only half of its 7 percent share in 1950. On the other hand, Africa's share will grow to nearly 30 percent by 2150 from 9 percent in 1950, while India will become the most populous country by 2050.

Table 9.1. Population of World Regions Projected Under the UN Low/Medium Total Fertility Rate Scenario, Earth, 1950–2150

Region	1950 (Mil.)	(%)	2000 (Mil.)	(%)	2050 (Mil.)	(%)	2150 (Mil.)	(%)
Europe	547	21.7	728	12.0	567	7.1	368	5.7
North America	172	6.8	315	5.2	310	3.9	217	3.4
Oceania	13	0.5	31	0.5	39	0.5	30	0.5
Group I	732	29.0	1,074	17.6	916	11.5	615	9.6
Africa	224	8.9	812	13.3	1,807	22.7	1,835	28.7
Latin Amer. & Car.	166	6.6	523	8.6	671	8.4	516	8.1
China	555	22.0	1,274	20.9	1,246	15.6	824	12.9
India	358	14.2	1,021	16.8	1,266	15.9	905	14.1
Other Asia	490	19.4	1,381	22.7	2,063	25.9	1,704	26.6
Group II	1,792	71.0	5,011	82.4	7,053	88.5	5,784	90.4
World	2,524	100.0	6,085	100.0	7,969	100.0	6,399	100.0 100.0

Source: UN, 1998, pp. 28–30

Age Distribution

Falling birth rates, coupled with increasing longevity, will reduce child dependency rates and raise aged dependency rates (table 9.2). Under the low/medium TFR scenario, the proportion of the world's population less than fifteen years of age declines from 30 percent in 2000 to 16 percent in 2150. Meanwhile, the proportion of population age sixty-five and over rises from 7 percent to 28 percent. Percentage shares will change less over time in the Western countries than in other countries (table 9.2).

Table 9.2. Projected Shares of Population in Selected Age Groups by Major Regions and the World, UN Low/Medium Total Fertility Rate Scenario, 1995–2150

Age	Year	North America, Europe, and Oceania	Other Countries	World
		(%)	(%)	(%)
Under 15	2000	18.9	32.4	30.0
	2050	14.3	18.0	17.6
	2150	15.1	15.6	15.5
65 or over	2000	13.9	5.4	6.9
	2050	28.0	16.4	17.7
	2150	29.7	27.7	27.8
Combined	2000	32.8	37.9	37.0
	2050	41.3	34.4	35.3
	2150	44.8	43.3	43.3

Source: UN, 1998, pp. 17–19

Partly due to rising incomes and more schooling, along with widening opportunities for females in countries with standard-model policies, birth rates fall, especially in formerly poor parts of the world. Compared to the rest of the world in 2000, the West has nearly half the incidence of population under fifteen and over twice the incidence of persons sixty-five years of age and over. The picture changes by 2150. With modernization, the rest of the world looks more and more like the West demographically. The West and the rest of the world are projected to have about 15 percent of their populations under fifteen years of age and about 30 percent aged sixty-five and over.

A world of high dependency rates will be a world of conflict between age groups for power and resources. The elderly will have growing socioeconomic and cultural influence and will be in position politically to demand a large share of a government's budget. Fewer working-age persons per retired person will strain pension funds and government finances. However, a less gloomy picture emerges for the working-age population when the perspective is relative to the total dependent population; *i.e.,* those under fifteen plus those sixty-five and over. This overall dependency ratio increases only a little, from 37 percent in 2000 to 43 percent of global population in 2150, and it doesn't differ much between the West and elsewhere. Improved health and economic necessity resulting from longer life will push the working lifetime beyond sixty-five, further reducing the burdens of dependency on the economy.

Shortages of workers will bid up wages and induce public and private initiatives to raise labor efficiency. Robots guided by computers will dominate assembly lines. It is important to note that the substitution of capital for labor cannot just focus on manufacturing. In the United States, for example, manufacturing accounted for less than 10 percent of jobs in 2005 and will account for a much smaller share by 2050. It has been much more difficult to improve labor productivity in service occupations than in manufacturing and agriculture. With nine of ten workers in service industries in the future, science and industry will devote considerable genius to raising productivity in service work. That effort will bear impressive fruits.

Stage IV: Implications for Future Food Supply/ Demand Balance

From 1961 to 2000, growth in world food production outpaced growth in world population. The result was an average annual increase of 0.5 percent in per capita food production and a decline of 1.8 percent annually in real food prices.[34] Production per capita has increased more slowly since the 1980s, but real food (farm commodity) prices at the farm level have continued to fall.

The food supply-and-demand balances since 1961 can be divided into three subperiods. Growth in food demand is measured by growth in population and in per capita consumption due to income.[35] The first subperiod, from 1961 to 1970, featured a rapid rise in yield, with no increase in area. In the second subperiod, from 1970 to 1990, yield and demand increased at almost the same rate,

---

34 The changes in real U.S. food prices at the farm level are taken to be measures of global real food price changes based on the assumption of relatively open U.S. markets. The U.S. real food price is the index of prices received for crops and livestock, adjusted for inflation by the implicit GDP deflator (Council of Economic Advisors, pp. 310, 420, and earlier issues).

35 Food demand includes population growth plus per capita food demand rising about 0.3 percent per year because of income growth per capita (see annex table 9.1). The formula for demand is $Pop(1+r)^t$ where Pop is population, r is annual growth rate in food demand per capita due to income, and t is year from the base.

but production increased relative to demand as global cropland area rose. In the third phase, since 1990, area in crops has been nearly static, while yield has continued to increase. The millions of cropland hectares added in Brazil and a few other countries have been offset by the millions of hectares worldwide converted to development and other non-crop uses. Also, millions of hectares have been lost to soil erosion, salinization, and waterlogging. Thus, since 1990, increased world food output has depended on increased yields to meet growing food demand.

Especially notable is the fact that from 1961 to 2004, aggregate cereal yields have increased at a remarkably linear rate of 440 hectograms (forty-four kilograms) per hectare (figure 9.2). Predicted yield increased from 1.4 metric tons in 1961 to 3.3 metric tons per hectare in 2004. Cereal yield trends were very close to total food yield trends (measured, for lack of data, as food output divided by area in crops), mainly because cereals account for two-thirds of all food sources. Yields of other major crops and livestock also increased at nearly linear rates; except for oil seeds, they increased on average more slowly than cereal yields.

Figure 9.2. Actual (dots) and Predicted (line) World Cereal Yield from 1961 to 2004

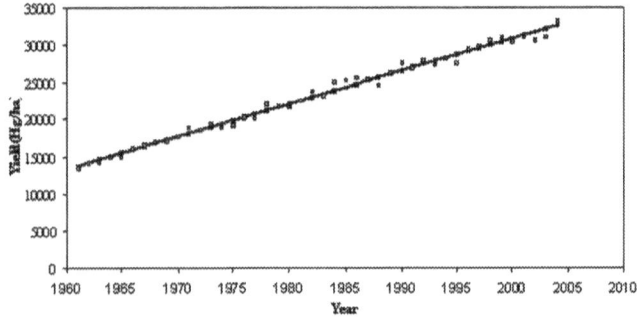

Source: FAO

The annual percentage increase in food yield is compared to the annual increase in global population in the following table:

	1961	1971	1981	1991	2001
			(%/yr.)		
Cereal yield	3.18	2.43	1.95	1.63	1.40
Population	2.57	2.04	1.70	1.45	1.30

Population growth slowed, but not as rapidly as cereal yields. The excess growth rate in cereal yield relative to population narrowed from 0.61 percentage points in 1961 to only 0.10 percentage points in 2001. If the per capita annual growth rate in food demand being generated by higher per capita income is added to the increase due to population, overall food demand has grown at least as fast as yield in recent years.[36]

Production of ethanol and diesel biofuels from crops is not included in food projections herein, but it adds a critical new dimension to demand for agricultural resources. At issue is whether biofuels can compete with oil to power vehicles. The OECD (von Lampe, p. 11) estimated that a gallon of ethanol produced in the United States from corn cost $1.09 and in Brazil, from sugarcane, cost $.83 in 2004. The same study calculated that the production of a gallon of biodiesel from U.S. soybeans cost $2.08 and from Canadian canola cost $1.72. Biodiesel lacks competitiveness. Given a transportation cost of seventeen cents per gallon to ship ethanol from Brazil to the United States, Brazilian imports at $1.00 per gallon could be highly competitive with domestic-source ethanol in the U.S. market, in the absence of an import duty.

The OECD (von Lampe, p. 13) calculated that ethanol in 2004 was competitive with gasoline in the United States at an oil price of forty-four dollars per barrel and in Brazil at an oil price of twenty-nine dollars per barrel. With oil at thirty-nine dollars per barrel in 2004, Brazilian ethanol was clearly competitive with oil for fuel, whereas U.S. ethanol from corn was marginally competitive without subsidies.

Another set of estimates of prices of oil (dollars per barrel) at which alternative energy sources become economically viable in 2006 are as follows ("Special Report: The Oil Industry," p. 67):[37]

36 The contribution of income to demand based on income level, growth rate, and income elasticities by groups of countries is shown in annex table 9.1).

37 At least three factors need to be but were not fully considered by analysts quantifying the oil price at which ethanol breaks even with gasoline to power vehicles. One is that a gallon of ethanol contains only two-thirds the energy of a gallon of gasoline. A second is that the price of ethanol is a function of oil price, because nearly a gallon of oil (or other fossil-fuel equivalent) is required to produce a gallon of corn-based ethanol. Third, ethanol is not well suited for shipping in pipelines, hence transport costs are greater than for gasoline. With full accounting for the three factors above, oil

Tar sands, Brazil ethanol, and natural gas-to-liquids, coal-to-liquids: $40/barrel
Shale oil: $50/barrel
Ethanol from U.S. corn: $60/barrel
Biodiesel: $80/barrel

The tar sands of Alberta, Brazil ethanol, shale oil, and natural gas or coal converted to diesel fuel or other liquid fuel are cheaper sources of energy than American biofuels and together constitute a massive energy reserve. Whether corn-based ethanol or biodiesel can compete with these fuels and oil in a twenty-first-century energy market without subsidies, tariffs, or tax breaks remains in doubt. The argument that ethanol subsidies are justified, to avoid reliance on risky oil imports from politically volatile regions, overlooks the fact that production of biofuels depends heavily on oil imports. Furthermore, the use of corn for ethanol reduces farm exports and hence enlarges America's dependence on food imports.

Above an oil price of sixty dollars per barrel, biofuels constitute a virtually unlimited demand for agricultural resources. One-third of U.S. cropland in cereal, oil-seed, and sugar crops would have been required to supply just one-tenth of U.S. transportation-vehicle fuel needs in 2004 (von Lampe, p. 15). In other words, using all land in these crops for biofuels would supply only one-third of the U.S. market. Thus biofuel demand seems destined to place a floor under food prices in the twenty-first century. That floor could end farm price and income support programs, but it constitutes a potential severe burden on soil and water resources and on low-income food consumers.

Twenty-first-century oil prices may average above sixty dollars per barrel, but expectations are flawed. Future portents for food consumers of very high energy prices would be ominous indeed in the absence of falling fertility rates. Global food demand would increase faster than food supply, elevating real food prices. Table 9.3 optimistically projects aggregate food supply based on a continuation of 1961–2004 cereal yield trends, but with no increase in crop or irrigated area, along with alternative aggregate food (excluding biofuels) demand projections from 2000 to 2100. Fish is assumed to supply only 2 percent of calories. Rising fish output will come not from oceans, but from fish that are fed crops on fish farms. All food trends assume the continuation of year 2000 food prices. Aggregate food supply, based solely on the optimistic cereal yield trend, and assuming no increase in cropland area or irrigation after 2004, is up only 60 percent from the 2000 level by 2050 and up 126 percent by 2100. If food

price needs to be as high as $60 per barrel for ethanol to compete, given equal tax treatment.

demand outpaces food supply, however, real food prices will rise and bring in more cropland, irrigation, and other inputs, while restraining food consumption.

Table 9.3. Global Food Supply and Demand Scenarios to 2050 and 2100

Scenario	Year		
	2000	2050	2100
	(Percent of year 2000)		
Food demand			
High (1950–1980 rate)			
Population only	100	246	633
w/income 0.20%/yr.	100	272	773
Medium UN pop.			
Population only	100	140	156
w/income 0.20%/yr.	100	155	191
Low/medium UN pop.			
Population only	100	119	108
w/income 0.25%/yr.	100	135	137
Food supply			
Cereal yield trend	100	160	226

Source: UN, 1998; 2005. See annex table 9.1 for demand response to income gains.

The high-food-demand scenario in table 9.3, for illustration only, demonstrates how far food demand could exceed food supply in the twenty-first century in the absence of the econo-demographic transitions. If population and income maintained their 1950 to 1980 trend growth, demand expands 112 percentage points more than supply by 2050. Markets would clear, but at higher food prices. The resulting increase in real food prices would prompt major investments in production technology as well as conventional inputs, the latter at considerable cost to the environment. Higher commodity prices would restrain consumption. If instead the United Nations medium-population-projection demand scenario prevails, food demand is projected to grow slower than food supply, but the food supply-demand balance is expected to be tighter than in recent decades. Real food prices would change very little by 2050, in contrast to the sharply falling real food prices of recent decades.

The demographic transition brought about by socioeconomic progress is apparent in the United Nations' medium population projection in table 9.3, a projection many consider to be a sensible prediction for the twenty-first century. Under that medium population projection and with income increasing food consumption by 0.2 percent per year, total food demand is projected to be up fifty-five percentage points by 2050 and ninety-one percentage points by 2100 over demand in the year 2000. Food supply grows only slightly faster than demand to 2050, the balance between food demand and supply remains tight, and real food prices at the farm level display little trend.

If standard-model policies are followed widely and population growth slows as a result, the United Nations low/medium population scenario could be realized as shown in table 9.3. This scenario is consistent with the projections of some experts cited earlier. Food supply grows twenty-five percentage points more than food demand from 2000 to 2050. This outcome would allow real farm-commodity prices to continue to fall an estimated 50 percent by 2050 and by even more by 2100. Even with this most optimistic scenario for food consumers, real food prices could be expected to fall on average by only 0.8 percent per year to 2050, about half the historic rate of decline. It follows that standard-model policies can be a boon to food consumers in the twenty-first century. On the other hand, continuing biofuel subsidies coupled with inattention to agricultural productivity would bring sharply rising real food prices and extend farming to marginal lands, with unfortunate environmental consequences.

NPG and the Environment

The economic and demographic transitions are attended by a less well-known environmental transition. The stylized diagram of figure 9.1 can illustrate the temporal pattern of environmental degradation. Environmental degradation is minimal in traditional Stage I, but it increases with population and economic growth in Stage II. Sustained population growth leads to land-clearing and soil erosion with the expansion of food production. Even with some economic growth, low-income countries cannot afford costly pollution controls or conservation technologies. Low income per capita is accompanied by high discount rates favoring present versus future consumption, further discouraging investment in environmental protection. Deteriorating air quality and water quality are two of the more obvious manifestations of wide-ranging environmental degradation as the socioeconomic and demographic transitions move through Stage II and into Stage III.

The fortuitous interaction between declining population growth and high income ultimately saves the environment. Effective policies of affluent nations correct externalities by establishing appropriate incentives and institutions. Lower birth and population-growth rates, brought about in part by higher income, reduce pressure on the environment. Higher income allows saving out of current income that is no longer needed to provide necessities, which in turn can be used to finance investment in science and technology that reduces pressure on the environment. Rapid productivity gains of agriculture in Stage III, made feasible by agricultural research financed out of economic growth in Stages II and III, enable the cropping of fewer and environmentally safer acres while freeing cropland for grass, trees, recreation, and biodiversity.

Education and research made possible by economic progress promotes awareness of environmental hazards, which in turn generate effective policy responses. Their basic needs being met, ever more affluent consumers demand greater efforts to protect the environment. They are willing to pay taxes if necessary to do so. Furthermore, as their incomes rise, consumers spend a larger share on services, whose production and disposal in general are less detrimental to the environment than are goods. The net result is a trajectory of increasingly less environmental degradation, as explained earlier in chapter 6. However, perhaps the most important contribution to the environment of economic progress accelerated by standard-model policies is reduced—and eventually negative—population growth.

NPG and International Migration

Individual countries will enter Stage IV at different times. Declining population, coupled with continued (though modest) income growth in Stage IV countries, could further widen the gap between per capita incomes in developed and developing countries. That gap will narrow and pressures for migration will be diminished if poor countries embrace the standard model. Some once-poor countries such as Taiwan, South Korea, and Singapore already are developed countries. With proper policies in place, China, India, and other countries will eventually join the ranks of developed countries. Countries rejecting standard-model policies will continue to have high birth rates and population growth but slow income growth. Many such countries will be in Africa, the Middle East, and South America and Central America. Internal population pressures will build. Underemployed and unemployed workers in poorly run economies will seek employment and income elsewhere. An obvious example is undocumented workers and their families entering the United States from Mexico and Central America.

High dependency rates and worker shortages will characterize North American and Western European countries in Stage IV of development. Migration, pulled by the shortage of workers in developed countries and pushed by the shortage of good jobs in developing countries, will be massive. In labor-short developed countries, firms and households alike will seek immigrant labor. Households in developed countries have the wealth to pay for household cleaning, health, gardening, and other labor-intensive services, and they will seek workers from home or abroad to provide them. Some wealthy countries in Stage IV will have on average only one worker per retiree, prompting their governments to look to immigrant labor for payroll tax receipts to pay retirement benefits.

Firms in developed countries having difficulty competing in global markets will seek skilled and unskilled labor from developing countries to fill jobs at competitive salaries and wages. To keep per capita income from falling, Stage IV countries will especially seek educated, highly skilled immigrants. That strategy causes a "brain drain" from poor countries of able citizens who are most needed to provide the skills and leadership essential for reform and development at home. The financing of higher education and training of students from poor countries by Stage IV countries can mitigate some of the regressive redistribution of human capital caused by this brain drain. Remittances by migrants to relatives and friends back home totaled $250 billion in 2005, multiples of official development assistance.

Intense migration pressure will make the influx of foreigners into some Stage IV countries uncontrollable and divisive. Much of that migration seems destined to be illegal—given powerful incentives to seek better jobs and with long borders impossible to control. Each year, up to one million undocumented aliens enter the United States and another one million enter the European Union, seeking economic opportunity. Imprisonment or the forced export of masses of established illegals is politically and socially unacceptable in a liberal society. Amnesty is inevitable.

To reduce the influx of illegals, countries have tried guest worker programs and penalties on employers of undocumented workers. The United States sponsored the *bracero* program from 1942 to 1964 for Mexican workers, and Germany sponsored the *Gasterbeiter* program after World War II for Turkish and Balkan country workers. In both cases, the programs did not stop migration—workers and their families stayed in the host country and served as cover for millions more illegal migrants ("Illegal Immigration," pp. 18, 86). The lesson is that immigration is difficult to stop when workers from poor countries and employers in rich countries need each other. The most effective long-term tool to slow immigration is for poor countries to follow standard-model policies, thereby providing more jobs at home and slowing population growth.

Legal and illegal immigrants bring religions, lifestyles, and birth rates quite unlike those of the recipient countries. The culture of recipient countries can be viewed either as enriched or threatened. If the latter view predominates among natives, tensions between natives and newcomers will be intense and will generate radical political movements and violence. Natives will fear that terrorists will be among the new arrivals. Some countries could be seriously destabilized, with global repercussions.

On the other hand, multiculturalism fostered by migration can enrich cultures in ways that defuse social and cultural tension. Immigrants will bring some aspects of culture from their homelands to the country of their employment, but they also will return home with some of the culture of their host country. Increased heterogeneity within cultures will be accompanied by less heterogeneity among cultures. One result will be the spread of standard-model policies.

Conclusions

Demographic and economic transitions that are underway, but capable of being accelerated by standard-model policies and institutions, portend falling fertility rates and declining global population within the next century for the world and for all major regions, except perhaps Africa. Of course, projections are hazardous when they extend 100 years, and they must be viewed with caution. Major shocks can and will intervene.

The likely implications of falling global population are numerous and mostly felicitous:

1. Falling fertility rates will avert a global food crisis. If population and food demand continued to expand at the 1950–1980 rate, the world would be headed for expanding regions of hunger, along with sharply higher real farm-commodity prices, to draw more land and other resources into food production.

2. If actual global population follows somewhere between the UN medium and low/medium scenarios, food supply growth could outpace food demand growth, resulting in the continuation of the historical decline

in real prices at the farm level. However, rapid economic growth in East Asia and South Asia, coupled with growing dependence on agriculture for energy, is a credible scenario. It could easily tip the balance to rising real farm and food prices as farm-commodity demand exceeds supply expansion. The conclusion is that the future food supply/demand balance is destined to be tighter than in recent decades.

3.   Even under the UN's low/medium scenario, the population of Africa will continue to increase and approach two billion people in 150 years. Food production there is not expected to keep pace with growth in food demand. Cereal imports by sub-Saharan Africa are projected to be triple the 1990 level as early as 2020 (Rosegrant *et al.*). Building buying power within Africa to purchase needed food imports will be challenging indeed. Rejecting standard-model policies and institutions will be lethal to millions of Africans in the face of disease, food, and environmental problems.

4.   The low-input, sustainable agriculture practiced in Stage I of the environmental transition depicted in figure 9.1 contrasts sharply with environmental deterioration at an initially low but increasing rate in Stage II, and at a high level though decreasing rate in Stage III. In Stage IV, however, the accumulation of wealth, science, technology, and knowledge during the earlier stages, coupled with declining population, permits a turnaround in natural-resource depletion and environmental degradation. Thus Stage IV provides optimism for the environment. The *environmental dilemma* is how and whether developing countries, including China and India, can pass through Stages II and III of high environmental degradation and natural-resource depletion to the higher per capita income of Stage IV—when environmental preservation predominates—without irreversibly damaging the local and global environment in the process. A slowing birth rate, coupled with economic development under standard-model policies, can minimize the environmental dilemma.

5.   A trade transition attends other transitions depicted in figure 9.1. From little to no international trade in the traditional society (Stage I), agricultural and general trade increases in Stage II and remains high in Stage III, as higher incomes and population growth encourage food imports. While lower demand growth due to negative population growth tends to slow trade in Stage IV, intra-industry trade among nations increases to realize economies of size and specialization. For food products, price ceases to be the major determinant of demand, as food selection becomes driven more by its compatibility with each

consumer's chosen lifestyle. Thus, agricultural trade remains high in Stage IV, to supply the diversity of food products demanded by high-income consumers.

6. International migration, legal and illegal, will become pervasive. It will involve both high-and low-skilled workers. It will lead to greater cultural diversity within a nation and narrow cultural gaps among countries. As cultures collide, the potential for strife will be real. That strife could negatively affect food production and trade. Poor countries adopting standard-model policies can create rewarding local jobs and reduce birth rates to reduce emigration and attendant social frictions.

7. Negative population growth will lower labor supply and raise the relative cost of labor, as well as of management and entrepreneurship. Science and technology will replace labor and human intelligence, especially at lower skill levels, with computer intelligence and robotics. However, ethical questions regarding how far machines should be allowed to replace workers will abound and drive a significant component of policy debates in the NPG countries.

8. The family farm will be threatened by lower birth rates. To be sure, having fewer heirs will facilitate intergenerational capital transfers. But labor shortages and high costs coupled with huge outlays to replace family labor with capital and hired labor will slowly shift farm ownership to a public corporate structure.

9. Negative population growth will tend to shift medical research from "young" to "old" diseases. Already, much progress is being made in understanding the aging process and the replacement of worn-out body parts. More people living to an older age will slow the rate of population decline, but more importantly, it will redefine the working lifespan, solidify the concept of lifetime learning, and increasingly replace a youth-culture orientation with an elderly-culture orientation. Enough success in health research could reduce death rates and raise longevity to retard, if not negate, the occurrence of NPG.

10. A declining global population and the transition preceding that decline raise ethical questions. Continued world population decline, while helping the environment, constitutes what some may regard as a collective international suicide. Given that reproduction is one of the more powerful instincts of humankind, what, if anything, has gone awry in a population whose members individually and subconsciously have chosen to phase themselves out of existence? What, if any, political dialogue and national education will emerge to sustain humankind? Countries following standard-model policies will have sufficient

wealth to create generous economic incentives for more children. If such inducements become commonplace and large, the future population could take an unexpected upturn, especially in affluent countries.

11. A Stage IV world not only is well-fed, it is overfed. Obesity is becoming a growing problem even in poor countries, but it especially troubles rich countries because of plentiful, low-cost, tasty, high-calorie foods coupled with sedentary lifestyles. Two-thirds of U.S. adults age twenty years or older are considered overweight or obese according to Centers for Disease Control.[38] Nearly one-fourth of American adults are obese. Overweight people are prone to health problems of cardiovascular diseases, some types of cancer, and diabetes, all of which shorten life. Obesity is a problem for more than just the overeater: U.S. taxpayers spent $39 billion in 2003 on treatments for obesity-related conditions. Issues of blame—the food industry or personal irresponsibility—will be contested, along with policies for remediation.

12. Food prices will increasingly depend on the value of farm commodities in nonfood uses. It is conceivable that nonfood uses will exceed food uses in the not-too-distant future. Nonfood uses for energy, plastics, pharmaceuticals, and the like will place a floor under farm commodity prices. Nonfood uses make for a more price-elastic demand, thereby diminishing perennial problems of price instability in agriculture. Favored tax treatment for biofuels stems from the widespread myth that energy from agriculture poses no threat to the environment or to food supply. The use of crops and crop residues for energy raises food costs and depletes soil organic matter, accelerates soil erosion, and deteriorates water quality. Crops are not as strong a candidate as grasses and forests for sequestering carbon as soil organic matter (cf. Tweeten, 2005, pp. 272–276). The world awaits new biotechnology able to turn crop biomass, grass, and trees into ethanol at lower economic and environmental cost.

References

Avery, D. "Why the Food Summit Failed," *Global Food Quarterly*, 18–3,1996.

Bos, E., M. Vu., E. Massiah, and R. Bulatao. *World Population Projection, 1994–95 Edition,* Baltimore, Maryland: Johns Hopkins University Press, 1994.

---

38 Adults with a body-mass index of thirty or more are considered obese. An overweight adult has a body-mass index of twenty-five to 29.9.

CBO. *Global Population Aging in the 21st Century and Its Economic Implications.* Washington DC: Congressional Budget Office, U.S. Congress, December 2005.

Council of Economic Advisors. *Economic Report of the President*, Washington DC: U.S. Government Printing Office, 2000.

Crenson, M. "World Population Reaches 6 Billion." New York: The Associated Press (rgray117@aol.com), October 10, 1999.

Diamond, Jared. *Guns, Germs, and Steel.* W. W. Norton, 1997.

Emmott, Bill. "A Survey of Japan." *The Economist*, October 8, 2005, pp. 3–18.

FAO. *FAOSTAT Statistics Database*, http://apps.fao.org. Rome: Food and Agricultural Organization, 2000.

"Illegal Immigration." *The Economist*, May 8, 2005, pp. 18–86.

Lutz, W., W. Sanderson, S. Scherbov, and A. Goujon. "World Population Scenarios for the 21st Century," Chapter 15 in Wolfgang Lutz, ed., *The Future Population of the World*. Laxenburg, Austria: International Institute for Applied Systems Analysis, 1996.

Mosher, S. "Too Many People? Not By a Long Shot," *Wall Street Journal*, February 10, 1997, p. A1.

Rosegrant, M., M. Agcaoili-Sombilla, and N. Perez. *Global Food Projections to 2020: Implications for Investment.* Food, Agriculture, and the Environment Discussion Paper 5. Washington DC: International Food Policy Research Institute, 1996.

Seckler, D. and M. Rock. "UN 'Low' Projection of Population Most Accurate." *News and Views*. Washington DC: International Food Policy Research Institute, October 1997, p. 5.

Shiptsova, R. *Linkages Among Agricultural Trade, Development, and the Demographic Transition*. PhD Dissertation. Columbus: Department of Agricultural, Environmental, and Development Economics, Ohio State University, 1998.

"Special Report: The Oil Industry." *The Economist*, April 22, 2006, pp. 65–67.

Tweeten, Luther. "Dodging a Malthusian Bullet." *Agribusiness*. 14: 15–30, January/February 1998.

Tweeten, Luther. "Confronting the Twin Problems of Global Warming and Food Insecurity." Chapter 27 in R. Lal, N. Uphoff, B.A. Stewart, and D. Hansen, eds., *Climate Change and Global Food Security*. Boca Raton, Florida: CRC Press, 2005.

Tweeten, Luther and Carl Zulauf. "Feeding the World: The Long-term Outlook." *Futurist*, September-October 2002, pp. 54–59.

UN. *World Population Projections to 2150*. ST/ESA/SER.A/173. New York: United Nations, 1998.

UN. *World Population Projections: The 2004 Revision*. New York: United Nations, 2005.

von Lampe, Martin. *Agricultural Market Impacts of Future Growth in the Production of Biofuels*. AGR/CA/APM (2005) 24. Paris: OECD, February 2006.

Annex Table 9.1. Calculation of Annual per Capita Increase in Food Demand

Country Classification	Population	Income per capita		World income share	Income elasticity of demand	Per capita food increase from income	
		Total	Increase				
	(Million)	*($)*	*(% incr./ yr.)*			*(%/yr.)*	
		1994				Un-weighted	Weighted
Low income	3,185	380	3.0	0.048	0.6	1.80	0.0869
Middle income	1,570	2,520	1.8	0.158	0.3	0.54	0.0853
High income	850	23,420	1.2	0.794	0.1	0.10	0.0953
				1.000			0.2675
		2050					
Low income	6,206	1,989	2.1	0.189	0.5	1.05	0.1985
Middle income	2,075	6,843	1.3	0.217	0.2	0.26	0.0564
High income	850	45,677	0.8	0.594	0.05	0.040	0.0238
				1.000			0.2787

Source: Tweeten, 1998, annex table 1.

10

Summary Synthesis

Previous chapters clearly show that means exist to improve the lives of people throughout the world. This chapter's seven-step logical summary synthesis disciplines and focuses our thinking regarding causes and cures, especially for hunger, disease, and poverty in developing countries (see also Tweeten *et al.;* Tweeten).

1. Transitory and chronic food (and health care) insecurity is caused mainly by *poverty*. Since World War II, the world has had sufficient food available every year to provide every person with an adequate diet. People with buying power obtain food. Even in areas enduring famine, food is available to those with sufficient income. Nobel laureate Amartya Sen observed that food was available to those who could afford it even during the great Bengal famine of 1943.

The 815 million undernourished people in 2000–02 noted earlier in table 1.1 are mostly part of the world's 1.1 billion people who live in abject poverty, defined as persons living on less than one dollar per day. People with adequate buying power overcome the frictions of time *(e.g.,* unpredictable, unstable harvests from year to year) and space *(e.g.,* local food shortages) to be food-secure. Working together as a community, people with buying power also have access to sanitary water, clothing, shelter, environmental protection, and preventable disease control and health care.

2. Poverty is best alleviated through broad-based, sustainable *economic development.* Altruism is laudable and motivates feeding members of the family. But where poverty is widespread, families cannot rely on others to protect themselves from hunger and disease. When there is no "pie" to divide, issues of redistribution are moot.

In the early 1990s, I chaired a task force examining operational changes needed in the United States Agency for International Development (USAID) after the U.S. Congress shifted the agency's mission from promoting economic development to promoting food security in poor countries. The members of the task force (including John Mellor, director general of the International Food Policy Research Institute, and perhaps the world's leading economic development expert at the time; Schlomo Reutlinger of the World Bank and at that time a premier world food security expert; and Jim Pines, one of the world's foremost nutrition experts and consultants) agreed unanimously that the most effective means to food security was broad-based economic development. Thus, aside from the food safety net issue, Congress's mandate for USAID to focus on food security did not justify a major redirection of resources from economic development.

The Food and Agriculture Organization of the United Nations (FAO, 1997, p. 3) is perceptive in its statement:

> The need is for policy measures that address all aspects of food insecurity with a view to providing safety nets for the vulnerable and to creating the conditions that can lead to an eradication of endemic hunger. *This has to mean economic growth.* [Emphasis added.]…Improving the equitableness of the income distribution can only achieve so much [in countries with low and falling income], and, as seen time and again, will be strongly resisted by the potential losers. So growth is necessary, and against a background of economic growth, experience shows that it is easier (although never easy) to implement measures that increase equity, particularly if the growth is broadly based to include the agricultural sector.

Interregional and international charity to redistribute food is commendable and has a proven record of responding to acute hunger (famine); however, it will never be a dependable source of food for the chronically undernourished and poor, because of donor fatigue and because food aid destroys market incentives facing farmers in poor countries. Few families or countries would wish to become dependent for their long-term daily sustenance on the caprice of fickle, distant donors. Higher incomes from economic development and not from food or income transfers, account for the vast majority of the millions of persons lifted out of poverty and hunger in recent decades. Charitable sources of medication for disease also are commendable, but a lasting solution requires economic development in poor countries so that people can afford to make their own decisions regarding how to prevent and control disease.

3. The most effective and efficient means to broad-based economic development is to follow the *standard model,* assuring an economic "pie" to divide among people and among functions such as human resource development, agricultural research, infrastructure, health care, family planning, a food safety net, and environmental protection. The standard model, outlined in chapter 2, is applicable to any culture and provides a workable prescription for economic progress, ensuring buying power for food self-reliance and for other needs (see footnote 32). Eventually, in conjunction with family planning, economic progress brings zero population growth, as explained in chapter 9. The model is not prized for its ideology but because it works. It is not a rigid, static, one-size-fits-all grand plan. It helps in identifying key restraints to be lifted for economic success. All components of the model need not be followed, but some key features are essential for a sound economy. It is a checklist of economic measures that will offer a different policy-reform prescription for each failed economy, depending on which items on the checklist a country fails. Although no country has adopted every component, many countries have adopted enough components of the standard model to bring economic success.

4. *Governmental or political failure* is the proximate reason why some countries do not adopt enough components of the proven standard model to end poverty and food insecurity. Only part of governmental failure is due to economic illiteracy. Individuals and groups with power and authority often lose with political change—even if current policies egregiously compromise the public interest. Regulations, red tape, licensing, quotas, subsidies, and the like are sometimes appropriate, to correct for externalities and provide a safety net, as explained in chapter 4. But such market interventions create what economists call *economic rents*, defined as the income stream generated either by creating or ending market interventions. Persons in power control interventions to receive economic rents. Market participants seek favors by paying off authorities who bestow licenses and enforce regulations. Such rents are so attractive that persons in power create excessive interventions, more properly called economic distortions. Inefficient state-owned enterprises (parastatals) or a bloated bureaucracy destroying value are retained to provide employment for friends and relatives of power brokers. Resources that could be used for productive work instead are devoted to obtaining or retaining economic distortions. Real output of the economy is diminished.

In short, governments need to provide public goods and services that correct externalities—to the extent they can do so while raising real national income. Beyond that, government interventions impose direct and indirect costs that reduce real national income. A modest-sized government doing a few things well (few distortions) offers little economic rent. Such government is unappealing to corrupt bureaucrats and politicians but is consistent with the standard model, as outlined in chapter 2.

5. Political failure is inseparable from *institutional failure*. Unresponsive institutions protect political leaders and bureaucrats pursuing failed policies from accountability to the public. Food insecurity and economic stagnation are not the result of limited natural resources, lazy and fecund people, greedy corporations, environmental degradation, or rapacious rich nations. Rather they are the result of misguided domestic public policies, which in turn are the product of weak, mismanaged, and corrupt institutions—especially central government. Thus the standard model is inseparable from institutional change. Institutional success is not synonymous with responsiveness to every demand of the people. One role of representative government is to subject populist appeals to the filter of facts, analysis, and informed judgment. Politicians responding to populism, defined as appealing and simple but wrong answers to complex problems, have wreaked havoc with the economies of numerous countries. South America offers notable examples. Thus institution-building means the creation of analytical expertise in government along with the education of voters and decision makers to help governments act in the public interest.

6. Poorly structured, inadequate institutions often can be traced to *cultural factors,* such as tolerance of the public for unrepresentative, corrupt, incompetent government, and for indifference to the broad-based involvement of citizens in government. Government leaders, products of the nation's culture, often view their position as an opportunity for personal aggrandizement rather than to serve the public interest. Socio-institutional change is blocked by cultural characteristics such as tribal and sectarian animosities, providing a fertile climate for dystopian governments to play one group against another. Preserving culture is indeed laudable, but people may decide that cultural change away from political corruption and from sectarian or tribal hatred and violence is a price worth paying to secure food and health.

Implementing the Synthesis

The message of the *summary synthesis* is that the standard model *economics* of development is the easy part. Politics, institutions, and culture—anything but straightforward—are the principal impediments to the adoption of standard-model policies and hence to development itself. In this context, economic development is not about economics; it is about politics, institutions, and culture. Ample evidence shows that institutions and culture can be changed, although time and patience are required.

Social scientists are not unaware of the role of culture in development. Rao and Walton (p. 3) state, "[In] the world of policy, culture is increasingly viewed as a commonplace, malleable fact of life that matters as much as economics or politics to the process of development." Culture ordinarily is not viewed as an instrumental variable to be changed to promote economic progress. Nonetheless, most people can cite examples where education has changed culture. When, as in the case of Africa, a continent is locked in chronic poverty, hunger, and disease due to lack of economic development which in turn is caused by a culture of tribalism, sectarianism, corruption, and economic illiteracy, shouldn't schools be teaching children a better way? Shouldn't clergy and other leaders as well as teachers be educating people toward ethnic tolerance, mutual trust, and peaceful means to settle disputes?

How and whether to bring about cultural change deserves attention, not just by laypersons, but also by the best minds in sociology, political science, and anthropology. These latter disciplines often seem as clueless as economists when dealing with institutions and culture. Clearly, collaboration of economists with other social scientists, long interred, needs to be exhumed, with the hope of new vitality.

It is my belief that outsiders should not force cultural change on any country, however poor. Bad policies are an addiction, and addictive behavior is rarely changed unless the addict wants to change. Cultural change can be informed by outsiders, but it must be home-grown. Thus the appropriate strategy is to help inform leaders and others in poor countries of the promise of sound policies and to have the patience to wait for poor countries to initiate changes in institutions and culture. Ethical questions remain, such as the proper extent for indigenous governments to intervene to change culture, such as the treatment of women.

Looking Critically at Development Aid

Concluding that the burden of making decisions to end poverty and hunger rests largely with poor countries themselves does not absolve rich countries from helping poor countries. Before examining how to help poor countries, it is useful to point out that experts are not of one mind about aid. Some experts contend that rich countries already have done too much. Economist James Shikwati, Kenya-based director of the Interregional Economic Network, an African policy research group, observes that:

> When aid money keeps coming, all our policymakers do is strategize on how to get more. They forget about getting their own people working to solve these very basic problems. In Africa, we look to outsiders to solve our problems, making the victim not take responsibility to change [see Pitman, p. A6].

A review (Heller, p. 9) of the payoff from ODA concluded that "empirical studies offer only mild (and not uncontested) support for aid boosting growth." To make aid more effective, Heller called for more predictable and longer-term aid commitments, for more aid as grants rather than loans, for building capacity for sound governance, and careful sequencing to overcome human capital and infrastructure bottlenecks. Investment in human resources is one reason why Asia, despite less aid, is making much greater economic progress than is Africa.

Rajan (p. 53) in a recent review of studies going back to the seminal work of Burnside and Dollar in 2000 revealing the (lack of) impact of foreign aid on economic growth concluded:

> Yet one point about which there is general agreement among economists is that there is little evidence of a robust unconditional effect of aid on growth.

Another review of literature by Radelet *et al.* (pp. 16–20) found that, not surprisingly, developmental aid such as investment in infrastructure contributed more to economic growth than did humanitarian aid such as food and medicine. The authors found support for the point made repeatedly in this volume that development aid is of little help without supportive domestic policies and institutions.

In his 2006 book, William Easterly (p. 11), drawing from extensive experience with the World Bank and other institutions promoting development, charged that most of the $2.3 trillion of foreign aid dispensed over the past sixty years was wasted. He favored going back to the "drawing board," assigning aid agencies fewer objectives, making agencies accountable for achieving objectives, and testing small-scale development initiatives by trial and error before unleashing them on the world's underdeveloped countries.

Easterly's proposal too has drawbacks. One is the question whether small-scale efforts that successfully work with highly motivated individuals in controlled, unique situations can be generalized. Successful pilot programs often fail when applied to larger populations and different regions. Another drawback of small initiatives is that many problems of poor countries are nationwide and macroeconomic in nature. Policies, by their very nature, cannot be taken piecemeal. In such cases, it is best to do as this volume does—examine the historical evidence and use the tools of logic, statistical inference, and the overall weight of evidence to judge how donors can best help poor countries. It is inappropriate for donors to force change, but they can work with recipients to learn what has worked in the past and is likely to work in the future. Donors can help to analyze, educate, cheerlead, and (sometimes) to finance such efforts.

Reforming Multilateral Institutions

Multilateral international finance, trade, and development institutions such as the International Monetary Fund, the World Bank, and the World Trade Organization have been the target of numerous critics and protestors in recent years. These global institutions, funded and directed mostly by rich countries, have been accused of giving bad economic advice, of overextending credit to poor countries, and of forcing austerity that has hurt poor people and the environment.

By the 1990s the World Bank and IMF were being widely criticized for implementing the Washington Consensus without regard to social consequences. Some of these criticisms were justified and some originated from privileged persons and organizations no longer able to benefit from the corruption and mismanagement characterizing pre-Consensus policies. Whatever the source of criticism, the World Bank implemented worthy reforms designed to involve recipient-country stakeholders in the development planning and implementation process, to recognize environmental needs, and to pursue a pro-poor economic growth strategy.

In the face of such criticisms, in November 1998, the U.S. Congress established the International Financial Institution Advisory Commission (IFIAC) to consider the future roles of six international quasi-public financial institutions and the World Trade Organization. In 2000, after extensive hearings and analysis, this "Meltzer Commission" (named for Allan Meltzer, the chair), composed of distinguished professionals with extensive experience in international economic development and finance, released several worthy recommendations (IFIAC).

The commission called for the International Monetary Fund, the World Bank, and related quasi-public regional development banks (African Development Bank, Asian Development Bank, etc.) to write off all claims against heavily indebted poor countries that implement an effective economic and social development strategy in conjunction with these development institutions. The commission recommended that the International Monetary Fund restrict its lending to the provision of short-term liquidity to deal with balance-of-payments problems. The commission contended that the IMF had given too little attention to improving financial structures in developing countries and too much to expensive rescue operations. In keeping with its role as lender of last resort to emerging economies, the IMF would be limited to the provision of short-term loans to solvent member governments at a penalty rate (above the borrower's recent market interest rate) and with loans secured by a clear priority claim on the borrower's assets. IMF would act only where a balance-of-payments crisis poses a threat to the global economy. Loans would be made only to countries in crisis that have met preconditions engendering financial soundness. Thus IMF would depart from its past practice of detailed "conditionality," which often called for numerous policy reforms by loan recipients. Promised reforms were often not delivered by loan recipients after credit was advanced. Examples of worthy preconditions that must be met prior to extending "bailout" credit include limiting corruption and allowing freedom of entry and operation for foreign financial institutions.[39] The IMF has a habit of extending new loans to cover payments on "past due" loans. With eventual debt forgiveness, borrowers have learned to be irresponsible with loan funds, because repayment will not be required.

Recurring official pronouncements call for countries to demonstrate better governance as a precondition for financial assistance. The theme stretches from the Meltzer Commission through at least two major reports in 2005 alone. One of the latter was the report of the Millennium Project, entitled "Investing in Development: A Practical Plan to Achieve Millennium Development Goals." The other was the report of the Commission for Africa, entitled "Our Common Interest." Both reports concluded that foreign aid would be wasted in Africa without improved governance, but in seeming contradiction, they argued for substantial additional aid (Teal, p. 19).

The commission was critical of multilateral bank performance in general and not just of structural adjustment programs of the IMF. The World Bank, evaluating its own project and program-funding performance in Africa, found a 73 percent failure rate (IFIAC). Only one of four programs, on average, achieved satisfactory, sustainable results. In keeping with its mission to alleviate poverty in the developing world, the World Bank claims to focus its lending on the countries most in need of official assistance because of poverty and lack of access to private sector resources. The reality is quite different. Seventy percent of World Bank non-aid resources flow to eleven countries that enjoy substantial access to private or domestic government capital markets.

The Meltzer Commission called for development banks to narrow their focus to the eighty to ninety poorest countries of the world that lack capital market access. To avoid again overextending credit to poor countries, the commission

---

39 Several East Asian countries have amassed billions of American dollars in exchange reserves by maintaining an undervalued currency, ostensibly to avoid a 1997-type financial crisis. Such neomerchantilist imbalances instead pose the threat of international financial crisis if the dollar collapses in value. If the IMF stood ready to assist in case of balance-of-payments problems, East Asian neomerchantilist governments would be deprived of one of their arguments for accruing outsized exchange reserves.

called for the quasi-public development banks to shift assistance from loans to grants—with "bank" dropped from their name to reflect the new direction. Thus a worthy infrastructure project in a poor country might be financed by a loan from private banks made attractive by a modest grant from the development "bank."

The commission observed that billions of dollars of private credit are available to private or public borrowers who can make the case that, through sound management of their affairs, they are credit-worthy. In part due to lending by public multinational banks, most balance-of-payments crises in the past quarter-century involved not too little but too much lending, particularly short-term lending that proved to be highly volatile.

Unfortunately, the sensible and widespread requirement for sound governance and economic policies in a poor country before economic development aid is extended has been given mostly lip service. Multilateral banks and agencies have not implemented the recurring call for aid recipients to show policy reform *before* they are extended development aid credit or grants. (Humanitarian assistance is another matter, of course.) The World Bank, if it continues to exist, will provide grants to expand the provision of global public goods such as knowledge and technology transfer, infrastructure, protection of the environment, and prevention of AIDS and tropical diseases.

In short, developing countries need to rely more on private sources of credit rather than on multilateral public banks. Private banks are less subject to political manipulation and have more incentive to avoid deadbeat borrowers. The supply of private financial credit is now virtually unlimited to those who can show they are responsible, credit-worthy borrowers.

Foreign Aid Outlays

Net aid to developing countries totaled $79 billion in 2004. The United States was the largest donor. America doubled its ODA from year 2000 to 2004, going from $10 billion to $20 billion. Still, its share of national income devoted to ODA was only 0.17 percent. Only Italy made less effort among industrialized countries. Scandinavian countries contributed from 0.8 to 0.9 percent of their national income to ODA. The United Nations recommends that developed countries contribute 0.7 percent of national income to poor countries, but on average, countries give only 0.2 percent.

Looking only at ODA, the aid story is incomplete. Americans excel at private giving. Carol Adelman (p. 3) reports that Americans gave $71 billion to poor people abroad in 2004, nearly four times ODA. Data are inadequate to compare this number to private giving for earlier years by Americans and for other countries. More controversial is whether some American military expenditure, such as for keeping the peace in the Formosa Strait, Korea, and other parts of the world should be added to the "foreign aid" account.

Major new foreign-aid initiatives in the twenty-first century have arisen from rich countries, the United Nations, the Bill and Melinda Gates Foundation, and many other entities. These initiatives to poor countries include canceling of debts (mostly uncollectible anyway), providing treatment for HIV/AIDS and other pestilence, and funding of research on tropical diseases and pests. Of special interest is the Bush administration's so-called Millennium Challenge Account, which promised to boost basic assistance by $5 billion annually by 2006, nearly 50 percent above the past level. Of particular note is the word "challenge," implying conditionality. The account was directed at countries that "get their house in order" by reducing corruption and by promoting human rights, education, health care, and liberal economic policies. Runge *et al.* (p. 197) commented approvingly, "The aid is conditional but the conditions are precisely those advocated by nearly all those involved in ending hunger and poverty in the developing world." Such conditionality is consistent with this volume and recommendations of the Meltzer Commission.

One problem with the Millennium Challenge Account as of 2006 is that its administrators had trouble finding worthy developmental targets—poor countries following sound economic policies and where an infusion of aid would provide quick, recognizable payoffs. The private sector and the poor-country representative governments are in the best position to identify high-payoff investments. Given their premium on consuming now rather than later (high discount rate), poor countries most need help with investments that offer high returns but only after several years. Education, agricultural research, and infrastructure investments are candidates.

In short, it makes little sense to set rigid development assistance targets as a percentage of donor GDP. It makes much more sense to provide development assistance where it has a high, sustainable payoff in raising real earning power—and that means in poor countries that follow sound economic policies. A major challenge is to provide assistance that does not "make the patient worse" but instead provides a lasting remedy for poverty. The following section elaborates.

Priorities for Assistance

This volume concludes with a summary of priorities for more developed countries (MDCs) to help less developed countries (LDCs).

- Provide humanitarian food and medical support to deal with crises of hunger and disease in LDCs. Public foreign aid needs to be timely and adequate, but it is best when not long-term. Rather, the priority is for poor countries to attain sufficient economic progress so that their people achieve decent living standards without perennially depending on donor charity.

- Help build institutional and intellectual capacity in LDCs so they can diagnose and treat—or better yet, avoid—economic, social, and environmental problems. In many instances, this will mean bringing students from LDCs to study in MDC universities. Increasingly, education at all levels will be in LDC institutions, assisted as needed by modern electronic communication with institutions of education and research in MDCs. Of critical priority is for LDCs to be made aware of the importance of the standard-model policies (with refinements and adaptations as needed) for economic progress.

- MDCs can set an example and provide a growth-friendly world economy by following standard-model policies. Economic recessions and depressions are created by imbalances built up mainly by failure to follow standard-model policies. Economic progress becomes unsustainable, sometimes on a global basis, when economies chronically over-or undervalue their currency, run persistent large budget and current account surpluses or deficits, erect trade and investment barriers, or tolerate "bubbles" from excessive speculation in asset markets. Some environmental solutions must come multilaterally through international agreements, given the "free rider" problem and the global consequences of air, water, and land degradation. Oceans and species have global public goods properties. Runge et al. (pp. 173–177) propose that such goods require remedial policies best coordinated by an international agency patterned after (say) the World Trade Organization.

- Chapter 8 made the case that one of the highest-payoff standard-model policies is open international trade and investment markets. Open markets give coherence to a central proposition of the standard model—that economic progress is facilitated by reliance on private markets operating in a supportive public institutional environment.

Freer trade, in most cases, pays off, whether done unilaterally, bilaterally, or regionally, but it is best done multilaterally. All countries would do well to end farm commodity price and income support programs that restrict access to local markets or that dump commodities abroad at subsidized prices.

- Once a poor country has demonstrated a commitment to standard-model policies, development assistance is warranted, not least because recipients of aid will be able to maintain the provided infrastructure and human capital investments. The debt problems that have plagued poor countries for years can be avoided by providing grants, rather than loans. Foreign direct investment also will flow. Private capital flow potential is enormous and will allow official development assistance from MDCs and multinational agencies such as the World Bank to be phased out.

- Sub-Saharan Africa and many other poor regions desperately need improved technologies to raise agricultural productivity. Although agricultural and environmental technology has been found to have a high payoff, poor countries (aside from notable exceptions such as Brazil, China, and India) do not have the economic means or political will to sustain the necessary research. Africa spends only 0.5 percent of its agricultural GDP on agricultural research, in part because they don't recognize the high payoff from investing more, and in part because they can't afford more. Rich nations spend 2 to 4 percent of their agricultural GDP on agricultural research, a growing part of that by the private sector. MDCs do a great service by performing basic research, often in the home country. Considerable adaptive research development and dissemination are required to apply results of basic research in MDCs to the disparate agricultures and environments of LDCs. Small, developing countries can afford adaptive but not basic research. The sixteen institutions of the multilaterally supported Consultative Group for International Agricultural Research (CGIAR) are strategically positioned around the world to integrate basic and applied research from rich and poor countries, applying results to the unique environments of LDCs. Dependable, stable funding is essential for successful research. Funding has lagged for the CGIAR system in recent years, and needs to be restored and expanded in critical areas.

Improving agricultural production technology in LDCs depends heavily on support from MDCs, because much agricultural technology is a public good and most LDC countries and farms are too small and poor to sustain needed investments. Falcon and Naylor (pp. 1119–21) document the alarming shift of international support away from agricultural research and development (R and D): Globally, the real value of R and D aid to agriculture in the late 1990s was down one-third from its level a decade earlier. USAID reduced its agricultural staff by over two-thirds from its peak in 1990 (p. 1120). The budget of the CGIAR system, the institutional father of the green revolution estimated to save one billion lives, stagnated at about $350 million in nominal terms from 1992 to 2001, implying that annual funding fell in real terms (p. 1120). CGIAR's comparative advantage, productivity-enhancing agricultural research, accounted for just one-sixth of its budget, and expenditures fell 6.5 percent annually in real terms from 1992 to 2001. The authors note that in Africa—characterized by so called "orphan" crops, countries too poor to fund R and D, and largely bypassed by the green revolution—agricultural R and D expenditures from all sources total only $1.5 billion annually. Given the high returns to public agricultural R and D, these trends imply missed opportunities that warrant reexamination of MDC assistance priorities. Additional, perhaps substantially more, funding of the CGIAR system may be warranted, but only after careful review of funding priorities.

Concluding Comments

The standard model is a development framework, not a grand plan. The model calls for the market to make most economic decisions. People, by their spending decisions, rather than bureaucrats, decide how to allocate resources. National planning has been discredited by past experience, and only a few high-profile utopians still preach it.

The good news is that today's natural resources, technology, and economic knowledge are adequate to end abject poverty and its attending pathologies in every country in the world. Abject poverty is not destiny, but the result of unfortunate choices capable of being changed. Bad policy choices will not soon go away, but it is useful to remember that man, not nature, is the villain or hero in this drama.

Humanitarian assistance by donors is critical to helping poor countries avert famine and to address diseases such as HIV/AIDS, malaria, tuberculosis, and the like. The ideal, however, is to promote policy change, so that currently poor countries in the not-too-distant future will have buying power to address their own humanitarian needs.

The standard model has triumphed as a coherent policy for economic progress, in part by absorbing competing ideologies such as Keynesianism and monetarism. The standard model is not the "end of economics," and it will be revised as new knowledge emerges, but it promises the economic "pie" that is essential for people to serve basic needs in any poor country willing to embrace it.

Critics attack the standard model for too much emphasis on economic efficiency and neglect of economic equity and public goods, such as protecting the environment. The model is fairly rigorous in specifying the provision of public goods, but it does not dictate a proper height of the safety net. Each country decides how to divide its economic pie. Economists can facilitate decision making by quantifying the tradeoffs between economic equity and efficiency.

Nobel laureate T. W. Schultz lamented the discrimination against agriculture in developing countries (see also Runge *et al.*, pp. 98, 142–146). That discrimination was apparent in taxes on agricultural exports and overvalued currency that made food and other imports cheap but exports noncompetitive in world markets. Discrimination also was apparent in underfunded agricultural research, schooling, and infrastructure. Discrimination against agriculture cannot be justified. Neither can discrimination against industry.

The standard model recognizes the synergism between sectors for economic progress. Every developing country currently has more people in agriculture than can be sustained at the much higher income levels that will prevail eventually under the standard model. Light (labor-intensive) manufacturing and eventually capital-intensive manufacturing and service industries must grow to absorb labor freed from agriculture as development progresses. That metamorphosis requires balanced growth.

The standard model offers more than a workable *economic* prescription for improving the quality of life for people. Needed progress in alleviating hunger, treatable disease, and abject poverty in hard-core underdeveloped countries awaits more than food, infrastructure, or public service assistance from donors. Poor countries often need institution-building and cultural change to reduce corruption, gender bias, and ethnic and sectarian animosities. Rich donors can assist in the education of leaders and the public at large in institution-building and cultural change, but the principal responsibility rests with underdeveloped countries themselves.

Finally, how do we reconcile this volume's call for better policies with William Easterly's extensively documented claim (p. 157) that aid donors' utopian planners have failed miserably and that foreign development aid has largely been wasted and "coddles (and probably worsens) bad governments"? Easterly overlooks two important facts. First, humanitarian aid, as called for in this volume, has saved countless lives. It continues to be needed. Second, Easterly fails to note that the numerous economic development successes of our time—ranging from the Baltic countries and Ireland in Europe, to Chile in

South America, to Botswana in Africa, to China and India in Asia—originate not from development aid, but from local initiative and *domestic policy reform*. These reforms were not forced by aid donors, but were of domestic origin from decision makers who, observing local policy failure, learned from economic successes of other countries. This book is intended to further publicize that message of policy reform that has freed hundreds of millions of people from poverty and raised the living standards of additional hundreds of millions. Donors may have a long wait for change in poor countries, but they can educate to speed reform. And donors can be prepared to assist development projects offering a high probability of success and sustainability in poor countries that have made reforms.

References

Adelman, Carol. "Director's Welcome." Pp. 3–4 in *Index of Global Philanthropy*. Indianapolis, Indiana: Hudson Institute, 2006.

Easterly, William. *White Man's Burden: Why the West's Efforts to Aid the Rest Have Done So Much Ill and So Little Good.* New York: Penguin Press, 2006.

FAO. *Food Security: Some Macroeconomic Dimensions.* Rome: Food and Agriculture Organization of the United Nations, 1997.

Falcon, Walter and Rosamond Naylor. "Rethinking Food Security for the Twenty-First Century." *American Journal of Agricultural Economics.* 87: 1113–27, December 2005.

Heller, Peter. "Making Aid Work." *Finance and Development.* Washington DC: International Monetary Fund, September 2005, pp. 9–13.

IFIAC (International Financial Institution Advisory Commission). *Report.* Washington DC: Joint Economic Committee, U.S. Congress, 2000 report. http://www.house.gov/jec/imf/meltzer.htm, 2004.

Pitman, Todd. "Helping to Feed Africa's Hungry Tied to More than Foreign Aid." *Columbus Dispatch.* July 31, 2005, p. A6.

Radelet, Steven, Michael Clemens, and Rikhil Bhavnani. "Aid and Growth." *Finance and Development*. Washington DC: International Monetary Fund, September 2005, pp. 16–20.

Rajan, Raghuram. "Aid and Growth: The Policy Challenge." *Finance and Development*. December 2005, pp. 53-55.

Rao, Vijayendra and Michael Walton (eds.). *Culture and Public Action*. Stanford, California: Stanford University Press, 2004.

Runge, C. Ford, Benjamin Senauer, Philip Pardey, and Mark Rosegrant. *Ending Hunger in Our Lifetime: Food Security and Globalization*. Baltimore, Maryland: Johns Hopkins University Press, 2003.

Schultz, T. W. *Transforming Traditional Agriculture*. New Haven, Connecticut: Yale University Press, 1964.

Sen, Amartya. *Poverty and Famines: An Essay on Poverty and Deprivation*. Oxford: Clarendon Press, 1981.

Teal, Francis. "The Commission for Africa and Economic Research on Growth." *Research Summary 2004/05*. Oxford, UK: Center for the Study of African Economies, Oxford University, 2005, pp. 19–24.

Tweeten, Luther. "The Economics of Global Food Security." *Review of Agricultural Economics* 21(2): 473–488, 1999.

Tweeten, L., J. Mellor, S. Reutlinger, and J. Pines. *Food Security Discussion Paper.* PN-ABK-883. Washington DC: Agency for International Development, 1992.

INDEX

978-0-595-39967-3
0-595-39967-3